Y0-BRJ-045

best sports stories 1974

best sports stories 1974

A PANORAMA OF THE 1973 SPORTS WORLD INCLUDING THE 1973 CHAMPIONS OF ALL SPORTS WITH THE YEAR'S TOP PHOTOGRAPHS

Edited by Irving T. Marsh and Edward Ehre

E. P. DUTTON & CO., INC. / NEW YORK / 1974

FIRST EDITION
10 9 8 7 6 5 4 3 2 1

Published simultaneously in Canada by Clarke, Irwin & Company Limited, Toronto and Vancouver

ISBN: 0-525-06620-9
Library of Congress Catalog Card Number: 45-35124

To Eva and Gerry, the missuses, who helped

Contents

Preface 15

THE PRIZE-WINNING STORIES

BEST NEWS-COVERAGE STORY

Peter Pan's Unexpected Birthday by David Klein,
Newark Star-Ledger 25

BEST NEWS-FEATURE STORY

Larry Brown: King of the Hill by Ray Didinger,
The Philadelphia Bulletin 29

BEST MAGAZINE STORY

Baseball's Wildest Owner by Jim Hawkins,
True Magazine 36

THE WORLD SERIES

All Runs Unearned by Joe Heiling,
The Houston Post 48

Mays Has the Last Laugh by Lou Chapman,
Milwaukee Sentinel 51

History Is Relived by Bob Stevens,
San Francisco Chronicle 55

The Unbelievable Happens by Maury White,
The Des Moines Register 58

The Mets Run Out of Miracles by Phil Pepe,
New York Daily News 61

OTHER BASEBALL

Little Boy Lost by Hal Lebovitz,
The Cleveland Plain Dealer 65

Baseball's Tenth Man by Joseph Durso,
The Saturday Evening Post 68
What It's Like in the Bushes by Dave Hirshey,
New York Daily News 74
The Smell of the Ball by Ira Berkow,
Popular Sports Magazine 78
Super Hero by Wells Twombly,
San Francisco Examiner 87
The Drive on the Record by Al Cartwright,
Wilmington News-Journal 90

FOOTBALL
Nightmare for the Longhorns by Blackie Sherrod,
The Dallas Times Herald 93
17 in a Row on a Shoestring by Jay Searcy,
The New York Times 97
Penn State's Joe Paterno by Charles N. Barnard,
Signature 100
The Vikings Mine the 49ers by Dwayne Netland,
Minneapolis Tribune 108
The Horrors of Training Camp by Edwin Pope,
The Miami Herald 112

BASKETBALL
"Very Bad, Very Rough, Damn Dirty Basketball"
by Tony Kornheiser, Newsday 118
The Giant Among the Champions by Dick Lien,
The Peoria Journal-Star 121
Nate Archibald Is Ten Feet Tall by Bob Greene,
Sport 125
The Nicks Upset the Form Charts by Dwain Esper,
Pasadena Star-News 138
The Recruiting of Kent Benson by Dave Kindred,
The Louisville Courier-Journal 141

GOLF
Tommy Aaron Is Finally No. 1 by Phil Taylor,
The Seattle Post-Intelligencer 146
Weiskopf Conquers Himself by Bob Addie,
The Washington Post 149

A $500,000 Tournament . . . And Who Cares? by Hubert Mizell, Golf Digest 154
Where's Ken Venturi? by Phil Jackman, The Baltimore Evening Sun 163
Golf Paralysis . . . Form Analysis by Ted Green, Los Angeles Times 167

BOXING
It Took Him 4 Minutes 35 Seconds by Eddie Muller, San Francisco Examiner 172
The Greatest Is Now the Tiredest by Dave Anderson, The New York Times 178
The Square Who Became Champion by Will Grimsley, The Associated Press 180

HORSE RACING
The Saga of Secretariat Lights Up Again by Nelson Fisher, The San Diego Union 184
1,001 Sure Fire Ways to Lose a Race by Mark Shrager, Turf & Sport Digest 188
The Greatest Horse Race in History? by Neil Milbert, Chicago Tribune 196

AUTO RACING
What Price Indy Glory by Bob Feeney, Buffalo Evening News 199
Speed, Sex and Heroes by William McIlwain, The Atlantic Monthly 203

HOCKEY
If Ken Dryden's So Smart, How Come He's a Goalie? by Nick Seitz, Sport 218

TENNIS
The Bitter Lessons of Wimbledon '73 by Barry Lorge, Tennis 223

OLYMPIC GAMES
The Olympics: End of a Dream by David Wolf, True Magazine 232

OUTDOORS

Dash—Profile of a Dog by H. A. von Behr, Outdoor Life 249

GENERAL

On the Mountainous Appalachian Trail by George Solomon, The Washington Post 256
Myths and Misses by Furman Bisher, Atlanta Journal 259
Yeah, But What Was the Score? by Melvin Durslag, TV Guide 262
A Day in the Press Box by D. L. Stewart, The Dayton Journal Herald 268
The Day of the Jackals by Stan Hochman, Philadelphia Daily News 271
FTC: Truth or Consequences by Paul Kaplan, Washington Star-News 274
The Song and the Fuss by Ray Fitzgerald, Boston Globe 277
The Love Life of a Private Secretariat by Dick Young, New York Daily News 279
On Coming in First by George Ross, The Oakland Tribune 282

FOR THE RECORD

Champions of 1973 284

WHO'S WHO IN BEST SPORTS STORIES—1974

Writers in Best Sports Stories—1974 302
Photographers in Best Sports Stories—1974 312

THE YEAR'S BEST SPORTS PHOTOS 317

Illustrations

Innocent Bystander by Bill Serne, Tampa Tribune 319
Double Play by Joseph Baker, Passaic Herald-News 320
Up the Wall by Anthony Bernato, Philadelphia Bulletin 321
Flying High by Dick Yarwood, Newsday 322
Alphonse and Gaston Are Brewing a Boo-Boo by John E. Biever, The Milwaukee Journal 323
Game Called on Account of Mud by Ernest W. Anheuser, The Milwaukee Journal 324
Play Ball! by Michael A. Andersen, Boston Herald-American 325
Where Is that Marker? by Ronald E. Schifferle, Buffalo Courier-Express 326
Vaulting a Viking by Donald Black, Minneapolis Tribune 327
Mud Pack by Charles G. Kirman, Chicago Sun-Times 328
Nothing Corny about This Cornhusker, by Kent Kobersteen, Minneapolis Tribune 329
A Study in Frustration by John Long, Hartford Courant 330
A Rare View of a Rear View by Richard Olsenius, Minneapolis Tribune 331
The Clock Tells the Whole Story by William Meyer, The Milwaukee Journal 332
Technical Talk Is Not Nice Talk by Jim Vincent, The Portland Oregonian 333
The Stackup by Al Roberts, The Knoxville Journal 334
The Windup by Paul Tepley, Cleveland Press 335
Break My Jaw, Will Ya! by Richard Mackson, Santa Monica Outlook 336
Pro and Progeny by Ray Matjasic, Cleveland Plain Dealer 337
Three on a Wave by John Titchen, Honolulu Star-Bulletin 338
Mane Event by Fred Matthes, San Jose Mercury-News 339
Georgia Poetry by Al Stephenson, Atlanta Journal-Constitution 340
Hang Gliders by Seymour Snaer, San Francisco Examiner 341
Behind the Eight Ball by Clint Grant, Dallas Morning News 342

best sports stories 1974

Preface

This is "the year of the maiden" in the *Best Sports Stories* series.

For in this 30th (pearl anniversary) volume of the annuals, each of the No. 1 selectees gained the winners' circle for the first time, although each has been represented in *Best Sports Stories* before. More, each of the winners was named No. 1 by two of the three judges and thereby racked up, in our system of scoring, six points.

Thus David Klein of the *Newark Star-Ledger* captured the top spot in the news-coverage division and the $250 award that went with it for his story of the Bobby Riggs–Billie Jean King tennis match which agitated the entire nation late in the year. And Ray Didinger of *The Philadelphia Bulletin* took the news-feature award with his piece on Larry Brown and his struggles to the top. The magazine award was won by another newspaper man who was moonlighting in *True Magazine* as Jim Hawkins's article on Charles Finley of the Oakland A's took the diadem. For Hawkins it was the fourth appearance in *Best Sports Stories* and for Didinger and Klein the third.

It is interesting to note that of the 50 stories in the book, 23 were tapped by the judges—John Chamberlain, John Hutchens, and Red Smith—for a first, second, or third in the competition. It is also interesting to note that only one writer, Dick Young of the *New York Daily News,* who appeared in the initial volume of this series back in 1944, is again represented in the current volume.

It should also be mentioned that the stories went to the judges "blind"—that is, they were identified only by a word or two (with no indication as to the writer or his publication) which is known in newspaperese as a "slug." You may note that's how the stories are identified by the judges in the box score and in their comments.

So, to the box score and the comments:

THE BOX SCORE

News-Coverage Stories	Chamberlain	Hutchens	Smith	* Total Points
Billie [*Peter Pan's Unexpected Birthday* by David Kline]	3	—	3	6
Foreman [*It Took Him 4 Minutes 35 Seconds* by Eddie Muller]	—	3	—	3
Footrace [*On the Mountainous Appalachian Trail* by George Solomon]	—	1	2	3
2d Game [*Mays Has the Last Laugh* by Lou Chapman]	2	—	—	2
Triple [*The Greatest Horse Race in History?* by Neil Milbert]	—	2	—	2
Indy [*What Price Indy Glory* by Bob Feeney]	1	—	—	1
7th Game [*The Mets Run Out of Miracles* by Phil Pepe]	—	—	1	1
News-Feature Stories				
Brown [*Larry Brown: King of the Hill* by Ray Didinger]	3	—	3	6
Pedro [*Little Boy Lost* by Hal Lebovitz]	—	3	—	3
Aaron [*The Drive on the Record* by Al Cartwright]	2	—	—	2
Love [*The Love Life of a Private Secretariat* by Dick Young]	—	2	—	2
Tennessee [*17 in a Row on a Shoestring* by Jay Searcy]	—	—	2	2
Dolphins [*The Horrors of Training Camp* by Edwin Pope]	1	—	—	1
Bush [*What It's Like in the Bushes* by Dave Hirshey]	—	1	—	1
Benson [*The Recruiting of Kent Benson* by Dave Kindred]	—	—	1	1
Magazine Stories				
Finley [*Baseball's Wildest Owner* by Jim Hawkins]	—	3	3	6
Olympics [*The Olympics: End of a Dream* by David Wolf]	3	—	—	3
Daytona [*Speed, Sex and Heroes* by William McIlwain]	2	—	—	2
Race [*1,001 Sure Fire Ways to Lose a Race* by Mark Shrager]	—	2	—	2
Paterno [*Penn State's Joe Paterno* by Charles N. Barnard]	—	—	2	2

Archibald [*Nate Archibald Is Ten Feet Tall* by Bob Greene]	1	—	—	1
Dash [*Dash—Profile of a Dog* by H. A. von Behr]	—	1	—	1
Pinch Hitter [*Baseball's Tenth Man* by Joseph Durso]	—	—	1	1

JUDGES' COMMENTS

John Chamberlain
News-Coverage Stories

1. Billie [*Peter Pan's Unexpected Birthday* by David Klein]
2. 2d Game [*Mays Has the Last Laugh* by Lou Chapman]
3. Indy [*What Price Indy Glory* by Bob Feeney]

As has usually been the case in recent years, the news-coverage stories are pretty well bunched from a technical point of view. I enjoyed all the World Series selections. But they are mostly what you expect—good, dramatic evocations of goatdom (Felix Millan's failure to kneel for a ground ball, Jerry Grote's passed ball) or a miracle denied (the Mets' final capitulation). You have the feeling that the forms of both baseball and football coverage have become stereotyped.

This naturally gives an edge to the offbeat subject. I found myself getting the most pleasure out of "Billie," the story of Billie Jean King's remorseless demolition of Bobby Riggs, the male chauvinist pig of tennis who couldn't get his fifty-five-year-old legs working when he needed them. Billie Jean's victory proved nothing about feminine superiority or equality (I'd like to see her take on Rod Laver or Ken Rosewall before we talk any more about a triumph for Women's Lib), but it did demonstrate that a middle-aged ham can ham it up once too often. The writer got the most out of a circus situation that did have its elements of drama. I pick "Billie" for No. 1.

No. 2 choice is "2nd Game" mainly because it gives you a fond farewell look at Willie Mays, which takes a bit of the stereotype out of it. The fact that it is a World Series story is incidental.

No. 3 has to be "Indy," with its mixture of triumph and tragedy. Again, the author of "Indy" has a most dramatic subject handed to him, but he knew how to make the most of it.

---

* Based on 3 points for a first-place vote, 2 for a second, 1 for a third.

News-Feature Stories

1. Brown [*Larry Brown: King of the Hill* by Ray Didinger]
2. Aaron [*The Drive on the Record* by Al Cartwright]
3. Dolphins [*The Horrors of Training Camp* by Edwin Pope]

The literary crowd goes on writing learned essays about the ability of such big-time writers as Tom Wolfe and Truman Capote to make fact as absorbing as fiction. Indeed, when Tom Wolfe visits Leonard Bernstein's "radical chic" party that was held in New York to raise money for the Black Panthers, his ability to track down the last bit of unintentionally comic conversation is hailed as genius. What the literary crowd does not realize is that the sports feature and magazine writers were out-Wolfing Wolfe long ago. And they are continuing to do it.

Take the story about Larry Brown Jr., which is my choice for No. 1 of the features. This is a magnificent account of how a talented young fellow, a black athlete who happened to be blessed with an understanding father, found his way out of the shambling Hill district of Pittsburgh to become the National Football League's most valuable player. The Hill district scene, with its atmosphere of violence stemming from dope addiction and endemic gang warfare, is most ably conveyed. So, too, is the different sort of violence cultivated by Vince Lombardi to test the rookies' hearts at training camp. This is the raw side of America—but there is nothing raw about Larry Brown's personal story. Clearly the best of this year's crop of features.

For No. 2, it has to be the pitcher's view of Hank Aaron. The guy who wrote this got a good perspective on Babe Ruth's challenger by going to Robin Roberts for his memories of pitching to Hank.

No. 3 choice, for me, is the story of the football training camps (Dolphins). It brings together a lot of material to make a generalized picture of the grind it takes to become a good pro football player. I had a hard time choosing "Dolphins" over the story of a sixteen-year-old boy, Pedro Guerraro, the baby of the Cleveland Indians' system (*Little Boy Lost* by Hal Lebovitz). But, unlike the story of Larry Brown's emergence from a Pittsburgh slum, the comparable climb of Pedro from a one-room-shack childhood in the Dominican Republic is presented a bit sketchily.

Magazine Stories

1. Olympics [*The Olympics: End of a Dream* by David Wolf]
2. Daytona [*Speed, Sex and Heroes* by William McIlwain]
3. Archibald [*Nate Archibald Is Ten Feet Tall* by Bob Greene]

With the magazine stories, we are back to the "new journalism" that brings novelistic exactitude and amplitude to writing about factual situations. I pick the saga of the Olympic shot putters, "Olympics," for No. 1, even though I wince at some of the more naturalistic language used by the athletes. What good characterization is here. And what a beautiful setting of a scene in which three comrades try to psych themselves and each other. Finally, what a commentary is here offered on the Olympics as an institution, with their orgiastic display of "nationalism, commercialism, administrative bungling, outright cheating and, finally, bloodshed."

My No. 2 choice is more "new journalism"—the story of the stock-car racers and their hangers-on at Daytona. There is more good sociology here than you could find in a score of books by professional social anthropologists, or by any of our contemporary fiction writers, most of whom have forgotten that novels used to be about society as well as about the people who live in it.

For No. 3, I pick the close-up of Nate Archibald, the unlikely basketball player from the South Bronx, "Archibald." Again, this story has the characterization and the detail that used to be the desired qualities of our best novels and short stories.

JOHN HUTCHENS

News-Coverage Stories.

1. Foreman [*It Took Him 4 Minutes 35 Seconds* by Eddie Muller]
2. Triple [*The Greatest Horse Race in History?* by Neil Milbert]
3. Footrace [*On the Mountainous Appalachian Trail* by George Solomon]

1. The title-winning, highly professional demolition job that George Foreman did on Joe Frazier was a classic performance to which this clean-cut story does equally professional justice. A tersely written piece that brings you right to the ringside of a heavyweight championship fight, that event which has about it a tension like no other in sport.

2. The Man of the Year—and never mind about all those politi-

cians, artists, and other aspirants—was the great Secretariat, and you have only to read this chronicle of his Triple Crown triumph to know just why. Considering the ease of his climactic Belmont victory (by 31 lengths), it may seem extravagant to call it "the greatest horse race in history," but the vividly presented details support that estimate.

3. A first-rate account of an offbeat spectacle, the annual John F. Kennedy 50-mile jogging race that attracted some 1,700 entries, including a jogging dog. It surely is a tribute to the writer's descriptive skill, and his art as an interviewer, that the armchair observer will congratulate himself on not having been a contestant.

News-Feature Stories

1. Brown [*Larry Brown: King of the Hill* by Ray Didinger]
2. Love [*The Love Life of a Private Secretariat* by Dick Young]
3. Bush [*What It's Like in the Bushes* by Dave Hirshey]

1. A truly moving portrait of a boy who came up the hard way from Pittsburgh's black ghetto to become not only a top professional football star but a man of character with a concern for those less fortunate and less talented than himself.

2. I have to say that I had never given much thought to the sex life of a thoroughbred horse, and so I am grateful for this highly informative and funny piece as a contribution to my education. Which is to say, all of us may now follow with appreciation the post-track careers of such mighty champions as Secretariat, and wish them all happiness in their parenthood.

3. Now and then it's well to get away from Shea, Fenway, Candlestick and other stadia of the big-leaguers and have a look at the youngsters on the way up. Here is a warmly remembered visit with a group of them, a New York Yankees farm club, making the long bus rides from one town to another, playing to small-town crowds of 400 in dimly lighted parks, somehow subsisting on $6-a-day meal money, and dreaming always of the big break that will find them the baseball heirs of DiMaggio, Mantle, Gehrig.

Magazine Stories

1. Finley [*Baseball's Wildest Owner* by Jim Hawkins]
2. Race [*1,001 Sure Fire Ways to Lose a Race* by Mark Shrager]
3. Dash [*Dash—Profile of a Dog* by H. A. von Behr]

1. You might not have bet that anyone could write an objective piece about the most controversial of current sports tycoons, Charles O. Finley, but here it is: the ego that drives all and sundry, notably his employees, up the wall, and the daring and intelligence that accounted for two successive World Series winners, his Oakland Athletics. This personality study may not convince you of the Finley charm, if any, but it will leave you understanding him, for better or worse.

2. Another educational item, lively and ironic, to give pause to those who rush confidently to the pari-mutuel windows, this being nothing less than an amazing compendium of all the ways a horse can lose a race—from neurotic behavior at the starting gate to the unfortunate effects of the brassy music played at the Kentucky Derby. Read it and ponder.

3. The man-and-dog story is rich in tradition, but here is one with a difference, tender but unsentimental, a deeply touching remembrance by a small-game hunter of his life with a friend.

RED SMITH

This job gets more difficult each year because you keep collecting better stuff each year. This time I'll offer no comment with my votes before I'd feel a compulsion to go on and explain why I eliminated so many other good ones.

Here we go:

News-Coverage Stories

1. Billie [*Peter Pan's Unexpected Birthday* by David Klein]
2. Footrace [*On the Mountainous Appalachian Trail* by George Solomon]
3. 7th Game [*The Mets Run Out of Miracles* by Phil Pepe]

News-Feature Stories

1. Pedro [*Little Boy Lost* by Hal Lebovitz]
2. Tennessee [*17 in a Row on a Shoestring* by Jay Searcy]
3. Benson [*The Recruiting of Kent Benson* by Dave Kindred]

Magazine Stories

1. Finley [*Baseball's Wildest Owner* by Jim Hawkins]
2. Paterno [*Penn State's Joe Paterno* by Charles N. Barnard]
3. Pinch Hitter [*Baseball's Tenth Man* by Joseph Durso]

As far as the photos are concerned we think you will agree that they merit the prizes of $100 for the best action photo and the best feature photo. Both winning photographers are making their first appearance in *Best Sports Stories.* One of them, Bill Serne, the action photo winner, is a youth of twenty-four who has been working for the *Tampa Tribune* only since 1972. Joseph Baker, winner of the feature photo award, is a free lance.

This, therefore, is *Best Sports Stories—1974.* Which brings us to a quote from *Best Sports Stories—1944:* "It is our hope that it will be the first volume in what may eventually become a library of sports writing."

It is our hope that we have.

IRVING T. MARSH
EDWARD EHRE

THE PRIZE-WINNING STORIES

Best News-Coverage Story

PETER PAN'S UNEXPECTED BIRTHDAY

By David Klein

From the Newark Star-Ledger

Peter Pan had an unexpected birthday last night. He suddenly turned fifty-five, and he looked every year of it.

Thus did Bobby Riggs, the Master Hustler of Tennis, meet his humiliation in the ballyhooed Battle of the Sexes. He was trounced, soundly and decidedly, by twenty-nine-year-old Billie Jean King, who proved to be not only queen of women's tennis in this world, but of fifty-five-year-old hustlers as well.

The three-set victory was carved out in scores of 6–4, 6–3, and 6–3, as a crowd of 30,472 in the Astrodome first murmured, then chuckled in expectation, and finally raged and roared at the dramatic impact of the rout.

It was a winner-take-all challenge match for $100,000 which, of course, Billie Jean took gladly. But it was worth far more, both financially and in prestige.

Billie Jean, a lean, lancet-quick dancer on the court, won half of the ancillary rights, estimated at another $200,000. Equally valuable to her was the accomplishment of putting down Riggs, the self-proclaimed Male Chauvinist, before a national television audience and in the process avenging a Mother's Day defeat administered by Riggs to her comrade-in-arms, Margaret Court.

In defeat, however, Riggs might console himself with the near $100,000 he will realize from his share of the ancillaries.

And it was entirely possible he placed a hefty bundle on Billie Jean, too—just in case.

He would have been well-advised to do just that. Billie Jean, who perhaps plays more like a man than any woman pro, was too much for him. He couldn't keep up with her speed and her footwork.

Her backhand returns, especially when the point was critical, were near-flawless. She was in on the net, which Court had not done, and she was able to put away several winners from there.

Riggs, whose stock in trade is "garbage" shots—spins, lobs, chops and drops—was not able to make Billie Jean run. Indeed, he found himself going from side to side, chasing her marvelously well-placed shots, and his stamina—despite the 415 vitamin pills he so publicly takes daily—was obviously going fast.

The match began with lavish fanfare. Riggs presented Billie Jean, attired in a menthol green tennis dress with a huge "Sugar Daddy" which she immediately donated to a Houston orphanage. Then she clearly won this first battle of nerves by taking the cover off a live baby pig—her gift to the Male Chauvinist Pig dressed in yellow with red trim.

Finally, they began to play tennis, and through the first four games both held their service. But in the fifth game Billie Jean weakened and Bobby broke through to take a 3–2 lead. It was to deuce twice before she blew an overhead smash.

Yet Riggs, with an opportunity to simply hold on, immediately saw Billie break his service, double-faulting the decisive point to tie it again, 3–3 in games.

Billie Jean held her service, Riggs held his, and at 4–4 she won hers 40-love and then broke his, as he again double-faulted on set point.

Billie Jean had the old man running now and as the second set began she fell behind as he broke through her service. But again she immediately turned the tables and tied it at 1–1. and then went up 2–1.

The fourth game, longest of the night, went 24 points before Bobby won it, but it was costly in that he might have spent the final reserves of energy. They were at deuce 10 times before Billie Jean hit the tape on a backhand return and then was long with a service return.

But she won her serve to move ahead, 3–2, lost the lead when he won his serve, and then played out to win the set, 6–3, and go up 2–0.

The third and final set went to 3–2, King, when she broke Riggs' service in the fifth game on four straight points. She made it 4–2, he rallied once more to cut it to 4–3, and then she rode in to her stunning victory.

The last game went to three match points and five deuces before Billie Jean did it. Riggs was serving. He went into the net on his first offering—indeed, he had had trouble all night on his first services—and then sent her return weakly into the net. It was over, and he used his final bit of energy to hurdle the net and shake her hand.

Afterward, in a mob scene press conference that saw several skirmishes erupt between reporters and TV cameramen, King was kind to her victim—"Roberta Riggs," as she called him.

"I feel Margaret had one of the worst days of her life when she played him, otherwise she might have beaten him, too," said the queen of the kings. "She helped me a lot. She told me to attack his backhand, because he can't roll off it. I'll tell you, I feel this is the culmination of 19 years of tennis. It's different from winning the Wimbledon and U.S. Open titles, but it's just as important."

King said she felt confident after winning the first set. "I hadn't known what to expect," she explained, "but when I won that first one and saw what he was doing, I felt if I just held my services I couldn't lose."

Billie Jean's backhand, tremendously strong, seemed to be tailor-made last night. "His style of play hits to my backhand," she said, "and I wasn't going to argue with that. It's my strong point, and I feel my backhand, as well as my game at the net and my mobility, beat him."

She said she has played "lots of men" who are better than Riggs, but added that "none of those matches made this kind of money. Now I'd love to go and drink some beer."

Then Riggs arrived, looking disheveled and worn. "I just feel I have to have a return match to make it right for the guys again," he said. "But she was much too quick for me. I don't know how I'd be able to play her any differently. She was too good tonight, too good.

"She won and Women's Lib won and that's that. But I'll be looking and hoping for a rematch."

A smiling Billie, sitting at his elbow, said about the rematch request:

"Give me 24 hours and a beer—and I'll think about it."

Riggs was a crestfallen figure after the match in the air-conditioned arena which is a world showplace of sports.

"I'm going to the bridge," he said.

Billie added charitably:

"Be sure and get a parachute first."

Riggs had boasted in one of his public appearances that if he didn't beat Billie Jean, the five-time Wimbledon champion, in their ballyhooed spectacular, he would jump off of Pasadena's "Suicide Bridge."

Billie, who had called Bobby a "creep" before the match, had said that she would insist that he carry out his vow.

Billie was ecstatic.

"This is a culmination of 19 years of tennis for me," she said. "I've wanted to change the sport and tonight a lot of non-tennis people saw the sport for the first time."

She said she was inspired by the boisterous, cheering crowd, the blaring bands, and circuslike atmosphere surrounding the match.

"This was a dream come true," she said. "I've always wanted people to scream at matches."

"I have to eat a lot of crow," Riggs said. "I was wrong and I'll have to be the biggest bum of all time. I have to take it and I will, but I want a return match."

At the close of the news conference, photographers wanted Riggs to give Mrs. King a victory kiss. Riggs accommodated, but some photographers didn't get the shot and asked them to repeat, which they did, after which Riggs told Mrs. King: "You better be careful, I'm going to turn you on."

Best News-Feature Story

LARRY BROWN: KING OF THE HILL

By Ray Didinger

From The Philadelphia Bulletin

It's not hard to find the Hill district in Pittsburgh. Just follow the trail of abandoned ambitions and transparent dreams leading from the center of town. Keep going until you see the streets begin to crack from neglect and look for the mountains of trash to rise up on either side, spilling over sidewalks bearing chalk-scrawled names from other generations. The nearer you get to the bottom of the Hill—where Kirkpatrick crosses Fifth Avenue—the chalk is too often replaced by blood.

Lawrence Brown Sr., a crew-caller at the Conway railroad yard, and his wife, Rose Lee, lived at 2525 Fifth Avenue, where the thick white smoke from the Jones and Laughlin steel plant mixed dangerously with the combustible fury of a black ghetto.

Lawrence Brown was aware of the Hill's environment of hatred and hopelessness and he worried about his three sons, especially the oldest, Larry Jr. Lawrence Brown figured if he could keep Larry from stumbling into the neighborhood's dead-end way of life, that would be enough direction for his two brothers, William and John.

Lawrence Brown noticed immediately that Larry had a physical gift for athletics. It wasn't hard for him to detect because he, himself, had much the same skill when he was growing up. There are folks who will tell you today that Lawrence Brown Sr. could have been a big-league ball player, except that when he was in his twenties, black baseball players were still condemned to a bush-league life. Jackie Robinson didn't come soon enough to free men like Lawrence Brown, who put their gloves and bats away like broken boyhood dreams and scattered to the big city's railroad yards and steel mills.

But the future had now opened for black athletes and Lawrence Brown looked in his son's eyes and dreamed his dreams all over again. He would take young Larry out to a nearby lot almost every afternoon and hit baseballs to him until dark. Often the grounders would kick crazily off hunks of brick.

"He got into the Little League and, right away, he was the best," Lawrence Brown will tell you to this day. "Why, at ten he was stealing bases even though you weren't allowed to take a lead."

Larry Brown played baseball and in his spare time he took on odd jobs to help bring additional money into the house. In the summers, he washed cars and cleaned the windows for an elderly lady who lived up the block.

"Window washing was a good deal," Larry Brown recalls. "In Pittsburgh, with those factories, the air was so filthy you'd wash a window one day and it would be black the next morning."

In the winters, he prayed for snow so he could shovel the sidewalks in more affluent neighborhoods. He'd go off with his shovel before 8 A.M. on non-school days ("you had to get the jump on your competition") and wouldn't return until dinner time. A day like that might be worth as much as $8 or $10. "Larry was such a good boy," Rose Lee Brown said. "He was the one that wanted to work, no one asked him to. He insisted it was his responsibility to help out since he was the oldest son."

He landed one steady summer job as an orderly at Presbyterian Hospital. The pay wasn't too good but he supplemented that with more after-hours window and car washings.

Larry Brown was carefully sidestepping the drugs, the crime, and the gang violence that lurked at each corner. Oh, there was an urge to succeed among the young people of the Hill all right, but the price of success and the means of making it were frightfully high.

"The guys wanted out but they didn't want to struggle like their parents," Larry Brown said. "They dreamed of being black Al Capones. Who could be the baddest dude? Who could be the richest pimp? Who would be the first one to drive his own El Dorado? The hell with how you make it, just make it. The guys I grew up with thought the only way to make money was to rip off somebody else.

"Some of them were pathetic, even comical. I knew one guy who just walked into a bank alone and robbed the joint. He ran out with the money in a bag and flew into high gear. Well, the cops came and you know where they caught up with him? Two blocks from the bank. Here's this black dude who just ripped off a bank in all-white end of town and he's sitting on the curb two blocks away, holding the money.

"The Man (the police) walked up to him and said, 'Well, you planned a good robbery, boy. In fact, it was great. But your getaway wasn't too cool.' The guy told the cops he started running and had an asthma attack. 'It was the money or my life,' he told them, 'so I sat down.'

"I think he's still sitting down, in jail somewhere. Hell, I guess most of the guys I grew up with are either in prison or dead or hopeless junkies, which is probably the worst of all."

Through it all, Lawrence Brown Sr. clung tenaciously to the belief that Larry would be a big-league ball player. That dream didn't even survive Larry's sophomore year at Schenley High, when he became disgusted with sitting on the bench and quit the team. He went out for football.

His family did not like the idea of Larry switching sports. Football at Schenley had a tragic history. Just a year or so before, two neighborhood boys were slaughtered in a savage gang rumble after a game.

The tense expectation of violence hung constantly over the Pittsburgh City League. Once Schenley was rolling up a big score over predominantly white Allderdice High and the hatred which had festered so long at last erupted. A husky senior from Allderdice ripped a rotting five-foot plank from the bleachers and began swinging it back and forth in a murderous arc.

"Come on!" he shouted, daring any Schenley players or fans to disarm him, "I'll rip your damn heads off!"

The police hustled the Schenley team into a bus but it was several blocks later before the rocks, bricks, and bottles finally stopped clattering off the sides and smashing through the windows. Larry Brown remembers hunching under a seat on that bus, listening to his young heart pound with fear, his mind bending under the strain of a people's sickness. "It came clear to me," Larry Brown said, "what the Hill was all about. We're here and the whites are there—simple as that. It wasn't one country at all. The history books were lying to me."

But instead of enlisting in the endless madness of gang warfare, Larry Brown rededicated himself to sports. He stuck with football because he knew it could help him earn a college scholarship and lift him above the Hill and everything it had come to represent.

First, he went to remote Dodge City Junior College in Kansas for two years ("My first day there, they had a cattle drive right through the center of town . . . honest.") and then transferred to Kansas State University where he spent two years blocking for a speedy wingback named Mack Herron. He didn't think any pro scouts would notice a 5-foot-11, 195-pound back who did nothing but bury his face in the numerals of a linebacker, play after punishing play. However, he was wrong. Mike McCormack, then a Redskin assistant coach, was watching from the spotter's booth one afternoon.

"Larry proved time after time that he was a contact player," McCormack reported. "That's the kind of back that's made to play pro football."

So the Redskins grabbed Larry Brown on the eighth round of the 1969 draft. When he reported to training camp, he found himself face-to-face with the famous—and feared—Vince Lombardi.

Lombardi was starting his first season with the Redskins after having transformed a dog-meat franchise in Green Bay into the National Football League's undisputed power in just three years. The Redskins, a team with a heritage mixing dreary mediocrity with outright futility, represented another massive challenge.

"I was prepared to break my back but I wasn't too sure about my chances," Brown admitted. "Here I was, an obscure rookie, working under a coach who always had great backs like Hornung and Taylor. Besides, he had about 32 running backs in camp at one time or another. Everytime I turned around, there was a new face next to me in the huddle."

But those new faces kept coming and going. Larry Brown stayed. He earned his place on the team in Lombardi's infamous "nutcracker drill," that ultimate test of a runner's heart. In the nutcracker, Lombardi would set two foam rubber dummies four feet apart and through that narrow chute a runner would have to crash into two linemen and a defensive back positioned five yards apart. There wasn't, Lombardi observed, any place to hide.

The first day of nutcracking was almost barbaric. Rookie linebacker Roger Jarvis suffered a broken arm. Veteran tight end Pat Richter had his nose broken twice and was ordered back into the pit again and again. Several linemen limped away with bad legs. Weak-hearted runners begged off repeated thrusts into the nutcracker, whimpering about the heat and assorted cramps and bruises. Lombardi carefully noted each of the malingerers and marked them for an immediate ticket out of Carlisle. But he also noted one pleasant surprise. This unheralded kid, Larry Brown, was splitting the other side of the nutcracker almost every time. And he kept scrambling back into line to carry the ball some more. His mouth was open and he was sucking in his air in the labored gulps but he never slowed down.

"On one particular carry, I blasted by both linemen before they could raise up," Brown said. "Right there, in front of God, Sonny Jurgensen, and everybody else, Coach Lombardi stopped practice and said, 'Nice going.' It was the most extravagant praise anybody heard from Coach Lombardi the whole first month of camp.

"He never let you get your balance," Brown said. "One minute you were in with him, the next he would be whipping you with that baseball cap of his. I remember one night, I was packing my bags to leave camp and my roommate, Harold McLinton, talked me out of it. The next night, he was packing and I was the one telling him to stay."

Lombardi growled and snarled at the rookie from Kansas State but whenever it came cutdown time, he always spared him. It was Lombardi who discovered that Brown was deaf in one ear and had a special helmet devised with a hearing aid to help him pick up the quarterback's signals. It was Lombardi who stuck with Brown until he became adept at catching passes, something he'd never done in college. And, in the end it was Lombardi who gave Larry Brown the confidence he needed to survive.

It was Lombardi who made Larry Brown a starter as a rookie and watched him gain 888 yards, including 105 in a game against the Giants (the first 100-yard game for a Redskin runner in eight years). But Lombardi died before the 1970 season and was not there to share in the triumph when Larry Brown hammered out his 1,125 yards. The tough, determined kid from Pittsburgh's gloomy Hill exceeded that last season when he rushed for 1,216 yards, scored 12 touchdowns, and was named the NFL's Most Valuable Player by an overwhelming margin.

Now Larry Brown is a wealthy young man. He has negotiated a new contract which earns him perhaps as much as $100,000 per year, not including assorted fringe benefits like endorsement and appearance money. Yet, according to Brown's attorney and advisor, John Perazich, Larry spends more time speaking in ghetto areas and schools for delinquent boys for free than he does traveling the lucrative banquet tour.

"As a criminal lawyer, I've dealt with any number of Larry Browns," Perazich said. "Guys with great potential who grew up in a bad end of town and blew their futures. To see this guy make it is an inspiration to me. I was up to here with the legal cycle. Every case seemed alike. A kid started at sixteen, lifting petty crap from a department store. Four years later, the kid is holding up a gas station. Two years after that, he shoots somebody. Before I met Larry, I thought justice was nothing more than a revolving door.

"That's why Larry is so involved with young people. He made it and he wants to impress on today's kids that they can make it, too. This morning we were in the worst-looking elementary school you could ever imagine. No windows—just cardboard where the glass should be. Larry sat there and talked to those kids for four hours. When it was over, a little boy said to him, 'I wish I had a father like you, Mr. Brown.' You should have seen Larry's face light up. We walked out and he said to me, 'Wow, man, after that who needs the Super Bowl?' "

Last year, the Redskins played Atlanta in a Monday night TV game and Lawrence Brown Sr. watched it at the train yard, crowded into a room with 300 other workers. That night, Larry Brown gained his 4,000th career yard, a first for a Redskin. The game was stopped while they presented him with the football and the D.C. Stadium crowd poured out their hearts in an emotional standing ovation. Back at the train yard, 300 guys lined up to shake the beefy right hand of Lawrence Brown Sr., who needed his left to brush away the tears.

"At that moment," Lawrence Brown Sr. said, "no man alive could have been prouder."

And perhaps at that moment back in Pittsburgh's crumbling Hill district, one more father could see past the frustration and despair outside and find hope for the future of his son. If so, it would be the one record Larry Brown would cherish most of all.

Best Magazine Story

BASEBALL'S WILDEST OWNER

By Jim Hawkins

From True Magazine

He staggered the length of the clubhouse, groping through the wall-to-wall maze of writers and well-wishers. His eyes, red and wide; his voice, taxed by two weeks of screaming, barely able to rise above a hoarse whisper.

"Champagne . . . somebody get me a bottle of champagne!" rasped Charles O. Finley, proud owner of the Oakland A's—the World Champion Oakland A's. "I want a bottle of champagne!"

He struggled for a moment with the cork, then lurched forward, spraying California brut over the head of the first reporter he recognized. Then another. And another.

They cringed, they covered their heads, they tried to escape, to hide from their bushy-browed assailant in the kelly-green blazer. But Charlie relentlessly stalked his prey, savoring every splash. One by one these men, who had poked so much fun at Finley for the past 12 years, retreated to a distant corner to dry off. The bubbly-over-the-head, the traditional victory baptism, had been reduced to a one-man ritual.

For the most part, the players sat idly by, sipping Paul Masson and watching the wild scene in the middle of the room with mild amusement. It was, after all, *his* World Series, *his* World Championship. No man had ever dominated baseball's blue-ribbon special the way Charlie had—without once swinging a bat.

Leading the cheers from his field-level box, waving a pennant in each hand while his personal Dixieland band blew in his ear . . .

dancing with his wife on the roof of the dugout, covering her face with exuberant, wet kisses while half the world watched on TV . . . parading his prize mule—also called Charlie O.—around the hospitality room, grinning as the beast gobbled roast beef right off the top of his master's bald head . . . everywhere you looked, Finley seemed to be the center of attention.

When his seventeen-year-old son Marty attempted to answer one of the more inane questions that were inundating his dad minutes after the final win, Finley silenced his son with an icy stare. "You just nod," admonished Charlie. "I'll answer the questions."

Among themselves some of the A's had conspired to come up with a scheme that would let them win the World Series and at the same time send Finley home a loser. Failing there, they now did the next best thing and looked the other way while Charlie celebrated.

In years past, when the A's had won a game, it was always "in spite of Finley." Now even Charlie's critics had to concede that A's ruled baseball "because of him." The players had defeated the Cincinnati Reds—but the victory belonged to Charlie.

He was the man who paid the big bonus money to Reggie Jackson and Catfish Hunter. He was the man who sat in the front row of the auditorium at an all-black high school while Blue Moon Odom graduated. He was the man who brought Matty Alou, Dal Maxvill, and Don Mincher to Oakland for the final run to the title.

"Nobody knows, nobody will ever know what he put into this season," raved Jimmy Piersall, the former major-leaguer who served as Finley's good will ambassador and all-around errand boy last year. "I saw it. I lived with him. I know what he went through. Up until 4 A.M. Up again at 8. On the phone all the time. Talking to a million people. Trying to do whatever he could. Nobody will ever know—nobody."

"I sweated blood for 12 years," admitted Finley. "I lost sleep. I lost my hair. My family suffered. My business suffered. All for this. I'm damn proud of my team. And, frankly, I'm damn proud of myself."

Commissioner Bowie Kuhn handed Finley the elegant trophy, symbolic of world supremacy, but the commissioner's heart wasn't in it. Kuhn represents baseball's establishment, and Finley—the rebel, the maverick—has never really been accepted into the fraternity, not even at the moment of his greatest victory.

"That's what hurts the most," remarked one Cincinnati club official, "not so much that we lost, but the fact that *he* won." That gray October day, 100 high-ranking baseball people in Cincinnati felt exactly the same way.

But Charlie couldn't have cared less. For quite possibly the first time in his entire life, the former bat boy, frustrated ballplayer, self-made millionaire felt fulfilled.

"We showed 'em," he finally croaked triumphantly. "We showed 'em all!"

In the entire spectrum of organized sports, there's not another operator who compares with the pompous, persuasive, powerful owner of the Oakland A's.

Logically, there is no explaining his actions, no anticipating his next stunt. Totally unpredictable, often self-contradictory, Finley marches to a drummer all his own. He has vilified and defied (and been fined by) Commissioner Kuhn. He has ridiculed American League president Joe Cronin. He has clashed with the Players Association and the Oakland city government. And he doesn't give a damn who likes it, or who doesn't like it. Or who gets in the way. In the words of one former Finley worker, "Charlie is like the Fourth Marine Division. He rolls right over you."

Despite his antics, he is one of the shrewdest, most successful businessmen in sports today. The A's made a profit of $1.3 million last season and insiders say Charlie's Chicago-based insurance agency cleared at least twice that much in commissions.

Yet Finley can be stubborn to the point of self-destruction. He has blasted the Oakland fans he is trying to lure to the ball park; and he has engaged in bitter, petty contract struggles that have threatened the careers of his most valuable young players, Reggie Jackson and Vida Blue. His response to a 1967 players' revolt was to fire the manager, suspend his best relief pitcher, fine the player representative, and release the team's leading hitter.

While Charlie has loaned players as much as $100,000 to go into business, he wouldn't budge another $5,000 in his salary dispute with Jackson and, later, Blue. When Vida, a sensational newcomer in 1971, won 24 games and the Cy Young Award, Finley bestowed a new Cadillac upon him, all the gas he could burn, and a closetful of clothes. But the owner heatedly rejected any compromise when the time came to talk contract in 1972. Finley conceded that Blue had brought more than $1 million extra into the A's treasury—and that Oakland would lose at least $500,000 if Vida didn't pitch—but he told Blue's attorney, Robert Gerst: "He's worth what you're asking, but he's not going to get it. It's a matter of principle. Nobody is going to tell me how to conduct my business."

Today, Finley's A's are a huge financial success, but the franchise was little more than a midwestern outpost of the New York Yankees when Charlie forced his way into the American League in 1960—on his fifth try—buying what may have been the worst club in baseball history.

With phone in one hand and his wallet in the other, he began to build. It wasn't easy, or inexpensive. "For every one dollar I made in insurance I lost a dollar and five cents in Kansas City," admits Finley. But by then Charlie was accustomed to overcoming adversity.

He wears his humble origins like a coat of arms. He has told the tale of his Horatio Alger climb to the top so many times it doesn't vary more than a word or two from telling to telling. "Sweat plus sacrifice equals success," says Charlie over and over. "Sweat plus sacrifice equals success."

Born on Washington's Birthday 55 years ago, he followed his father and his grandfather into the steel mills of Gary, Indiana, starting as a machine-shop apprentice at 47 cents an hour and working his way up to foreman of the maintenance department while playing semipro baseball on the side.

He rose to superintendent in a munitions factory during World War II and sold insurance at night. After the war, peddling policies full time, he set all sorts of sales records until he almost died of pneumonic tuberculosis. But it was then, while he lay ill in a sanitarium, that Finley, flat broke, dreamed up a group health plan designed especially for doctors. That idea made him a multimillionaire.

Then, while the premiums poured in, he started shopping around for a big-league baseball team he could call his own. It took him six years—six years of haunting hotel lobbies at the baseball meetings and watching first the Athletics, then the Chicago White Sox, Detroit Tigers, and California Angels sold to somebody else. The baseball establishment looked upon Finley as just another rich eccentric. But finally, in 1960, he outbid a group of Kansas City businessmen and became the owner of 52 percent of the Athletics.

Vowing to keep the club in Kansas City at any cost, Finley spent half a million dollars redecorating dilapidated Municipal Stadium in turquoise, yellow, and orange, adding a zoo behind the bleachers and sheep on the right-field slope.

In a ceremony on the steps of City Hall, he supposedly burned his contract with the city for the rental of the stadium—a contract that contained an escape clause in case attendance ever dipped below 850,000. "I will not only give you my word of honor, but I'll give you the names of some prominent people around the country who will vouch for my word," announced Finley. "Now that I've found a place to roost here in Kansas City, brother, I mean to tell you I'm here to stay."

That was in February.

In July he inspected the Cotton Bowl in Dallas to see if it was suitable for baseball. In August he admitted he had never really burned that contract at all—the city was, in fact, still bound by that minimum-attendance clause. Within a year he would approach the league with the idea of moving to Oakland—an idea he had already discussed at length with Horace Stoneham, owner of the San Francisco Giants.

Eventually the league ordered Finley to stay in Kansas City through 1967, although he had threatened to play all home games in a cow pasture and actually signed a contract to perform at the Kentucky State Fairgrounds. But Finley served his sentence—kicking and complaining—then fled to Oakland. On the floor of the U.S. Senate, Missouri's Stuart Symington described Finley as "one of the most disreputable characters ever to enter the American sports scene"; and one Kansas City resident called Oakland "the luckiest city since Hiroshima."

But it didn't look like Finley was getting any bargain in the transfer, either. The Giants were already entrenched across the bay, with 10 years of black ink behind them, while Charlie had been losing more than $3 million in Kansas City. Finley demonstrated again, however, that he's no fool when it comes to a business deal. The contract he negotiated in Oakland was one of the best in baseball: it included a five-year, $5.5 million radio-TV package (compared with $156,000 a year in Kansas City); 25 percent of the concessions; 27½ percent of the parking; and the ball club only had to pay $125,000 a year in rent. Finley may complain about inadequate fan support, but since moving to Oakland, he has never made less than $600,000 in any one season, and last year's take was more than double that.

In 1970, after taking a long look at Finley's bankbook, the National Hockey League reluctantly let him buy the California Golden Seals, deciding even Charles O. Finley was better than roller-derby king Jerry Selzer. And last fall he added the American Basketball Association's Memphis Tams—who were on the edge of extinction—for a mere million bucks.

Now the rumor is that Charlie may move all three of his sports teams to the soon-to-be-completed Superdome in New Orleans. Finley vehemently denies that, just as he denied earlier rumors that had him relocating the A's in Dallas, Fort Worth, and Toronto. Furthermore, the NHL, wary of the gypsy image both baseball and basketball have earned, is reluctant to let Finley shift its franchise, even though the Seals have already cost him more than $2 million.

Still, there are skeptics. Bill Dauer (who was vice-president of the Kansas City Chamber of Commerce during Charlie's stay there and now holds a similar post in San Francisco) says, "Everything Finley has said and done in Oakland is like a record being played back to me. He's so crafty, so cunning—truly one of the last of the great characters. It will take some pretty smart guy to outwit those people in Oakland, and he may be just the guy."

The chain of command in Charlie's conglomerate begins and ends with Finley. His attention to detail, his fetish for total domination, extends from his family to the front office, to his ball clubs on the field.

When Finley sits down to dinner at a restaurant with his two daughters and five sons, he orders for everybody. Then he tells the busboy how to clear the table. During the five days the World Series spent in Oakland last fall, Finley himself sold tickets to the people who streamed into his office; and he attended to such items as how many chunks of fried chicken the visiting reporters would find in their box lunches.

"Charlie butts into everything," says veteran announcer Bob Elson, who used to broadcast Finley's ball games. "He'll hawk programs, sweep out the ball park, anything. He's the hardest-working man in baseball. But Charlie Finley feels that if Charlie Finley dropped over dead tomorrow, the world would stop turning."

A perfectionist, Finley pushes himself at a prodigious pace. And he expects his employees to keep up. Yet he surrounds himself with the brothers of his in-laws and the sons of his friends—then refuses to let any of them do anything on their own.

An emotional, impetuous man, he once fired, rehired, and fired manager Alvin Dark in a single evening. When the Athletics—as the A's were called in Kansas City—swept a series in Chicago, an overjoyed Finley beat the team bus back to the hotel and was waiting there with $25 in his hand for each man when they arrived.

He is addicted to the telephone, calling other owners and club executives at all hours of the day and night, often opening the conversation with, "Screw it, let's you and me make a deal." And, as one general manager who has been on the receiving end of a few of those calls reveals, "the sonofabitch will make a trade just that quick, too." In his own mind, Finley is convinced he can manipulate and outmaneuver his fellow owners in any war of wits. And he frequently does. Yet they look upon him as a whimsical gadfly to be watched with amusement and considerable caution—but never to be respected.

"Charlie Finley is a liar, and on top of that the man is chicken-s—," says Detroit manager Billy Martin, echoing the sentiments expressed in less graphic terms by a number of baseball people.

Martin, who agreed to manage the A's before he accepted the Tiger job three years ago, took on Finley in a name-calling contest that threatened to upstage last fall's AL play-off. Among other things, Charlie accused Billy of ordering Tiger pitcher Lerrin LaGrow to throw at A's shortstop Campy Campaneris. "I could have sued Finley for the things he said about me," claims Martin with contempt. "I had some prominent lawyers tell me I could have collected a lot of money, too. But there's an old saying: Never get into a pissing fight with a skunk."

Finley is an opinionated progressive in a corner of the globe saturated with stodgy, stand-pat conservatives. Many of his ideas—like brightly colored uniforms and World Series games at night—were years ahead of their time. Yet anything with Finley's name attached seems doomed to defeat when first put to a vote of the other owners.

This winter, while Finley was pushing for passage of his latest pet project, the designated pinch runner, one rival AL executive chuckled, "I can tell you right now what will happen in that meeting—it'll be 11 to 1 against." It was.

"The other owners," admits Charlie, "have just skunked the hell out of me." They have no compunction, however, about adopting one of Charlie's ideas after he no longer is in a position to claim credit: scheduling those middle three Series games at night last fall, for example. Finley had been campaigning for that for years—"Give the working man a chance to watch our biggest spectacle—but when the innovation was announced, it was Bowie Kuhn's idea."

"We in baseball know what our problems are," says Finley, as if he still can't quite believe all the opposition he encounters. "We know what they are and we could correct them, literally, overnight. Overnight! It's just stupid that we don't. And stupidity is something I can't stand."

But Finley seems to enjoy being on the "other" side, always at odds with everybody. "The man's capacity for turmoil is incredible," says reporter Ron Bergman, who has covered Finley for the last five years for the *Oakland Tribune*. "He thrives on controversy. If none exists, Charlie will create one. He yells at people for therapeutic purposes."

In 1971, as Oakland neared its first divisional title, Charlie cancelled "Fan Appreciation Day" in a fit of pique when it became apparent that the A's weren't going to draw a million people. He refused to let the players attend a victory party planned by some of Oakland's more prominent citizens; and snubbing the several spacious new motels within walking distance of the Coliseum, he selected the Mark Hopkins, across the Bay in hated San Francisco, as his play-off headquarters. But when his plans were exposed, Finley nimbly retreated behind a smokescreen of explanations and excuses, blaming the ball players and incompetent underlings for the "whole misunderstanding."

Usually Charlie loves to see his name in print. He will call reporters in the middle of the night with a "scoop" that invariably involves Charles O. Finley, then check the papers the next day to make sure it's there.

When the Oakland City Council considered a motion to rename the Coliseum "Charles O. Finley Stadium," Charlie claimed he was against the idea. But when the motion was defeated, Finley summarily cancelled the politicians' season passes. "If that bill had passed," scoffed an American League general manager, "Charlie would have been out there the next morning with a paintbrush in his hand."

Finley's attitude toward his players smacks of some feudal baron set down in the middle of the twentieth century by a time machine gone berserk. He dispenses favors and inflicts pain as he pleases.

Above all, he simply cannot stand to have his authority challenged or his paternalism questioned.

He showers his players with bonuses, expensive gifts, and tips on the stock market, and frequently invites them out to his 1,280-acre farm (it's across the Indiana border from Chicago) for steak or liver cooked by Charlie himself. When relief pitcher Rollie Fingers' jaw was fractured by a line drive while playing in the minors, Finley ordered Fingers and his wife to take a delayed honeymoon anywhere in Florida—all expenses paid.

Yet most of the Oakland players dislike the owner. Many, in fact, despise him.

"The man is insensitive and egotistical," says one of the A's. "He thinks nothing of messing up your personal life." At one point in Jackson's feud with Finley—which lasted nearly all of the 1970 season—Reggie told him, face to face, "I hate the way you treat me—I hate the way you treat people."

"There is confidence and there is cocky confidence," observes Blue. "I have confidence. Charlie Finley has cocky confidence." Blue has never forgiven Finley for the way he was treated during their 1972 debate—like "a damn colored boy" is the way Blue describes it. "Charlie Finley," says Vida, "has soured my stomach for baseball."

When Finley quotes Blue, he does so with a vague southern accent—which Blue doesn't have—injecting soulisms like *pacific* for *specific*. "Vida," says Finley, "is basically a good boy."

Even Charlie's habit of handing out bonuses whenever the spirit moves him annoys some of the A's. Although they accept the money, they grumble that such actions pull apart the already badly divided team, emphasizing individual achievement rather than team effort. Of course, the guys doing most of the grumbling are the guys who didn't get the bonus money.

On the A's chaotic cross-country flight between the second and third games of the Series, Finley paraded up and down the aisle, a straw skimmer on his head, his Dixieland band behind him, serenading the A's with his favorite song: "Sugar in the morning . . . sugar in the evening . . . sugar at suppertime. . . ."

As the procession passed his seat, catcher Dave Duncan grabbed one musician by the arm and asked if he was having fun. "No," was the terse reply.

"Then why do you do it?" inquired Reggie Jackson.

"For the same reason you guys do," the musician said. "Because Charlie calls the tune."

When someone doesn't sing along, Charlie reacts harshly. In the waning days of 1970, when it became obvious the A's weren't going to win the AL West in spite of their talent, reporter Bergman of the *Tribune* asked the players if they thought manager John McNamara had done a good job. "It doesn't matter who manages this team," responded catcher Duncan. "There's only one manager—Charles O. Finley."

The owner reacted by almost immediately firing McNamara because "he couldn't keep the players from popping off." Then—in his most scandalized tones—Finley informed the press, "I have found out Dave Duncan and [coach] Charlie Lau have been sleeping together." In fact, the two men had done nothing more sinful than rent an apartment together in Oakland to cut down on expenses.

As for managers, Finley's attitude toward them has always been quite simple. "It doesn't take a genius to run a baseball team," he says bluntly. "A monkey could stand out there on the field and wave at the pitchers." So far, he hasn't given his mule an opportunity to manage, but hasn't given his human managers much rein either.

In the dozen years that he has owned the A's, Finley has employed 11 managers—a dozen if you'd care to count Hank Bauer's two tours of duty—as well as eight publicity men, seven farm directors, six traveling secretaries, five general managers (including the incumbent, Charles O. Finley), four business managers, and assorted other hired hands whose assignments were never really revealed because they didn't stay around long enough. "I don't ask to be loved," explains Charlie, "but if a man accepts my money, I demand and expect his loyalty. If he doesn't extend it, I don't need him."

As a manager, Dick Williams always had been known as his own man. He was fired in Boston because he couldn't get along with the owner there. When Finley hired him, people immediately began trying to predict the date Williams would be canned. Two years and three retroactive raises later, he is still around—with another two years to go on his contract.

When Finley called a midnight press conference in the middle of the play-offs in Detroit, there was Williams lighting Charlie's cigarettes and mixing his drinks. In the eighth inning of the seventh game of the Series, there was Williams leaning over the railing, conferring with Finley in his private box.

Williams still claims to be his own man, but Finley follows the progress of most A's games—anywhere in the country—over the intercom in his downtown Chicago office (while traveling secretary Tom Corwin or farm director Norm Kosselke watches the contest in person) and he keeps a telephone in hand and a line open. "Call down and tell Dick Williams to have this next guy bunt," Charlie barked into the phone late one evening, checking to make sure the impressionable sports writer seated across the desk was paying attention. "What happened?" Finley asked after a few silent moments.

Kosselke's voice crackled back, via 2,000 miles of telephone wire, "Mangual bunted."

"I've been accused of meddling," Finley admits, "and that accusation is 100 percent right. Anytime I spend $8 million, I want to know what's going on."

The roster of his alumni association is longer than Harvard's, yet the A's actual office staff is the smallest in the major leagues. "If the other clubs want to clutter up their payrolls with a lot of useless employees, that's their business," explains Charlie.

Nobody in the organization dares do anything without first getting the go-ahead from Finley. "When he happens to be in Oakland for a ball game, he sits in his private booth—high above the field—giving orders to the public-address announcer over a phone in one hand and waving instructions to the organist with the other.

He once spent a full hour showing his publicity director, Bob Bestor, how to address an envelope. "He leaves you without a shred of dignity," recalls Bestor. "It gets to the point where you're almost brainwashed. If he doesn't chew you out one day, like a prisoner of war, you find yourself saying, 'How nice of him not to beat us us tonight.' "

Charlie's own cousin resigned as business manager because he couldn't take the interference. And after one year of running errands and wearing a T-shirt that labeled him as "Charlie's Bat Boy," Jimmy Piersall packed up and left, too.

For a while it seemed that even Charlie himself was considering a departure. While the A's were battling for the title last year, he repeatedly told reporters: "If we win the Series, the first guy I'm going to get rid of is Charles O. Finley!"

His health, never good, had taken a beating from all the hours he'd put in running his diversified empire; and it was common knowledge that his wife, Shirley, wanted him to slow down. After the Series, he went into semiseclusion, even skipping the major-league meetings in Hawaii—a week-long combination bull session and flesh fair that Finley never failed to enjoy. He sounded almost resigned to semiretirement when he announced, "I'll let my record speak for itself."

The retirement talk vanished, however, with the first signs of spring—and the renewed prospect of another good, old-fashioned contract fight with Vida Blue. "If he doesn't get in line," Charlie proclaimed, as rumors swirled that the super-talented Blue would be traded, "he'll find out that we can win just as well without him."

Meanwhile, to commemorate the A's first completely successful season in 42 years, Finley had purchased the most lavish rings in baseball history. Full-carat rocks for each player, costing Charlie $1,500 apiece—five times the amount normally spent on such souvenirs. They are marked "World Champions, 1972," of course. And the A's decision over the Reds is duly recorded. Each player's name is also engraved on his ring.

And just in case anybody might ever be tempted to forget who really was responsible, each ring carried the autograph of Charles O. Finley.

The World Series

ALL RUNS UNEARNED

(World Series Game I)

By Joe Heiling

From The Houston Post

Felix Millan usually kneels. In prayer, yes. He was raised that way. He also kneels in fielding ground balls, something else he learned at a young age.

In full view of 46,021 fans and countless millions on TV Saturday, Millan didn't drop to his knees.

Campy Campaneris' bouncing ball squirted between his legs and the error made all of the Oakland A's runs unearned in a 2–1 mugging of the New York Mets in the opener of the 1973 World Series.

Ken Holzman, Rollie Fingers, and Darold Knowles combined to four-hit the National League champs while the gallant loser in defeat was lefty Jon Matlack.

One hopping ball in the third inning means the Mets must start another battle from behind, something they've done practically the whole season.

The thing you must remember about Millan is that he is Mister Met of 1973—the Metropolitans' most valuable player. They wouldn't be in this October classic were it not for his outstanding play.

But here came that bouncing ball. Millan eyeballed it as he has all the others. Then it zipped through him and the guy they call Felix the Cat felt a sickening feeling in his stomach.

"I didn't go down on the ball," said the sad-eyed little veteran from Puerto Rico. "I stayed straight up. All year I've been kneeling on almost every ground ball. This time I didn't. I can't explain why. I just didn't do it."

On the error, Holtzman scored from second base. The A's pitcher had doubled inside the third base line with two out. It was only his second batting appearance in this, the year of the designated hitter in the American League.

Campaneris flashed his speed, stealing second, from where he hightailed it home on Joe Rudi's single to right. Another hit followed, by Sal Bando, and Willie Mays, starting in center field as the recuperating Rusty Staub sat this one out, bobbled the ball for the game's other error.

Nothing came of the momentary lapse, and those two runs were to withstand anything the Mets could produce on a day when excellent defense complimented the fine pitching.

After running the bases, Holtzman found he had left a bit of his steam behind. He was a trifle tired and his pitches began to come in higher than usual.

Thus Cleon Jones lashed a double to left center and John Milner whipped an RBI single up the middle and, suddenly, the Mets gave all the appearances of being a hot item.

What cooled them down was an outstanding catch by Reggie Jackson, running down Jerry Grote's long blast to center. The ball was over his head, but he caught up with it, almost stumbling as he hit the outfield track.

In the fifth, Millan got some extra clout in his bat and drove a pitch deep to left. Rudi was playing him shallow, and was forced to scramble for all he was worth to get back. The ball dropped for a triple.

Although Millan didn't score, Dick Williams, the A's manager, had seen enough. Fingers heated up in the bullpen and blanked the Mets into the ninth when Knowles secured the final two outs after a walk to Ron Hodges, a pinch hitter.

The A's had seized the opener and they'll send out Vida Blue (20–9) to deal with the Mets' Jerry Koosman (14–15) in Sunday's 3:30 P.M. CDT contest before the Series switches to New York.

"We certainly did expect this kind of pitching," Williams replied when asked about the low score, "and we expect it to be equally tough tomorrow. We expect it to be that way all through the seven games, which is what I expect the Series to go."

"We have outstanding starters, just like they do, and we have a tremendous bullpen, too. I saw Mister (Tug) McGraw today and I know he's equally tough. They have fabulous pitching and we'll scrounge for all the runs we can get."

They'll also play a spot of defense. Dick Green, the A's second baseman, sparkled afield along with Jackson and Harrelson, the little shortstop of the Mets.

Green stopped a hard shot off Wayne Garrett's bat and turned it into a seventh-inning double play. Also, he took a little looper over the infield away from the pinch swinger Jim Beauchamp in the ninth.

He stretched high as he could, like a guy trying to reach an object on a high shelf, to rob Beauchamp—first man to face Knowles—of a hit that might have fired up a Mets rally.

"After I caught the ball," said Green, "I should have planted my foot and thrown to first. I think I could have gotten him [pinch runner Ted Martinez] before he got back to the bag. But I was a little off balance and I might have thrown the ball away. So I held the ball."

When Garrett flied to right for the final out, Green was happy he hadn't gambled a throw.

He even felt a pang of sorrow for Millan, his opposite number in the Mets' infield.

"I've had those kind of errors," he said, "and I hate them. I know how he feels. I don't know what happened. Maybe he didn't charge the ball enough. He let the ball play him more than he should."

Whatever the reason, Millan couldn't be consoled afterward.

"I just want to go back to the hotel," he said, "go to my room and go to bed soon as I can. I want to forget it. The sooner I forget it, the better. I'm just glad this wasn't the last game."

MAYS HAS THE LAST LAUGH

(World Series Game II)

By Lou Chapman

From the Milwaukee Sentinel

Willie Mays may be a falling star but he's no buffoon—even at forty-two and in the twilight of his great career.

They laughed at Willie Sunday, which is like thumbing your nose at a deity or writing a vulgar graffiti on a national shrine.

The unflappable Mays, though, had the last chortle when he delivered the go-ahead run with a single in the 12th inning and his New York Mets exploded for three other tallies to outlast the Oakland A's, 10–7, and square the World Series at one game apiece.

You've got to trot out all the superlatives in putting this four hour and 13 minute marathon in the proper perspective among other classics.

It was the longest duel in Series history, one of the most exciting in the 70-year annals of baseball—and yes, just about one of the zaniest.

The fellow who used to write the scripts for the Marx Brothers' funnies in the old days must have come out of mothballs to prepare this one.

Mays was one of a number of characters who qualified for the comedy role during the wearisome, but thrill-packed, afternoon.

Willie turned in two horrendous maneuvers on balls hit in his center-field sector—one of which he didn't see.

There were two key pratfalls turned in unintentionally by a pair of A's—Sal Bando at third and left-handed reliever Darold Knowles —which proved particularly costly.

One record was broken as the game became the longest from the standpoint of time in Series history and tying a mark for the most pitchers used—11 by both clubs.

The previous record for longevity was the three-hour 28-minute ordeal on October 8, 1945, when the Chicago Cubs beat the Detroit Tigers in 12 innings, 8–7.

Each club took turns trying to give the other the game. The A's surrendered a 3–1 edge after three innings and the Mets refused to contain a 6–3 bulge after six.

It finally boiled down to the decisive 12th when the Mets rapped Rollie Fingers, the prize of the Oakland bullpen.

Bud Harrelson triggered the charge with a crashing double to right center and the Mets received a break when Bando, charging in for reliever Tug McGraw's bunt, slipped on the wet grass as the ball shot over his head.

Harrelson, who took off for third, of course, made it easily and McGraw was credited with a single.

"The groundskeepers did a terrible job," Bando complained later. "The infield was bad and the outfield was soggy."

Fingers reared back and struck out Wayne Garrett, who had homered in the third off A's starter Vida Blue. The mustachioed pitcher also got Felix Millan on a pop to first. Then, up came Mays, who has had a flair for drama since breaking in with the old New York Giants in 1951.

Willie flailed at a fast ball and bounced it up the middle to score Harrelson, and Cleon Jones singled to send Fingers to the showers. A funny thing happened, meanwhile, to Mike Andrews on his way to wearing goat horns as Paul Lindblad came on in relief.

First, the former Sox—Red and White vintage—let John Milner's grounder go through. Then he made a bad throw to first on Jerry Grote's high bouncer to give the Mets a 10–6 lead going into the A's half of the 12th.

McGraw, the fourth New York pitcher who came on in the sixth, turned in six strong innings. He finally gave way to George Stone, who managed to get the side out after giving up a run-scoring single to Jesus Alou.

Mays committed the first of two tragically funny defensive lapses when he misplayed pinch hitter Deron Johnson's drive to center and set the stage for the A's game-tying two-run ninth.

Willie circled under the ball, then fell on his face. The A's capitalized as they struck for the runs following a walk to Bando, Reggie Jackson's run-scoring single and another hit to left by Gene Tenace.

Again, in the 12th, Mays braced himself against the wall on Jackson's smash, but the ball bounced in front of him and Reggie ambled to third.

Jackson collected four hits in a row off left-hander McGraw, whose screwball was more effective against right-handed hitters.

"The first one [by Johnson] I didn't even see," Mays confessed later. "But on the one by Jackson I figured I wasn't going to kill myself. We were leading 10–6 and I thought, 'Why get hurt?' If the score was close, then I'd have gone for it."

Willie, whose trophies and list of thrills could stretch all the way to this former Candlestick playpen in St. Louis, was asked how the big hit compared with those.

"I feel great about it because I made these guys happy," said Mays, pointing in the direction of his jubilant Mets teammates. It's important winning a game like that and going into your own ball park 1–1 instead of 0–2.

"Look, it doesn't mean we're going to win it, but it sure gives us momentum."

Mays entered the game in the ninth, following a single by Rusty Staub, who started after missing Saturday's 2–1 Oakland win because of an injured right shoulder.

The Mets didn't want to risk aggravating the injury, hence the insertion of Willie.

The A's weren't about to concede after the Mets' big 12th inning. Tenace drew a walk and Alou singled Jackson in following Reggie's triple. Ray Fosse then forced Alou; but, Stone walked Andrews to load the bases with one out.

Campy Campaneris, who can hit the long ball, stepped up, representing the winning run. But he bounced out to end the game.

The Mets' miracle appeared to be taking another day off when the A's struck for two in the opening inning on Joe Rudi's one-out double, which Jones lost in the sun. Bando's triple and Alou's double.

The Mets wasted an opportunity to win it in the ninth when Harrelson was thrown out at home trying to score from third on Felix Millan's fly to left. From the vantage point of television, it appeared that catcher Ray Fosse failed to catch the oncoming Harrelson, who didn't slide.

"If I slide, I'd never get past him [Fosse] to the plate," said Harrelson.

Meanwhile, as the Mets' shortstop put it later, Mays's defensive misadventures "only proves he's human."

The scene now shifts to Shea Stadium, where it could become even whackier with those crazy, hopped-up Mets' fans.

HISTORY IS RELIVED

(World Series Game III)

By Bob Stevens

From the San Francisco Chronicle

One of the most stunning moments in World Series history, the infamous passed ball by Mickey Owen in 1941, was relived at Shea Stadium last night before a crowd of 54,817, few of whom could remember Mickey, none of whom will forget Jerry Grote.

A passed ball by Grote, normally a man of fluid movement behind the plate, sent Ted Kubiak scurrying to second base in the 11th inning, whence he scored on clutch-hitting Campy Campaneris' crisp and decisive single to center field to give the Oakland A's a scrambling 3–2 win over the New York Mets in the third game of the 70th World Series.

The triumph gave the defending champions a 2–1 bulge in this one, with the A's Ken Holtzman to oppose Jon Matlack in tonight's fourth game.

In the fourth game of the 1941 Series between the New York Yankees and the Brooklyn Dodgers at Ebbets Field, Owen let a Hugh Casey two-strike pitch squirt through his glove. Tommy Henrich fled to first base, a rally exploded, the opportunistic Yankees won and went from there to the world championship.

Brooklyn never forgave the ill-fated Owen.

Grote's misplay seemed to typify the Mets' defense last night. Outfielders turned the wrong way on fly balls and rallies survived. First baseman John Milner failed to go to second base for a force and the road to the finish was made just that much longer. Ray Sadecki failed to cover first base and the A's nearly won it in nine.

Tom Seaver struck out five of the first seven A's he faced, before leaving after eight, tied 2–2. Jim (Catfish) Hunter, who throws wild pitches with about the same frequency Neil Armstrong walks on the moon, threw one in the first inning and the Mets, ignited by Wayne Garrett's lead-off homer, charged out in front, 2–0.

Seaver was hit hard and for distance in the sixth, when the A's narrowed the margin to 2–1. Joe Rudi ran center fielder Don Hahn to the wall for the first out. Sal Bando ran Hahn to the wall for a misplayed double, and Gene Tenace ran Bando home with a howling double to the left-field corner.

Oakland's second run, in the eighth, was a classic in execution by both sides.

Campaneris, who collected three of the A's 10 hits, singled to lead off and a 2–2 deadlock was on the planning board.

Wary of Seaver's pick-off move to first, and with Joe Rudi at bat, Campy hugged the bag until the right moment, then took off. It was a fast ball, down, perfect.

Grote released it immediately upon reception, sending a low, perfect throw into the glove of the defending Felix Millan.

But Campaneris was ahead of the throw—barely.

Seaver's next pitch was away from Rudi and Joe went with it, slashing a dust-spraying single underneath first baseman Milner and Campy fled home for 2–2.

Hunter and Seaver, who were supposed to have decided who is the universe's finest pitcher, were long gone when the game came down to its pivotal point, the point at which Grote was to realize the anguish of Mickey Owen.

The "finest pitcher" problem has yet to be resolved.

First Sadecki and then Darold Knowles held their respective foes at bay, then Paul Lindblad of the A's and Tug McGraw of the Mets. Then, after surviving a near home run by Bando in the 10th, Harry Parker became the Hugh Casey in 1973.

Ted Kubiak, who might not have been playing had owner Charles O. Finley been kinder to Mike Andrews and not sent him home after Mike made two errors last Sunday in Oakland, walked with one out.

Parker went to 2–2 on Angel Mangual, a late game entry, and then broke off a pitch that roared in on Angel, below the knees. He missed the ball. So did the distraught Grote, Kubiak racing to second base and Mangual to first.

But, with less than two out and a runner on first base, the batter is out regardless. Kubiak was entitled to second base, however.

Campy then singled and a hush you wouldn't expect at a military funeral descended upon unbelieving Shea Stadium.

The Mets were not dead; however, Garrett, trying to check his swing, singled softly up the middle and A's manager Dick Williams waved in reliable Rollie Fingers from the bullpen.

Millan sacrificed. Rusty Staub went out to Mangual in center field, Cleon Jones grounded to the bracing Campaneris at shortstop and this one, not elegant, not particularly shabby—just exciting—was over.

Fingers was asked if he was prepared to duplicate last year's effort of appearing in six games.

"Once I get warmed up, the adrenalin starts flowing. I only faced three batters tonight so I'll be ready to come back tomorrow.

"As a matter of fact, I can go all seven if necessary—this is the World Series, you know."

The A's were smiling. Mike Andrews is due back and the Mets are behind.

THE UNBELIEVABLE HAPPENS

(World Series Game IV)

By Maury White

From The Des Moines Register

The unbelievable finally happened here Wednesday night.

There was a swift, logical baseball game that was "over" almost as soon as it started and the New York Mets won it, 6–1, to even the World Series at 2–2.

Rusty Staub, a redhead who once captured the city of Montreal by learning to speak French and hitting home runs, stepped to the plate as the third Met batter to face Oakland's Ken Holtzman.

The first two—Wayne Garrett and Felix Millan—were perched on various bases in sold-out (54,817) Shea Stadium as Le Grande Orange walked up to the plate, bringing along an aching right shoulder.

"I'm not going to get into that business of whether it pained or not," he said later. "Obviously it causes a little trouble, but it's not that bad. I hurt my shoulder and I try and compensate my swing."

Oh, did he compensate.

Staub, a left-handed swinger, pole-axed a towering driver over Joe Rudi's head in left field, thereby gaining great rewards for a solitary batting session Monday in trying to hit to the "wrong" field.

"It was a fast ball over the heart of the plate . . . Holtzman's stuff," said Staub. "The wind was blowing out to left field, just right. When I hit it, I didn't think it would go out."

Go out it did, setting up Jon Matlack with a quick 3–0 lead that he carefully tended by not giving any hits until the fourth and allowing only three singles until lifted in the ninth.

"It certainly was a relief to have Rusty get that early homer," said Jon.

Rusty couldn't have agreed more. He was getting worried. That shoulder got banged up when he ran into a wall making a catch in the play-offs. Ever since, he had not hit ONE ball over any fence even in batting practice.

"Concentration and a little bit of knowledge about their pitchers helped," he insisted.

"I feel our best lineup is with me in right field. I sincerely believe that. If I didn't I would not even try to play."

Would Staub be playing if this weren't the World Series?

"I wouldn't be playing if I thought there was somebody else who could do the job better," he said. "That applies to every day of the season, not only play-offs and World Series games," he said.

The homer was merely the most spectacular of Staub's four hits. And he drove across five runs, one short of the record held by many, and had the surprisingly light-hitting A's out-hit until Matlack departed in favor of Ray Sadecki.

Sadecki gave up two singles in his brief stint, striking out Campy Campaneris with the bases loaded to get a "save." Forget that the game wasn't even in peril until Matlack's shoulder tightened.

"I was reared in Pennsylvania and like to pitch when it's cold, but I had trouble getting warm tonight," said the young man who lost the opening game and now is 1–1 for the first Series he's ever attended.

Manager Yogi Berra jerked his young ace out when the arm started stiffening in the late innings. Not long before, with a big lead, he had taken out outfielder Cleon Jones, who has a touch of flu.

"I just hope Cleon Jones is feeling good tomorrow," growled Yogi. "Everybody had us dead yesterday and here we are, even again."

Yes, indeed, and the Series is sure of going back to Oakland for a sixth game after Vida Blue and Jerry Koosman hook up here tonight starting at 7:30 (Iowa time).

There was a particularly memorable moment when Mike Andrews, the second baseman fired by A's owner Charles Finley Sunday night and brought back by popular demand Tuesday, came to bat in the eighth.

When the reserve infielder stepped out of the dugout, the fans immediately started a roar. In a moment the ball park was a sea of sound and everyone was standing, whooping it up.

"All of us were pulling for Mike to get a hit. I got goose bumps just listening to the ovation," said Joe Rudi, who made another of his patented wall-climbing catches. "I was really pulling for him."

What did that ovation mean?

"There's a lot of working people come here. I think they were just happy that a guy who got the shaft . . . if that's what you call it . . . got his chance."

Andrews grounded out—and got an ovation.

"It was great. I don't think I'd had even one before," said Mike, a trifle misty-eyed. "I should have acknowledged the first one going to the plate, but all I was thinking of was trying to get a base hit.

"To me it meant everything to know that the people—and especially the ball players—were behind me. My mind's been so messed up the last couple of days, this was like a rejuvenation for me.

"I don't think I've ever had a standing ovation in my life," Andrews added. "It gave me chills. . . . It really made me feel good."

No cigar there, but it was worth the price of admission to see the dour countenance of Finley, the Grinch who has threatened to steal the World Series with his tasteless tactics.

The crowd's reaction made it clear that Finley was wearing horns and, as Charlie glowered, his wife sat alongside the owner, laughing merrily at something or other.

Once again, Oakland manager Dick Williams went through his bullpen like black plague, using five pitchers. He has employed 18 in four games, for an average of four and one-half per game.

There hasn't been a complete game on either side to date, although Matlack would certainly have had one on a warmer night. But who expects balmy breezes in New York in mid-October?

Fielding? The A's were brilliant, ripping off four double plays to tie a record. Actually, it just saved the score from getting more lopsided. And, of all things, sure-handed Dick Green fumbled a ball and erred badly.

Anyway, there is a tomorrow. And a day after—in Oakland.

THE METS RUN OUT OF MIRACLES

(World Series Game VII)

By Phil Pepe

From the New York Daily News

The Mets ran out of miracles today when Bert Campaneris gathered in a soft pop fly off the bat of Wayne Garrett. The end came at 4:07 Pacific Daylight Time.

Held without a home run by superior Met pitching for six games, it was inevitable that the slugging A's, who hit 147 out of the park during the regular season, would eventually explode.

They waited until today, the sudden-death seventh game, when Campaneris and Reggie Jackson each bombed two-run homers off Jon Matlack in a four-run third to lead the A's to a 5–2 victory over the Mets that gave them the 1973 world championship.

Moments after the victory, Dick Williams officially announced he would not be back as Oakland manager next year.

Williams leaves with two consecutive world championships, the first time that has been accomplished in 12 years. It was last done by the Yankees when they beat the Reds in 1961 and the Giants in 1962. The manager those years was Ralph Houk, who resigned last month and left a vacany in the Yankee managerial chair. So much for suggestion and coincidence.

As inevitable as the slugging A's explosion was the fact that the Mets' inability to score runs, thereby putting tremendous pressure on their pitchers, would eventually haunt them.

They had come back here from New York, leading three games to two, and needing just one victory in two games to complete their second miracle in four years.

But they scored only three runs in the two games here and Matlack, who had not allowed an earned run in 26 innings of pressure pitching, finally faltered.

Their offensive weakness exposed, the Mets fell behind, 5–0, after five innings, an almost insurmountable lead with their bats. But to their credit, the Mets never died. They scored one run in the sixth, driving Oakland starter Ken Holtzman out of the box for the third time, rallied in the eighth and went down swinging in the ninth.

One run was in and the tying run was at the plate, in the person of Garrett, when Dick Williams was forced to go to his bullpen for the last time. Darold Knowles came in, setting a record by appearing in his seventh game.

The miracle was still alive. The believers kept their faith. Then Garrett hit a little pop behind short and it was fitting that Campaneris, brilliant in the entire Series, should have the honor of putting away the final out, ending the miracle.

No sooner had the ball disappeared into Campy's glove then all hell broke loose. Fans swarmed all over the field. Seeking souvenirs in the modern-day form of celebration, they engulfed players, who had to fight their way to the Oakland clubhouse, tried to grab caps or gloves, attempted to steal bases, tore at the turf.

Then, in the Oakland clubhouse, the celebration continued. Charles O. Finley expressed a desire to make it three in a row next year and Williams said, "I'll miss not being with you, but I made a decision and I'm going to stick with it."

And Reggie Jackson, his arm around his manager, said, "I'm sorry, I'm sorry, I'm sorry, I'm sorry that he's leaving. I wish to hell he wasn't. But I understand."

They told Reggie Jackson he was voted the Most Valuable Player of the Series, but what did they tell Bert Campaneris? Jackson was great—in the last two games—with three hits Saturday and his two-run homer today. Campaneris was great for seven games, with his glove, with his legs, even with his bat.

He was the man the Mets admired, the one they thought had beaten them. And he had. He scored the winning run in the first game, drove in the winning run in the third game, and drove in the first two runs in today's game. And he was brilliant in the field.

If pitching match-ups mean anything, the edge today had belonged to the Mets. Ken Holtzman had been bombed for eight hits and four runs in five and one-third innings. He had been bombed out in the first inning of the fourth game. Matlack had held the A's without an earned run and to just six hits in 14 innings of World Series pitching.

For the last crucial month, he had been the Mets' best pitcher, in the stretch run, in the play-offs, in the Series. He was capable of throwing a shutout at the A's. He would have had to throw a shutout to win.

And he looked to have great stuff as he held the A's hitless through the first two innings, then got Dick Green looking at a third strike to start the third.

But Holtzman drilled a double down the left field line in his second Series at-bat. Both at-bats were against Matlack, both times on a Sunday, both times he doubled to left to start a rally.

They brought up Campaneris and you could have gotten big odds that he would be the one to hit the first A's homer. He had hit only four during the regular season, but hit three in post-season play, two in the play-offs, one today. It came on Matlack's first pitch, a high breaking ball away, hanging there invitingly.

Campy jumped on it, throwing all the force of his 160 pounds into his swing, driving the ball deep to right and, as it disappeared into the seats, Rusty Staub punched the right-field wall with his gloved hand. The Mets were down 2–0, and Staub knows what it's like to make up two runs.

But two runs weren't going to be all the A's would score. Joe Rudi drilled a single to left and Sal Bando popped out. Then Jackson was the batter. The count went to 1–1 and Matlack threw a curve ball, and Reggie hit the dog out of it as only he can. It soared into the air into deep right center and landed in the lap of somebody with a lousy seat, some 440 feet from home plate.

When he hit it, Jackson knew it was gone. He never moved. He stayed at home plate watching the ball disappear, then the little boy came out of the man again. He jumped up and down and threw his hands in the air, then soared around the bases, whirling and bouncing happily, clapping his hands and hopping as he ran. When he reached home, he landed on the plate with both feet and was engulfed by happy teammates.

The A's tacked another run onto their lead in the fifth, a run made possible by Campaneris with a single, a steal, and Rudi's single. Down 5–0, the Mets began to struggle back, an almost impossible uphill climb.

When Felix Millan and Rusty Staub crashed back-to-back doubles in the sixth, believers took heart. But Dick Williams doesn't believe in miracles and he brought in Rollie Fingers, who doesn't believe, either.

Fingers cut the Mets off without another hit. But they rumbled again in the seventh and Fingers left two more men in scoring position by slipping a 3–2 breaking ball past Wayne Garrett, who was tying a record for futility in a World Series of futility.

It was Garrett's 11th strikeout, tying Ed Mathews of 1958. He also made three errors at third, one less than the record. There were records for the most men left on base in a Series for two teams and one for the most strikeouts by one team when George Stone made Jackson the 62nd victim. And Gene Tenace, who tied a record for homers in a Series last year, walked for the 11th time in the third to tie Babe Ruth for the most walks in a Series.

But still to be determined was the money and when Fingers got through a one-two-three eighth, the Mets were about to breathe their last. First they would take one more stab at a miracle.

Miracles don't die easily and believers don't give up easily and John Milner walked to lead off the ninth and, one out later, Don Hahn pushed a single through the right side. Bud Harrelson's bunt was a great idea with disastrous results. Fingers got it and Buddy, late getting out of the box, was nipped at first, leaving the Mets down to their last out.

Eddie Kranepool hit for George Stone and bounced to first and people began pouring out onto the field, but Tenace bobbled it and a run scored and the tying run was coming to the plate and the believers believed once again. The gremlins were at work.

Williams got Fingers out and Knowles in, his seventh appearance, another record. Knowles threw a ball and then Wayne Garrett swung and hit the little pop to Campaneris. There would be no miracle. Players were running and people were swarming on the field. It was the end of a miracle, the death of a dream. And the clock on the scoreboard said 4:07.

Other Baseball

LITTLE BOY LOST

By Hal Lebovitz

From The Cleveland Plain Dealer

He is sixteen years old and lost.

Large, frightened eyes stare from his round, childlike, ebony face. His head recently had been shaved and the hair is just beginning to grow back.

Pedro Guerrero is the baby here, the youngest player in the Indians' system. He's lonely and bewildered.

He speaks no English. He fails to comprehend even a friendly hello. This is the first time he has ever been away from his home, San Pedro Demarcoris, of the Dominican Republic.

Everything he sees here—except a bat and a ball—is foreign to Pedro. Only when he is facing a pitcher does he feel relatively comfortable and even that has been a jolt.

The first day of batting practice each hitter was given five swings. Pedro dug in against veteran Vince Colbert.

Colbert jammed him on three successive pitches. Pedro hit each one on his fists, spraying the ball to right field, although trying to pull.

Without explanation he walked out of the batter's box, refusing the remaining two pitches.

That night he told his roomie, ex-major leaguer Marcelino Lopez, he never saw pitches like those before, that he never had to hit to the opposite field that way and that he quit because his hands hurt.

"Never, as long as I live, will I forget that," Lopez reported Pedro as saying.

Lopez was assigned as Pedro's roomie—baby-sitter, guardian, mouthpiece—because he came out of his native Cuba at the same age to make the majors. That was 14 years ago.

"Pedro came here with a big suitcase," said Lopez. "It was empty except for one pair of pants and a blue shirt. No underwear. No baseball equipment. He didn't even know what a supporter was."

Pedro had received $66 for initial expense money. Lopez took him on a shopping spree: underwear, socks, two shirts, baseball shoes, and other necessary equipment. Only $17 remained. A sympathetic and more affluent rookie gave him two pairs of pants.

"Pedro said it was the most money he ever spent in his life," said Lopez.

The boy was shivering. The weather has been cold here. "Buy him a sweater," said farm director Bob Quinn.

From Quinn and minor-league coach Joe Azcue, who acted as interpreter, the Pedro Guerrero story was pieced together.

He started playing ball, Little League variety, at age eight, as most kids do in the Dominican Republic.

At eleven, Pedro had to quit school to go to work; his family desperately needed financial help. He lived in a one-room house, inhabitated by ten, including his grandparents, aunts, uncles, two brothers, and a sister. (Now, sleeping with just two roommates, in one motel room, is like living in a palace to him, strange and unsettling.)

As a breadwinner, at eleven, he worked as a cement mixer and wheel-barrow-toter for $2 a day. When he grew a little taller—he is now 5-foot-11 and weights 164—he graduated to the sugar mills, carrying 200-pound sacks for $3.20 a day. His father, once a sugar-mill employee, is now an invalid, partially paralyzed.

Pedro, meanwhile, continued to play ball, moving up to what is similar to our American Legion League. The program in the Dominican Republic is headed by Pedro Gonzalez, once an Indians' second baseman. Gonzalez, noting the boy's talent, continually encouraged him.

A smooth-fielding, switch-hitting third baseman, the boy led the entire island in hitting, with a .438 average.

"He told me," said Azcue, "that he bats better right-handed, but he also bats left-handed just for practice. He said he was batting for a high average right-handed, then when he went to left-handed another kid caught up to him. So he went back to right-handed again and got way ahead of the other kid. Then he returned left-handed again because he needed the practice."

The Indians' Latin American scout, Reggie Otero, saw Pedro and was impressed with his raw talent. He offered the boy a $2,500 bonus to sign.

Gonzalez begged the boy to wait, telling him he was too young, that he would continue to improve and that the money would come when he was more mature and in a better position to handle himself in the United States.

But $2,500 was more than anyone in his family ever had seen. His parents signed for him.

The other day, Quinn took Pedro to the Federal Building here to get his social-security number. "Now we can pay your bonus," he told the boy through Azcue. "Ask him how much he wants us to send home and in whose name to write the check. The rest we'll put into an account here and tell him I want an accounting for every cent he spends. We've got to take care of our baby."

Azcue conveyed the message.

"He wants you to send $2,300 to his mother right away," Azcue translated.

"He is so, how do you say, frightened," said Azcue. "The other day we brought out the rubber pants for sliding practice. All of a sudden Pedro disappeared. I found him hiding in the lavatory. He never saw sliding pants before. He got scared."

Nor did the Indians' baby know how to slide. In the attempt he sprained his wrist and was taken to the hospital for X-rays, another bewildering experience.

"You have to put yourself in his shoes," suggested Azcue, "to know what he's going through. I went through it myself, although I was a little older when I left Cuba and I didn't come from as hard a home life as he did. But in a couple of years he'll be talking English good and he'll be all right. He's a good kid, just a baby with talent."

"Ask him about his family. Ask him if he's lonely," the interviewer suggested.

Azcue relayed the question.

The boy tried to reply. He couldn't. Huge tears rolled down his cheeks.

Azcue took the boy in his arms and hugged him tightly.

BASEBALL'S TENTH MAN

By Joseph Durso

From The Saturday Evening Post

Tuesday, March 6, was a nice sunny day in Orlando, Florida, the only city in the hemisphere that harbored both Mickey Mouse and Harmon Killebrew. The 26 million tourists who visit the state each year all seemed to be converging on the town. Disney World was alive with cartoon heroes and kids. The racing cars were spinning at Sebring to the east. The fishing fleets were plying the Gulf of Mexico to the west. The lady jockeys were booting home winners in Miami to the south. And, on all sides, the baseball camps were rustling after a delayed start induced by rigidity of the "whereas" clause at the bargaining table.

Over at the spring-training headquarters the Minnesota Twins were getting ready for the first exhibition game of the season and everybody was talking idly about Willie Mays' knees, Sparky Lyle's ankle, Leo Durocher's temper, and Richie Allen's salary. But before the afternoon was over, they would all be talking about a twenty-six-year-old retreaded outfielder named Larry Eugene Hisle—because he was about to become the pioneer in the most controversial experiment on the leisure-time scene. He was the first "designated hitter" of the baseball season.

As the 10th man on a traditionally nine-man team, Hisle wasn't sure that afternoon whether he was a pioneer or a guinea pig. He did know that he had had four shots at steady employment in the big leagues with the Philadelphia Phillies, for whom he once built a miniature batting average of .205, and that he had been passed from Albuquerque to St. Louis to Minnesota without playing any games during the previous winter. He also knew that manager Frank

Quilici had "designated" him to bat for the Minnesota pitcher all afternoon, and so Hisle—a good "glove man"—would spend his time marching from the bench to home plate without ever touching a glove.

History had to wait a few minutes before Hisle made his debut as the "dh" in the box score because the other team was the Pittsburgh Pirates, who play in the National League. The rub was that the Twins play in the American League, which had voted in January to try the new rule for three years, except in interleague games: the World Series, the All-Star Game, and exhibitions. So the Pirates put up a big argument when Quilici offered the umpires a batting order with 10 names. They finally subsided after the Minnesota management said it had advertised the experiment when selling tickets, grumbled that it wouldn't happen again, and then watched Larry Hisle whack a home run with two men on base and another with the bases loaded.

"It felt kind of weird sitting in the dugout while my teammates were on defense," Hisle reflected later. "I don't think I'd like the job full time since I enjoy defense almost as much as hitting. I killed the time by studying the Pittsburgh pitchers and by drinking a lot of water at the cooler."

Maybe it was caused by the seven-hour day, the five-day week, or the four-week vacation, to say nothing of the fact that earthmen these days stare at a quarter of a *billion* television screens in 100 countries from Albania to Zambia. But whatever the reason, the 1970s came hustling into sight wrapped in dollar signs surrounded by people with the time and money to lavish on something called "the entertainment buck." It took 200,000 of them to buy one minute of commercial time on the Super Bowl telecast; 5 million of them to syndicate a race horse, and 100 million of them to build a stadium.

It was a time when most ski-country families had two or more snowmobiles in the barn, when America added 300 golf courses a year, and when the National Hockey League expanded overnight from six teams to 12 and then to 14. You could watch Hungarian soccer players kick field goals from the 50-yard line or North Carolina basketball players heave three-point baskets from 30 feet out.

There were 16 teams in two divisions in one hockey league and 10 teams in two divisions in the competing league; 17 teams in four divisions in one basketball league plus 10 teams in two divisions in another; 26 teams in six divisions in two conferences in one football conglomerate, and 24 teams in four divisions in two baseball leagues. And as for the public: bewildered and bewitched maybe, but free-spending definitely. "They're really pouring it on," *The New York Times* observed as things heated up. "When the little guy suddenly gets a little money, he spends it."

To make a long story short, when he started spending it on something else, the baseball people started looking around for ways to recapture his interest and his wallet. Then, when 9 of the 12 clubs in the American League drew fewer than a million customers in 1972, the stampede was on. The villain: the 6-foot-4 pitcher with overpowering stuff. The victim: the man waving a baseball bat 60½ feet away. The reason, suggested Gabe Paul: "The pitchers and the stadiums grew too big."

Larry Hisle didn't realize it at the time, but that was his cue. Actually, the cue had been sneaking up on him. In 1895, the infield fly rule was adopted to keep smart infielders from tricking unsmart base-runners. In 1901, it was revised to protect the innocent. In 1920, the spitball was outlawed. In 1950, the strike zone was defined (armpit to top of knee). In 1963, it was defined again (top of shoulder to bottom of knee). In 1969, would you believe armpit to top of knee again?

Then men walked on the moon, the Mets won the pennant, and the red-ink wretches of the American League began clamoring for somebody, anybody, to put more clout into the old ball game. Enter the tenth man: the "designated hitter."

He arrived in 1969, during the same summer Neil Armstrong arrived on the shore of the Sea of Tranquility, but nobody paid much attention. Still, in places like Rochester and Syracuse and Toledo, he was often the talk of the town: the man who did nothing but bat for the pitcher, and Alexander Cartwright be damned. He was experimental that summer, his stage was the International League (highest minor) and his impact on the seas of baseball tranquility was immediate.

Batting averages in the league promptly rose by as much as 17 points for the first-place club. More runs were scored. The designated hitters collectively batted 120 points higher than the pitchers they replaced. The pitchers—who were allowed to stay in the game strictly as pitchers—began to stick around a lot longer. Few of them got to bat very often. And some of them—the eighth, ninth and tenth men on the staffs—didn't get to pitch very often, either.

Also, since nothing takes so much time in a baseball game as changing the pitcher, the games zipped along: 10 minutes shorter on the average. The fans, reported George Sisler, the league president, "overwhelmingly liked it" when polled.

One player named Jim Campbell spent the summer batting in the No. 9 spot in the lineup for Rochester, hit .295, drew admiring glances from the St. Louis Cardinals (who were looking for a pinch hitter) and made the big leagues as a specialist.

Choo-Choo Coleman, the little sign painter who had kept Casey Stengel in chuckles on the chuckling Mets a decade earlier, came out of retirement for the occasion. Laying aside his paintbrushes in Florida, he revived his baseball career as the lead-off batter for the Tidewater Mets—since his contributions as a catcher had always been suspect, anyway—and had such a heady time that he charged the team only for his busfare from Orlando to Norfolk.

Hal King, a catcher for Louisville, couldn't run or throw particularly—which was like having a quarterback who couldn't pass particularly. But as the designated hitter, he batted .330 while Bob Montgomery handled the catching chores. And *both* then made the big leagues.

Everything worked so well, in fact, that Tidewater sent only three pitchers to bat all season. As luck would have it, two got hits.

Now it's 1973, and the mail is pouring in to the American League. Suppose, people wanted to know, the Minnesota club has a weak-hitting shortstop. Can Harmon Killebrew be designated to bat for him? No, the experimenters answered patiently, he can swing only for the pitcher.

Does that mean the "dh" must always bat ninth in the lineup, where the pitcher usually bats? Not necessarily. Pitchers bat ninth most of the time because they're usually the weakest hitters on the team. But theoretically, they may swing anywhere in the lineup—and so may their "designated hitters."

Q. Suppose the manager wants somebody else to bat for the designated hitter later in the game; is that possible? *A.* Yes, but then that man becomes the official "dh" in the batting order and the original hitter is out of the game.

Q. Suppose Al Kaline is the designated hitter and, later in the game, manager Billy Martin wants to use him in right field on defense. Legal or not? *A.* It's legal, but then Kaline becomes the right fielder and Detroit plays the rest of the game without a designated hitter.

Q. Does this mean that in every American League game for the next three years, there will be 10 men in the lineup instead of nine? *A.* No, the manager may elect to use the designated hitter on any given day or he may not. He has three choices: Start the game without a designated hitter and go the distance without one. Start with one and stick with him (or his successors). Or, start with one, and then switch him to defense later in the game and revert to the old-fashioned rules.

A fine mixed bag of mail it was, too. The Governor of Pennsylvania, Milton Shapp, advised the commissioner that the game needed some punch. An American college student in Nairobi, Kenya, penned a 32-page handwritten letter reviewing the situation in the big leagues and suggesting changes. From a mission church at Fort Defiance, Arizona, a priest put it in scenario form: "Suppose one team starts a left-handed pitcher and the designated hitter. Later in the game, the lefty is replaced by a right-handed pitcher. Can the right-handed designated hitter be replaced by a lefty?" He enclosed two answer boxes to be checked off: one marked "yes," the other "no." And a stamped self-addressed envelope.

Joe Garagiola, who did not hit in the big leagues, said it was an innovation and he was looking forward to it. Tony Kubek, who did hit in the big leagues, believed you'd get more runs for your money but felt the rule would "take something out of the game, too." Billy Martin said he hadn't been in favor of it especially, but noted that his pitching staff had the worst collection of hitters in the league—they batted under .100 and struck out 50 percent of the time. Joe DiMaggio liked it, but doubted that the experiment would have prolonged his own career 20 years earlier. Mickey Mantle scoffed at himself as a "dh" and said: "If I could still hit, I'd still be playing."

The Boston Red Sox tried to sneak a 10th man (Orlando Cepeda) into the lineup in an exhibition game one day against the Philadelphia Phillies (wrong league) and, when the umpires blew the whistle, manager Eddie Kasko raged: "We've got a stupid rule that nobody wants to make a ruling on." Cepeda, forced to pinch hit once under the old rules, grounded out and the Phillies won. Two weeks later, in an unscheduled game against the Detroit Tigers, he hit an unscheduled home run and the Red Sox won.

Anyway, everybody was talking about it—even yelling about it—and that was probably the idea in the first place. The point was that the 10th man was here in the nine-man sport. Not even the lonely end or the pulling guard rated such commotion, and strong men began to wonder what might have happened in the old days if . . . well, if the 10th man had been around then.

"It's a shame the designated hitter wasn't in when I was playing," lamented Ralph Houk, manager of the Yankees, who got 43 hits during eight seasons on the back benches of baseball. "Then somebody else would've done more designated hitting and I would've done more catching."

The beau ideal, people guessed, would have been Smoky Burgess, who set records for pinch hitting with the Chicago White Sox. In his last couple of years, he didn't even own a catcher's mitt, though that had been his trade, and as soon as he pinch hit some days, he would skip the park and leave things to the nonspecialist troops.

Or it might have been Johnny Mize, who did nothing but pinch hit for the Yankees at the end of his career. Or Zeke Bonura, who did strange things at first base but not at home plate. Or Ernie Lombardi, the hulking catcher who never got an infield hit but who got plenty of outfield hits. Or Hack Wilson, who knocked in 190 runs one year. Or it might have been Jerry Lynch, who had all the qualifications: no glove but a home-run bat. He was a menace to his own team in the field and a menace to the other team in the hitter's box.

In the dim days before the designated hitter crept into the box scores of America, the Pittsburgh Pirates stationed Jerry Lynch in left field one day—just after his manager, Fred Haney, had received a pregame plaque from the National Safety Council. Then the game started, fly balls began to cascade into left field. Lynch misjudged three in a row, people sitting in the bleachers scurried for cover, and Haney finally pulled him out of the game, explaining: "I was afraid they'd take the plaque away from me if I left him in there."

But not anymore. Wherever you may be, Jerry Lynch, come back—all is forgiven in this enlightened day of electronic computers, microphotography, lunar modules, sophisticated missiles, laser beams, floating dollars, and the tenth man in the nine-man batting order.

WHAT IT'S LIKE IN THE BUSHES

By Dave Hirshey

From the New York Daily News

The bus roars down the Connecticut Turnpike, its passengers oblivious to the rolling countryside that flashes by. Some sleep, some play cards, some devour the sports sections of the local newspaper. All dream.

It is a four-hour ride from West Haven, Connecticut, to Reading, Pennsylvania, where the West Haven Yankees, the AA farm club of the New York Yankees, are to play four games that weekend. Yet only twice during the trip does any of the passing scenery evoke a response.

The first instance is when Danny, the bus driver, pulls up alongside a convertible with a leggy blonde and bellows into a microphone: "On your left, fellas." The whistling and raucous laughter start almost immediately, all but drowning out the mellow tones of Loretta Lynn belting from a tape deck . . . "I beg your pardon but I never promised you a rose garden."

After about 10 minutes, the cackling subsides and the players return to their card games. It is not until the bus rumbles through the Bronx that they are heard from again. "Across the water on the left, fellas, is Yankee Stadium," Danny announces. "You can't see it but it's there. Ain't that right, Doc?"

Doc Edwards, the West Haven manager, nods. He is a plain-spoken, affable thirty-six-year-old dude from Red Jacket, West Virginia, who wears white patent-leather boots and has reddish brown hair swept back in a modified pompadour that makes him look something like a middle-aged Fabian. For 19 years, he had been an itinerant catcher, playing for five different major league teams. One of his stops was Yankee Stadium in 1965. "You take that exit on your right for the Stadium," Edwards drawls. "It's about a mile and a half away."

A mile and a half. For most of the 22 West Haven players on the bus, that is as close as they have ever been to Yankee Stadium. For most of the West Haven players, that is as close as they will ever get to Yankee Stadium. Except in their dreams.

West Haven plays in the Eastern League, AA ball, two levels removed from the big time. When a player has an outstanding year at West Haven, he is usually promoted to Syracuse, the Yankees' AA farm team, or, in rare cases, to the parent club itself. In the past two years, three West Haven alumni have made the jump from the bushes to the majors—George Medich and Dave Pagan, both pitchers with the Yankees, and Charlie Spikes, an outfielder recently traded to Cleveland. They are what it is all about.

"The boys look at Davey [Pagan] pitching against Cleveland before 35,000 people and remember only four weeks ago he was pitching against Three Rivers before 400 people," says Edwards, "and they know there is a chance for them, too."

It is that chance, however slim, that keeps them going through bus rides, greasy meals, cramped motel rooms, and stadiums unpacked with 400 fans. "I want to make the big leagues so bad," says Alfie Rondon, a twenty-one-year-old reserve outfielder from Santo Domingo, "I do anything to get there." Rondon earns $600 a month playing for West Haven. To play professional baseball, you have to pay the price, as they say. As Rondon says, "The price doesn't pay the rent." And the bus keeps bumping along. . . .

"Welcome to Reading, Pa., the Pretzel Capitol of the World," the sign reads as the bus enters the town of many pretzels, much industry, and little else. The motel the players are staying at is on the outskirts of town, in West Reading, which is the drugstore next to East Reading. The bus pulls in at 1:30 P.M. and the players struggle off, stretching their legs and rolling their necks. Don Schroeder, a pitcher with a humming fast ball and a ready wit, remarks to a visitor: "If you like this trip, you'd love our 11-hour roadie to Quebec City."

The motel is shaped like the point of an arrow, a curious combination of Pennsylvania Dutch and highway modern. The rooms are clean and, of paramount importance, air-conditioned. The players generally seemed pleased with the accommodations save for one small detail. The rooms have two beds and three players assigned to each of them. Which means that the guy who cuts the lowest card gets the rollaway bed, his roommates' sympathy, and a sore back.

The players scatter to their respective rooms in their casual dress —blue jeans, ban-lon shirts (hence the name Ban-Lon League), sport shirts with the tails out, sneakers, high-heeled boots. Not exactly the kind of attire you'd expect to find, say, on Ron Blomberg or Bobby Murcer, but then Ron Blomberg or Bobby Murcer don't eat at roadside diners. I mean, do you get dressed up to go to McDonalds?

The diner is down the road apiece from the motel. "A typical place," says Billy Stearns, West Haven's gutty catcher. "Greaseburgers and greasefries doused in ketchup and what's this here sauce to kill the taste."

At West Haven, the players are allotted $6 meal money a day for overnight roadtrips and $3 for commuter trips, major leaguers get $19 a day, but their appetites are no bigger. Needless to say, it limits one's choice of restaurants. The waitress, a graying veteran of 20 years, shuffles over and delivers her customary monologue about the diner's specialties. Herm Schneider, the jovial, roly-poly trainer-traveling secretary, orders the turkey dish and then grimaces when it arrives, swimming in a sea of yellow gravy. "You have to wait for five minutes for it to gell, Herm," suggests pitcher Joe Blake.

Game time that night against the Reading Phillies being 7:15, the players have four hours to kill. Most go back to their rooms to sack or watch TV. The Yankees are on the tube against the Twins and in the bullpen is a familiar figure to the West Haven players. "Get a load of Pags in those doubleknits," Schroeder yells out loud. "That lucky *bleep*." Then a quick call and back into the bus. . . .

Reading Municipal Stadium is considered the best facility of its kind in the Eastern League, an impressive red-brick oval that rises high above a grassy knoll with eight light stanchions spreading bright light on a finely manicured outfield. "It's one of the few parks in the league where an outfielder can see the ball before it hits him," says Schroeder. "In most places you find better light in a hall closet."

You may also find better uniforms there. "Look at these things," says Stearns, sewing up a rip on the seat of his uniform. "I think they're hand-me-downs from Abner Doubleday."

When the Yankees finally decided to join the mod generation and switch to doubleknits, they resisted the temptation to give the old flannel uniforms to the Salvation Army and, instead, farmed them out to West Haven. This is not to say, however, that they sent West Haven the newer old uniforms. In fact, one player recently discovered the name of Bob Turley stitched in his pants. Turley pitched for the Yankees in the mid-fifties.

It is now 15 minutes before game time. A stadium cop spots two young boys, their faces streaked with dirt, sitting high up in the stands. He grins. "You boys crawl under the fence again?" he calls out. "I'll catch you one of these days."

"And then what would you do?" someone asks. "Oh, ask them to wait until I wasn't looking." He is told that at Yankee Stadium, the boys would probably be evicted from the premises. "Yeah, I know," he says. "They take things too seriously up there."

Refreshingly, in the bushes, sneaking into the park is as an accepted ritual as hob-nobbing with the players at the hotdog stands or giving away free dinners to the fan with the lucky number. Or as was the case at Reading, a free car. The prospects of winning the 1973 Dodge drew 2,500 to the park on a muggy Saturday night, some 1,800 over the average crowd. They sat through a 28-hit slugfest won by Reading, 11–7, abuzz with excitement over the impending drawing. Hundreds of tickets had been tossed into a box and now the time had come for manager Cal Emery to draw the lucky number.

The announcer approached the microphone with the ticket, looked at it, looked at it again, and then giggled nervously. "You wouldn't believe this, folks, but the winner is none other than Ken Tuckey, our local baseball writer."

He was right. The fans didn't believe it. They booed and threw pretzels.

THE SMELL OF THE BALL

By Ira Berkow

From Popular Sports Magazine

Big-league baseball is subtle; cloaked in summer languor, moving with the slow, supple grace of a ballerina practicing backstage, yet taut and technical in its skills. To view a baseball game and appreciate it takes concentration.

The setting is dramatic. This is especially so in the evening. Bright lights cut through the dew and illuminate the infield and outfield. Deep, brown dirt circles the bases and trims the outfield edge, in sharp contrast to the green. Slim, simple white foul lines slide along until they crawl up and over the outfield wall.

White-and-gray-flanneled figures dart and dive, swoop and slide, loop and leap; and sometimes they just stand, gloved hand on hip, dreamily watching the spike marks in the dirt as though waiting for them to crawl away.

There is much to see in a baseball game if one is not overly preoccupied with chasing down vendors or foul balls. The superior thing about baseball watching is that the maneuverings on the field are so easy to see (so easy to carry around in memory, too), as opposed to observing the baroque entanglements in football and the surrealistic postures in basketball.

Bowie Kuhn, commissioner of baseball, has said that he likes to take his wife and daughters to a game and point out how outfielders watch the way the wind is affecting the flags in center field, consider the power and precedence of the batter, take into account their own speed afoot and strength of arm, then step some steps this way or that. Computations worked out, they then wait.

There is no greater drama than the confrontation of pitcher and batter, this small white sphere being hurled at great speeds to a man who must have reflexes honed to decide in the split of a second whether to swing and, of primary interest, when to jackknife to keep his health.

A difficult aspect to cage in concentration is the strategy of the pitcher: a high inside fast ball, a low outside curve, another fast ball up, a slow breaking pitch that will twist a batter into a pretzel.

Reggie Jackson, slugger, said he revels in watching Joe DiMaggio in Old-Timers' games still able to stroke those "frozen ropes": line drives that come screaming off the bat and which can knock an infielder into the outfield.

And the catcher clanking like a fat knight after a foul pop; an outfielder smoothly moving at the crack of the bat, back, back to the wall, as the ball visits among the stars, then descends apace and culminates in a leather plop; and a runner tipping the edge of the first-base bag and barreling into second with a neat hook slide that stirs just a tuft of dust.

Of course, the double play with a pirouette by the second baseman, a split by the first baseman and, by the straining runner to first, an arabesque.

And the excellence of the athlete, who has spent uncountable hours getting the snap in his swing, tracking down a ball that has just fallen out of the sun, developing his throw to display before the deep-throated, insatiable world of the stadium.

"I have tremendous respect," essayist E. B. White has said, "for anyone who does something extremely well, no matter what." It is thrilling to see excellence, whether it be Brooks Robinson or Rembrandt or a plumber.

Baseball retains its appeal because it is not frenetically and self-consciously modern. Baseball is a link for the country in a way that no other sport is. Baseball was here with stiff collars and bustles, before the motor car, after man's landing on the moon. No other spectator sport in America has meant so much to so many for so long.

Though baseball officials have tried to "modernize" the sport—with artificial turf and artificial cleats—the game is still timeless. In fact, it is played without a clock. Unlike football and basketball, there is no timepiece in baseball ticking silently, hands pacing in relentless monotony, ending where it finished and informing the fans not to forget that they were in some vague rush.

Baseball has been in disrepute in some circles as a remnant of the past for its so-called slow pace. Yet former Senator Eugene McCarthy, who played first base long ago in Minnesota's semipro Sioux League, predicted that baseball will revive in popularity now that the Vietnam War has come to a close for us. The country, he said, is dog-tired of violence. Baseball, in contrast to football, represents sanity in a world gone haywire.

Strange how tight a grip baseball has on one's gentle boyhood. For a large slice of the male population in America, baseball is a very big deal in early years, is eclipsed in young manhood by other concerns such as young ladies and acne, and then slowly seeps back into interest as one grows toward senility.

One spring morning in 1971, when I was thirty-one, I stood behind the batting cage at Wrigley Field in my official capacity as sportswriter. I was faking it, for really I was eleven years old and I knew that at any minute an usher would escort me out of there by the scruff of the collar.

A ball rolled under the cage and I picked it up. It was still white but discolored by a bruise of brown and a stain of green. The red stitching stood out. For some unaccountable reason I smelled it. Pungent to the core. There is a distinct, unforgettable muskiness to the tanned horsehide of a baseball. Smell being one of the greatest memory devices, it was so easy to be transported several yards and 20 years away to the moment I got my first big-league baseball.

The day before, my friends and I had fought in the autograph jungle under the cool stands as the Cubs of those days, Andy Pafko, Roy Smalley, Hal Jeffcoat, and Hank Sauer, emerged like gods from the clubhouse after the game, big and leathery-tanned and hair-slicked.

Roy Johnson, whom everyone called "Hardrock," came out. He was a tough-looking coach, but pigeon-toed, which gave away the humor under his gruff veneer. He was in a hurry, he said, and had no time to sign. I continued in hot pursuit. No, no, he persisted. In desperation he said, "Come to the park tomorrow, kid, and I'll give you a ball," slamming his car door a millimeter from my finger.

I believed him. My friends were much too sophisticated. He was just givin' you the slip, dope. It was not all that easy to fall asleep that night.

Armed with my lunch—with the usual soft fruit my mother packed carving a soggy hole in the bottom of the brown bag—I was off to

Wrigley Field with my friends. They poked little jokes, even up to the time I left them in the grandstands. I ran down through the shadowy stands as the park began to fill, past vendors hawking peanuts, past the steamy hotdogs on portable grills.

I had come down to the short, red-brick wall along the first-base line. Straight out was No. 42, Hardrock Johnson, cracking fungoes into the bright sky. I watched a ball drop through the clouds, down past the Baby Ruth billboard on the building across the street, get lost momentarily in the scattering of white shirts in the sunny bleachers, and finally disappear silently into the outstretched glove of a fielder against the ivy-covered wall.

"Mr. Hardrock, sir," I called through cupped hands. No answer. I called again. "You promised me a ball yesterday, Mr. Hardrock, sir." Nothing, but the crack of his bat. "Just a dirty old ball, Mr. Hardrock." The few adults seated nearby tittered.

I'm not certain how long I kept this up, several minutes, surely. Soon, there was that predictable yank at the collar. I was explaining the situation to the grim usher when there came this great, throaty rumble, "Hey kid!" Hardrock Johnson tossed me a ball in a long, underhand toss. Up the stairs I flew.

They all wanted to see the ball, and I showed it to my friends. One by one—with me holding it. The ball created an uncomfortable but wholly welcome bulge in the right front pocket of my jeans. Home, I fondled the hard ball with the upraised stitching. I inspected the dirt and grass smudges closely, the Spalding trademark in a small baseball, the stars alongside "Official Ball, National League." The signature of Ford C. Frick, then League president. I smelled that tanned-horschide smell that has not changed in 20 years, that has not changed in 100 years.

Many suggestions were offered to get the ball as clean as new. The one that sold me was to put it in milk. I immersed the ball in a large bowl of milk for two days, periodically coming by and rolling it around with my finger to make sure no patch was left unmilked.

When I finally removed it, the ball had turned a sick yellow. I mounted the ball on a shelf in my room, for a while. But somehow it got out into the streets. Soon, one end was unstitched and became a flappy tongue and, shortly, the ball was reduced to a sphere of string.

At the batting cage now, I felt the red ridges against the smooth, off-white horsehide. I slowly tossed the ball in the air a couple of times. I smelled it. Then I casually squeezed the ball into my suit-pants' pocket.

As a sports columnist syndicated in 700 newspapers, I have had a chance to indulge my childhood fantasies. I have sat and talked with the heroes of my youth, such as Joe DiMaggio, Ted Williams, Casey Stengel. As a man, you see them now as men—warts and all, their ill-humors, their petty conceits (Williams wears a warm-up jacket on the hottest days to conceal his bay window)—yet they remain special in a romantic and probably foolish way.

But, as Roy Campanella has said, "To be good, you've gotta have a lot of little boy in you. When you see Willie Mays and Ted Williams jumping and hopping around the bases after hitting a home run, and kissing and hugging that goes on at home plate, you realize they have to be little boys."

I believed that to be true, and not just for athletes. Picasso is a prankster, Hemingway was a ham. Perhaps the most honest artists, in any field, see things with the fresh enthusiasm of their youth.

I once asked Tom Seaver, Mets' pitcher, about Campanella's remark. "I think the good professional athlete must have the *love* of a little boy. And the good players feel the kind of love for the game that they did when they were Little Leaguers." Seaver said he never tires of the game. "Baseball is so challenging and complex that the more you learn the more there is to learn.

"But what in life isn't a game? Look, when a bank president puts over a big deal, isn't that a game of sorts? He doesn't jump up and down like a ball player who has hit a homer, but that's only because of the difference of environments. If he were wearing a jock strap and sweat pants, he'd be clapping his hands and hopping on his desk, too."

Being a sports columnist has permitted me entree into ball parks in a way I had been totally unaccustomed to as a kid. In the past, I would scale a fence, jump over a turnstile, or fade angelically into a church group getting off a bus. Or, when workers' eyes were elsewhere, slide down the ice chute that stuck out like a long tongue from a beer truck through a ground-floor window of Wrigley Field. It was a chilling experience if you slid down on your fanny instead of on your heels.

And once my job permitted me to bat against a big-league pitcher. I went down to Lakeland, Florida, in June of 1970, to do a story on

Denny McLain. McLain had been suspended from baseball for the first half of the season, and was now preparing to return in July.

Every evening around suppertime, with the warm sun down, but still a couple hours left before nightfall, McLain pitched a nine-inning "Piggy Moveup" game to a ragtag of local high school and college players. His catcher was Jim Handley, the local high school baseball coach who had caught in the New York Met and Detroit Tiger farm systems.

The seven fielding positions were taken by the kids; Handley was permanently behind the plate. McLain stayed on the mound, throwing about three-quarters speed as the rotation continued.

That afternoon, when I had learned of the games, I asked McLain if I might play. "Why not?" he said with a shrug.

I confess I was rather excited about the prospect because I hadn't faced a big-league pitcher in some 20 years. It had been something like the 1951 World Series, Yankees versus Giants, played against the wall of the Bryant Elementary School on the West Side of Chicago. Jerry was Vic Raschi, and Allie Reynolds, too. And I, crouched with a bat and the rectangle of strike zone chalked on the dark wall behind me, waiting for Raschi to serve up that pink Spalding rubber ball, I was Willie Mays.

So now I stood, batting helmet and gym shoes and soft knees, facing the real McLain. As McLain, in Bermuda shorts, stooped in that classic pose, gloved hand on left knee to get the sign, I waggled my bat. Mostly for effect, for I was nervous. I gripped the bat tightly. McLain appears chunky, from 60 feet six inches away, but becomes formidable as he kicks and whirls and comes around in that graceful, smooth, grooved delivery and the ball popped into Handley's mitt. Strike one.

A breaking ball broke low and outside. I tried to watch the ball all the way, as I had read to do years before in *The Way to Better Baseball,* by Tommy Henrich, the "Old Reliable" of the Yanks. But how magnificently McLain hid the ball. You never saw the white of it until it was traveling plateward.

I fouled off a ball to the right that bounced down and almost into the hazy lake, fringed by mossy pine trees. The count went to 3–2 and then, staring and frozen, I struck out on an outside fast ball. I trotted head down to right field.

Next time up, on the second pitch, I hit it up the middle, past McLain's right, and I ran like hell. I knew I shouldn't watch where the ball was going, but I had to. The shortstop charged over but threw late. I had beaten out a hit!

The inning ended with me stranded on first. But I had another turn at bat. I was up second in the inning. And I was concerned. McLain's pride might be hurt. He told me once that he wants to win at everything, that he'd even whip his mother at Monopoly. (Later, he said with a smile when I bragged a bit, "That *hit?* It took 13 bounces.") His competitive fires burn bright.

At bat again in the darkening evening, the fielders seemed far away, while McLain loomed close. His tanned face and arms were dark with sweat, and so was his gray T-shirt with "Detroit Tigers" lettered across the chest.

Quickly, the count came to 2–2. A high, medium fast ball pushed me back. "Oh gee," said McLain, with feigned anxiety, "I wouldn't want to hit *him.*" Meaning a sports writer. Handley echoed a laugh from behind his mask. I swallowed. (At the time, I was only faintly aware that I had just experienced an authentic brushback pitch.)

3–2 count. McLain wound up and—my God!—he was coming in *sidearm.* "Where are you going?" asked Handley, as I strode into the bucket.

The ball came in and, as I swung awkwardly, creakingly, the ball kept coming in. A change-up! By the time it had reached the plate, I had crumpled to one knee.

McLain's smiling white teeth looked very bright against the dark of his face. Yes, I had struck out ignobly, but as I trotted out to right field in the warm haze of the Florida evening, I was absorbed in the already fading details of my hit. I was batting .333 against Denny McLain. I still am, and will be, forever.

There is, however, no evidence of my feat in Baseball's Hall of Fame, in Cooperstown, New York. I suspect there never will be. Though not long ago I drove the five hours to Cooperstown from New York City. I went up there because, well, because I hadn't been there since I was twelve years old.

The town itself is a harmless little hoax. Streets are broad and lined with shading elms and horse-chestnut trees and the homes are tidy and there is a most pure, placid lake. There are no Vietnams here. No race wars. Hardly even inflation. It is still the nineteenth century here and one fully expects that, to get out of town, you still go eight miles by steamboat across Lake Otsego and then seven miles to Richfield Springs by tally-ho.

To sports fans, the town is best known for the Hall of Fame and Museum, and, until recently, was generally accepted as "the birthplace of baseball," as it says on local oompah signs.

But the claim has been dispelled, even by Hall director Ken Smith, who said that "They made a mountain out of a molehill." Baseball, tradition has it, was supposed to have been invented in Cooperstown by Abner Doubleday in 1839. Actually, no one knows baseball's origin. Some historians have marked the beginnings in Pharaoh's Egypt. But even in the museum there is a painting of youngsters playing "rounders" in 1802.

Yet Doubleday, a Civil War general from Cooperstown, has his army footlocker laid to posterity in the museum alongside Lou Gehrig's historical vertical locker. A reluctance to disavow the past, no matter how patently apocryphal, is integral to baseball love and lore.

A letter I received about my column on the Hall-of-Fame visit brought this home to me. I wrote that baseball, though a dream world, has been corrupted by big business and bigotry. The arrogance of owners—which has resulted in players often being treated like serfs, and the economic fear of owners which resulted in the despicable delay in breaking the color line for players and still holds for blacks on a managerial level—has helped rend fans' interest to a degree. As a youth, one rarely sees this side or cares. And as a youth, one only sees heroes through the glow of the halo. Then I wrote: "The Hall of Fame with its revered plaques is set in an impressively austere, columned corridor, and how the great men of the game have changed for the man who was last here as a boy. You know now that Grover Cleveland Alexander was an alcoholic, that Babe Ruth's famous 'bellyache' was actually a case of social disease, that Cap Anson was a racist. Yet you are touched by the old favorites, by the memories of the effortless DiMaggio, the electric Williams, the daring Jackie Robinson. . . ."

The letter was from an army sergeant in Wichita Falls:

"You might take a look into your own past prior to slandering a giant like The Babe. I won't mention the things you failed to mention in your article, for these things would mean nothing to an individual who never participated in so much as a marble shooters game. . . . If you want some constructive advice as a sports writer—you stink. And you might try something more in line with Ann

Landers' column. The *girls* would love it. With a name like Ira it's questionable to which gender you belong."

This cut me to the quick. My manhood was impugned. Not only had I shot marbles in my time, but just a month before that letter I had belted a base hit off Denny McLain, a 30-game winner.

Like the sergeant, I am both male and a longtime baseball lover. And like those enshrined in the Hall of Fame, I have wanted to play baseball well, and have admired those who look good in the field. In this regard, I will always respect a Willie Mays, a Tom Seaver, a (yes) Babe Ruth, and a certain outfielder who played on a high school team against my team. I don't remember his name, but I will never forget him. A long high fly was hit his way. He wheeled back for it, ran, and his cap flew off. He halted in his tracks, picked up the cap, put it back on his head and, dapper again, resumed the chase for the ball that he would not catch.

SUPER HERO

By Wells Twombly

From the San Francisco Examiner

In nature, there are certain movements so swift and so graceful that no mortal can adequately describe what has taken place. In the upper branches of a fir tree, a squirrel goes bounding from level to level, his eyes focused on the horizon, his heart pounding gently with the vibrations of the earth itself. Beyond a copse of birches, a doe stirs. Somewhere inside her she knows that a hunter is waiting, hip-deep in the snow. Swiftly, she turns and goes leaping through the drifts.

No man living is skillful enough to describe exactly how Roberto Clemente moved through the meadows of our land for 18 summers. His was a special style and grace. It was a smooth motion, fluid and compact. Most of the people who bought tickets to watch him play right field for the Pittsburgh Pirates never seemed to appreciate what he could do. They accepted it. But they never appreciated it. Pay $3.50 and see Roberto do the impossible. He was brilliant, to use a phrase that doesn't really do justice to his memory.

No athlete of Clemente's quality has been taken for granted quite so shamelessly. The customers applauded him like human beings who had seen too much television. Magic was dead. The super-sensational was too ordinary. Perfection was their birthright. They paid their money and they sat there as baseballs went sailing off toward a glove that never made a mistake. It was far too easy, far too sweet. Roberto just couldn't make the game of baseball look hard enough.

Hit the ball to right at Pittsburgh and forget it. Try to run to second on that slim figure in the outfield and you could count on the ball being there ahead of you. It was so lovely, so automatic that God Himself must have designed the play. Offensively, Clemente was one of the best of his generation. He rated right there with Mickey Mantle, Stan Musial, Willie Mays, Henry Aaron, etc. He was a walking immortal. He ran. He threw. He hit.

Trouble was that Roberto Clemente could never communicate his true self. It was his opinion that newspapermen had a stringent pecking order. They regarded baseball players in the following way: On top were the American whites, followed rapidly by the American blacks. Next were the Latin whites. Way down at the bottom were the Latin blacks. They were nobody's children.

"I feel that I would be considered to be a much better athlete if I were not a black Latin," he told a newspaperman one sorrowful evening in Pittsburgh two years ago when the Pirates were winning the World Series.

"I play as good as anybody. Maybe I play as good as anybody who plays the game. But I am not loved. I don't need to be loved. I just wish that it would happen. There are many people like me who would like that to happen. I wish it for them. Do you know what I mean?"

Trouble was that few people truly understood what he was talking about. Even his colleagues on the Pittsburgh Pirates admitted that they weren't just sure how to take him. They didn't know if he was a self-serving egotist or a humanitarian who honestly loved his neighbors. Always Roberto Clemente seemed to be tiptoeing along a chalk line.

"This was the most decent man I've ever known," said pitcher Steve Blass. "And nobody ever seemed to understand him. Maybe there was a language barrier, I don't know. He was absolutely selfless. He'd talk about his physical problems and writers would make jokes. What he was trying to say was that Latins and blacks play hurt just like everybody else. They didn't get that. They said he was a hypochondriac."

When the Pirates got into the World Series, Clemente got a dozen hits. He was splendid beyond belief. After each game he would talk seriously to writers. Certainly he wanted credit for himself. Why? Not for personal glory, but because he wanted a forum for his beliefs. He had this wild notion about a sports city in his native Puerto Rico where indigent children could live. They could grow to manhood with the high ideals of competitive athletes to guide them. Their whole lives would be changed by the opportunity to play games, to get a decent meal, to wear clean clothes.

"This is my dream," he said. "I do not know exactly what this sports city will be like, but it will be beautiful. It will be open to everybody. No matter what they are. After I open the first one in Puerto Rico I will open others. I will do this thing because that is what God meant me to do. Baseball is just something that will give me a chance to do this."

And Roberto Clemente believed he had this mission to perform for mankind. When the Governor of Puerto Rico asked him to head the island's relief fund for the Managua earthquake victims, he threw himself into the project with a passion.

Here was one of the finest baseball players who ever lived and he went from door to door in the richer sections of San Juan, asking for donations. He raised $150,000 in cash and thousands extra in material goods. Roberto filled up the Santurce ball park with clothing and food. Clemente said he would personally take them to Nicaragua. He meant it.

The time came to transport those items. The airplane rose slowly from the runway, headed out to sea, made a desperate turn, and fell into the water. Thus died a humanitarian. Thus died a real man. Thus died a very fine baseball player. Not necessarily in that order.

THE DRIVE ON THE RECORD

By Al Cartwright

From the Wilmington News-Journal

"What do I remember about pitching to Aaron? I shoulda walked him, 400 times. I'da been better off."

I am a Henry Aaron man, as I was a Robin Roberts man. So I called the Phillies' old meal ticket to talk with him about Aaron's drive on The Record. It is the only pleasant topic in the land this depressing summer of infamy and inflation.

Bless you, Hank Aaron. You, too, Babe Ruth.

I had a frightening thought while I was dialing: Gad, it was 25 years ago this season that a collegian named Roberts came to Wilmington to pitch his first professional game. It can't be that long. Now there he is in the Philadelphia suburbs, retired long enough from the ball field to be eligible for the Hall of Fame; a broker of stock, and with a son freshly graduated from Delaware.

He made with the gruff, defensive greeting that is the Roberts trademark, and, also typically, warmed to the topic.

"How many of those 700 did I throw to Henry—seven, eight?" he asked. The answer was nine. "I remember four that really hurt me. The others didn't matter—I was either winning by six or losing by six."

Roberts reached back through the years and the pitches in meticulous detail. It was like he was telling the names of his children.

"The one that really sticks with me," he said, "was the day Spahn was going for his 200th win with the Braves. A doubleheader, in Philly. Bobby Thomson threw one of our guys out at the plate in the ninth inning of each game.

"I would have beat Spahn the second game, but Thomson nails

Ashburn at the plate in the ninth—Del Ennis hit the ball—and we go into extra innings.

"In the top of the 11th, Henry hit a line drive over the top of my head. I had no idea it was a home run—it wasn't that far above me. But I look around and it's still going and it is a 400-foot shot into the stands in center field. Henry never was known as a tape-measure hitter, but this must have been one of his longest.

"Anyhow, that puts them ahead 3–2. Kazanski hits one out in our half to tie it. By this time, I'm gone. They score in the 12th off Bob Miller, and Spahn has his 200th and I have my greatest memory of Hank Aaron."

Thus, I offered, it is no surprise to Roberts that Aaron is about to become the new Babe Ruth, accumulatively speaking.

"Now it isn't," he said. "But in his early years, I looked on him as the next .400 hitter, not as a home-run guy. He was a Musial-type hitter, but he was capable of doing anything he wanted on offense. Somewhere in his career, he made the decision to go for the home run and you have to say it was the right decision, as far as the record is concerned. Now I'll only be surprised if he doesn't hit 800."

I mentioned that the pitcher Aaron stroked the most for home runs was Don Drysdale. Aaron hit 17 off the tall, strong, mean, side-arming right-hander of the Dodgers. Drysdale was a villain of a pitcher, with a matching fast ball.

Roberts whistled. "I didn't know that. And to me, nothing explains any better what kind of a hitter Aaron is. That Drysdale, he'd go inside a lot and there are right-hand hitters who never hit nothin' off Drysdale, let alone 17 homers. Wes Covington, when he was with the Phillies, used to tell stories how Drysdale would knock Aaron right on his bucket and Henry would get up and hit the next pitch nine miles.

"I have nothing but admiration for Henry Aaron, and I'm pulling for him to make the record, and then some." The old ace laughed. "As long as he's not hitting any more off me, I don't mind at all."

I talked with Johnny Ogden, the retired scout. He worked for the Braves when they were in Milwaukee, Aaron years. Before that when he was pitching for the St. Louis Browns, Ogden had the honor of serving up one of Babe Ruth's 714 big ones. I thought he'd be an old-timer who would attempt to dilute the performance of the modern guy, but he wasn't.

"Hell, no, I'm not disturbed somebody is taking the record away from Ruth," he bellowed into the phone from Oxford, Pennsylvania. "It's like arguing whether a 1776 soldier is better than a World War I soldier. If Aaron can do it, he earns it. And it might be a little tougher on him because he is seeing more pitchers from the same side, the right-handers, than the Babe saw left-handers. Simply because there are more right-hand pitchers.

"The Babe wouldn't care about somebody passing him. There wasn't a jealous bone in his body. I can't see why any of the old-timers should resent it. This life wasn't meant to be like that."

Yes, John, but it is. Henry Aaron gets mail that says it is.

Judy Johnson of Marshallton, who is a man, remembers a young Henry Aaron so much it hurts. Judy scouts for the Phillies and was one of the great stars of the old Negro leagues. He played against the Babe in exhibition games.

"I tried to get the Philadelphia Athletics to take Aaron before anybody ever heard of him, and they wouldn't go for it," Johnson said. "Aaron came to Wilmington Park with the Indianapolis Clowns. Played against the Baltimore Elite Giants. He was the shortstop and he hit two balls high over the left-field fence and over Northeast Boulevard, too.

"I was doing a little work for the Athletics. That same night I called up a guy named Syd Pollock, who owned the Clowns. The barrier in the big leagues against colored players was down, but the A's had none. Pollock said he'd take $3,500 for Aaron. And you know what—Mr. Mack of the A's said it was too high. Imagine getting Aaron for $3,500. And the Braves didn't pay that much more for him."

Henry Aaron in North Philadelphia? If they had bought him, rescued him from the dusty, dim blur that was Negro baseball, the A's might still be in Philadelphia. But I have to believe the price was a cop-out, as stingy as the Mack family was. The color of the money wasn't as objectionable as the color of Aaron.

But that's history, the bad kind. Now this same Henry Aaron is making history.

The good kind.

Football

NIGHTMARE FOR THE LONGHORNS

By Blackie Sherrod

From The Dallas Times Herald

It was, you should excuse the expression, as one-sided as a barbecue.

Lightning bolts from beyond the Red River simply and starkly electrocuted the once-proud Texas Steers Saturday, searing the Longhorns beyond recognition in one half the time allotted. For the last portion of the game, it was a question of Oklahoma appetite for beef.

The total damage was 52–13 and by the time Steve Davis, Joe Washington, Tinker Owens, and their talented associates were through, superlatives dangled from the Cotton Bowl like weary streamers on New Year's morning.

Examples: It was the worst defeat ever strapped on a Darrell Royal team anytime, anyplace. It was the most points ever scored by the winner of this bitter interstate duel. It was the most points yielded by a Longhorn team since 1908. And so on.

"It was like a nightmare out there," said Texas quarterback Marty Akins.

The fury of the Oklahoma attack established the result so early that Texas fans began leaving the stadium in the third quarter. This probably also is a record. The northern half of the Cotton Bowl was almost bare in the fourth period, while the southern half was still crammed with red-coated and red-dressed fanatics cheering the third straight Oklahoma victory. The crowd of approximately 72,000 had recognized the fatal signs right after the second-half kickoff when Barry Switzer's swift youngsters swelled their advantage to 27–6.

And neither could the departing Texas supporters mutter wait till next year, for every one of the seven Sooner touchdowns was scored by a sophomore or freshman.

At least the backsliding Longhorn fans were spared the embarrassment of seeing Switzer flood the field with Oklahoma substitutes in the final period, who, incidentally scored with just as much effectiveness against a tired Texas team.

The first half was a weirdo. Texas monopolized the clock, keeping the ball almost 22 minutes of the 30. The Longhorns ran twice as many plays as the Sooners, 42 to 20. They rushed the ball with typical doggedness against the huge Oklahoma line. Yet their efforts could produce only two field goals, 36- and 44-yard boots by Billy Schott.

Meanwhile, Oklahoma reverted to the forward pass, a foreign weapon to the country's leading rushers, for three stunning long-distance touchdowns.

"Those three plays caught us totally asleep," said Royal.

The Sooners had thrown only 24 passes in their three previous games, completed just nine. Washington had never thrown a pass in his natural-born college life. Yet here was the whippet halfback taking a pitchout from Davis, faking a sweek, cocking and throwing 35 yards down field where Owens waited on the Texas 10-yard line, a furlong behind Longhorn safety Tommy Keel. It was a shocking 40-yards touchdown play on Oklahoma's first possession and led the Big Red partisans to a roaring that lasted the afternoon.

Schott's field goals pulled Texas to a 7–6 deficit before the next Sooner bolt struck.

This was a 63-yard heave from Davis to Owens, 33 yards in the air and 30 yards of gallop by Owens, outdistancing Keel and Jay Arnold. This score also seemed the responsibility of Keel, but halfback Terry Melancon had the primary responsibility of covering the tricky Owens.

Just before the half, Oklahoma struck again with the same sudden swiftness. This was a 46-yarder from Davis to the other wide receiver, Billy Brooks. The Oklahoma soph, a Navarro JC transfer, took the perfect pass on the Texas five, inches above the desperate dives of Keel and Arnold.

"If we could have put them [Texas players] in the defense we wanted 'em in, and if we call the pass we want them to call, that was it; yet they hit it," said Royal.

"We had a special scheme," Owens said afterward. "Their safety (Keel) keyed on our center for a pass or run. We noticed in films that he always came up fast when he thought it was a run. So we had the center fake the run."

Then, when Keel started toward the scrimmage, Owens slipped behind him. "It worked twice for touchdowns and one other time when they caught me," he said.

In the second half, Keel was replaced by a 138-pound freshman from Odessa, Joe Bob Bizzell. But by then the Sooners had had enough of that aerial foolishness. They just rammed the ball down the Longhorn gullet, aided and abetted by mounting Texas mistakes.

Oklahoma took the second-half kickoff and slammed the coffin shut. Mainly on Washington's darts, the Sooners marched 78 yards, with Davis's 15-yard spring accounting for the touchdown. The unfortunate Keel went back in the game for one play, and was promptly flattened by Washington's rolling block, clearing the path for Davis.

"We were lucky in the first half," said Switzer. "We had to take the opening kickoff of the second half and score. It was a challenge to our players. I think that drive was the turning point of the game."

From then on, the carnage went thusly:

A Clyde Powers interception of Akins' pass, a 30 return to the Texas 7. A touchdown plunge of two yards by Davis. 35–6.

An Akins fumble, recovered by Mike Struck on the Texas 7. A 25-yard field goal by Rick Fulcher. 38–6.

Another Powers' interception of a Mike Presley pass, a return of 32 yards to the Texas 10. Sub-quarterback Scott Hill almost scored on first play, fumbled as he reached the goal, and guard Jaime Melendez covered in the end zone for touchdown. 45–6.

With Oklahoma subs afield, Texas then drove 80 yards for its only touchdown late in the final quarter, Presley sweeping 31 yards for the score. 45–13.

On runs by reserve halfback Bob Berg and third-string quarterback Joe McReynolds, a freshman yet, Oklahoma moved 81 yards for its last touchdown. McReynolds scored on 11-yard run. 52–13.

Oklahoma did not outrush the Steers by a great margin, 283 yards to 209. Roosevelt Leaks got 82 of the Longhorn yards before leaving the game in the third quarter with a bruised back. But Oklahoma had a 225–79 edge in passing yardage. It was a most impressive all-around victory for the probationed Sooners, who should certainly improve their No. 6 national standing in next week's voting. The Longhorns will second the motion.

17 IN A ROW ON A SHOESTRING

By Jay Searcy

From The New York Times

There isn't a blade of grass on the Tennessee State practice field, and when it rains, practice is canceled because of the mud. When the weather is dry, the field has to be watered to keep down dust.

There are rarely enough helmets to go round at the beginning of fall workouts, the locker room is equipped with nothing beyond the bare essentials, and the athletes' dormitory is stark. This is home for the nation's No. 1-ranked college-division football team, which finished its season last Saturday undefeated and with the nation's longest winning streak—17 games.

"When a boy comes to Tennessee State," said Coach John Merritt by phone from Nashville, "we know he wants to play football because we don't have anything fancy here and we don't hide anything from him."

Tennessee State, or Tennessee Agricultural and Industrial State University, has lost only two games in four years, has a 28-game winning streak at home, has won three straight National Collegiate post-season games and has more graduates in the professional ranks than any other schools except Southern California and Notre Dame, according to Merritt.

"I know it's hard for people to believe this, but it's true," he said. "We have substandard facilities, to say the least; we purposely avoid the blue-chip athlete at recruiting time and we operate on a $4,000 recruiting budget."

Yet Merritt has won five national championships and 108 of his players have been drafted by the pros in his 21 years of college coaching, 10 at Jackson (Mississippi) State and 11 at Tennessee State.

Merritt expects eight of his nine seniors to be drafted by the pros, including Ed Jones, a 6-foot-9, 264-pound defensive tackle, who may be the No. 1 choice. Two Tennessee State graduates in the pros are sons of Merritt's assistant coaches—Joe Gilliam Jr., a backup quarterback for the Pittsburgh Steelers, and Alvin Coleman Jr., a defensive back for the Philadelphia Eagles.

Merritt shies from the most outstanding high school athletes because he says he can't compete financially with the big-money schools. And he dispels the theory that many top black athletes in the South attend Tennessee State because it is a black school.

"I've never heard a boy say he came here because of black pride or because it's a black school," Merritt said. "He comes here because he knows he'll be a winner. We guarantee it. And he knows he'll be scouted by the pros here."

Merritt and his staff spend most of their recruiting efforts in small towns throughout the South and Southwest looking for little-known athletes who are "certain body types."

"A lot of people will laugh at this," said Merritt, a native of Falmouth, Kentucky, and a graduate of Kentucky State, "but we recruit a lot by the way of player looks."

Here is part of Merritt's recruiting formula:

"We want the boy with the long muscle, the boy who has the short body and long legs, the tall boy.

"We like the boy whose skeletal system is developed well, but we'll take a pigeon-toed boy. Pigeon-toed boys, we've learned, make good athletes.

"Kids who are knock-kneed are not good athletes. They have trouble moving laterally so we stay away from them.

"We like a boy who's got a long neck. We don't go in for many of these kids whose neck and shoulder are all together, even though some are good football players.

"If you get a kid with a square chin, you've got yourself a hitter. We look for square-chinned boys because, for some reason, that's very true.

"We get a lot of kids who never played football. Jones had 52 basketball offers, but never played football."

Only one player on Merritt's 65-man squad was considered a blue-chip player at recruiting time, 260-pound Waymond Bryant, a linebacker from Dallas, now a senior. He said he had passed up the bigger schools "because my high school won only two of 20 games and I wanted to be a winner.

"They promised me that I'd be a winner at Tennessee State," he said. He is expected to go in the first round of the National Football League draft.

To keep his players lean, Merritt buys no football pants larger than size 34, and if a player requires a larger size, he must buy his own. Only one player on this year's team had to buy his pants, a size 38.

The Tigers' defensive front stands 6-4, 6-9, 6-5, 6-6 and 6-5, all with 34-inch waists. "We want them lean and quick," said Merritt, "and if they get a little heavy, we have what we call the T-day diet—no food on Tuesdays or Thursdays. We're serious about football. It's tough to play for us, but don't get the idea that we're a football factory, because our kids graduate."

The predominantly black school of about a 5,000 enrollment (Merritt has had only five white players) draws about half its players from out of state. There are 16 states represented on this year's team.

"We don't have any racial problems anymore," said Merritt, "although we still have trouble with scheduling enough games, and nobody's asking us to go to any of those bowls." The Tigers played 10 games this year and have only seven scheduled next year.

"Not because of race," said Howard Gentry, the athletic director, "but because we win we can't get a team to stay with us very long."

Merritt, who credits his staff for outstanding teaching jobs, has a record of 93 victories, 13 losses, and three ties at Tennessee State. The Tigers have beaten Grambling, another southern black power, four times in the last five years.

"We don't have any problems that money wouldn't solve," said Merritt. "We have to travel all over the country to play our games and that's all right except it costs money. Until two years ago, we took buses to all games, including an 830-mile trip to Houston—play the game, eat, load up, and drive straight back another 830 miles. But we're flying more now.

"I don't know how much longer we're going to hold out without more money, but we say that every year and we're still in business."

PENN STATE'S JOE PATERNO

By Charles N. Barnard

From Signature

The wind had turned cold and dark rain clouds moved across the sky toward the rim of the Allegheny Mountains. On a football field in the valley, young men in the practice uniforms of Pennsylvania State University were beginning a scrimmage. A third-string offensive team, mostly freshmen, was trying to run against a first-string defense which in 1972 had forced opponents to fumble 20 times, had made 17 interceptions, and was one of the best in the nation. The eighteen-year-olds were showing effects from the shock of battle against seasoned regulars.

For a series of downs, the young men crashed against the dark blue wall, fumbling once, penetrating nowhere. They came back to the huddle time and again, tugging down their chin straps, elbows bleeding, hands trembling from exertion, protective mouthpieces left hanging from gasping lips like broken fangs. For most of them, it was a nightmare in which 11 bigger, older, and tougher men were making every effort seem futile.

Then a little man with owlish eyes behind thick glasses stepped into the huddle with them. His hands were shoved into the pockets of a blue jacket, his shoulders hunched slightly forward. The wind whipped thin gray pants against his skinny legs. The players towered over him. His voice, Cagneylike, slapped them.

"You guys are scared!" he shouted. "Look at you! You're turning pale! You're shaking! You think that defense is a lot better than you are, don't you?" His finger pointed like a pistol at the distant wall of blue shirts.

"Let me tell you something about them," he went on, shifting his feet like a fighter. "They're no better than you are! You can run all over them if you *want* to! Now let's move out of here!" He whispered a play up into the quarterback's ear and moved back to watch the results of his directive.

"This is where I find out which players are willing to pay the price of football," the coach said to a visitor. Then he added, "It's also where the players find out the difference between being injured and just being hurt."

The freshmen gulped their mouthpieces, clapped their hands, and wheeled once again to face the big defenders. The ball was snapped, the lines lurched at each other once more, helmets and shoulder pads clattering with the bursting power of the drive. Off tackle. Five yards.

The little man behind the glasses taunted the defense now. "You guys can't stop 'em!" he hollered across the lines as he gave another play to the quarterback. A sweep. Four men in front of the ball-carrier. Ten yards.

Finally, an end-around play produced a touchdown. The youngsters bounded up from the goal, arms raised, fists shaking victoriously. It was only a practice session but they had done what had seemed impossible. They had shoved the big guys back, all the *way* back!

The little man now had no more to say. He looked at his watch, scribbled some notes on a piece of paper, and directed his attention to the next problem. He is Joseph Vincent Paterno. He produces small miracles every day, bigger ones almost every fall—and he still dreams of the biggest one of all: an undisputed national championship for the Penn State team he coaches. The fulfillment of that dream would mean nothing to Paterno if he could not do it on his own rather unique terms. At Penn State this is sometimes called Joe Paterno's Grand Experiment—to be No. 1, but to reach that summit while adhering to a code of ethics that would make some other football powers look like organized crime. Paterno's basic philosophy says that young men should be in college to get an education first and to play extracurricular games like football second.

Even though a Penn State team has yet to be universally accepted as the best in the nation (they've been ranked second twice), there is little argument that Joe Paterno is the premier college-football coach. In a merely statistical sense, no one can touch his record: 63 wins, 13 losses, and one tie in only seven years; ranked in the top 10 in five of the last six years; five consecutive bowl games resulting in three wins, one loss and one tie; 12 unanimous All-America players in six years.

"If you're talking about my statistics," Paterno says, "remember that out of 109 seniors who have played on my teams, 108 have *graduated.*" He didn't add that this compares with less than 50 percent for players at most big football schools.

A body of legend has begun to grow around Paterno. Some of it is, admittedly, his own creation. Unfortunately, Joe Paterno doesn't yield to quick and easy characterization. Indeed, much of his "legend" simply fails to reveal the true man. When you replay Paterno, he surprises you.

When he was a spindly-legged quarterback at Brown in 1949, a famous sports writer said of young Joe, "He can't run, he can't pass, he can only think and win." It was a reasonably apt appraisal at the time, but it has so often been quoted in later years that it has led almost automatically to another label: "the thinking-man's coach." Paterno shrugs this off. "All coaches are thinking men," he says, "or else they wouldn't survive today."

Paterno has come into demand as a speaker with a reputation for candor, disarming humility, and a repertoire of funny stories. Accused of favoring a certain young player on his squad, Paterno quipped, "I don't like the boy because he's Italian. I like him because *I'm* Italian." It gets a laugh, but it's out of character. Part of Paterno's success as a coach is due to his even-handedness and his sensitivity, which helps him get the best out of players from diverse ethnic and socio-economic backgrounds. Other coaches have had to deal with serious racial flare-ups on the athletic field; Paterno has kept Penn State cool.

Yet Paterno's players don't seem to exhibit anything like the blind loyalty—bordering on worship—that other coaches have seemed able to instill. Some former Penn State standouts, in fact, have taken pains to make it clear that they respected the coach, but genuinely disliked the man. Thus, the nation's premier coach eludes the Knute Rockne characterization and offers paradoxes instead. It's because Joe Paterno isn't just a football coach who happens to be a success: he is a complex and unstereotyped man who happens to be a football coach.

The forty-six-year-old Paterno was born in Brooklyn. Joe and his younger brother George (now head football coach at the U.S. Merchant Marine Academy) grew up to play football together at Brooklyn Prep; then in 1946, they allowed themselves to be recruited to Brown University in Providence, Rhode Island, where a coach named "Rip" Engle was trying to revive the Ivy League school's sagging football fortunes.

For three seasons at Brown, Joe Paterno played doggedly both at quarterback and on defense. His passing arm was, indeed, substandard, and his running was only slightly better, but his field generalship was impressive.

The Paterno football saga might have ended with Joe's graduation after an 8–1 season in the spring of 1949. Encouraged by his late father, a clerk in the New York Supreme Court, he planned to go on to law school, then return to a practice in Brooklyn. But Rip Engle was suddenly offered the head coaching job at Penn State and after searching for an assistant coach who would willingly accompany him to the hills of Pennsylvania, he finally decided he could do worse than invite his feisty senior quarterback.

Paterno took the job only because he thought it wouldn't last. He still wanted to be a lawyer like his dad, but, what the hell, another year with Engle couldn't hurt. Now, 23 years later (he became head coach in 1966, when Engle retired), everyone agrees that Joe Paterno has a permanent love affair with Penn State.

If this affair has shaped and directed his life, it must also be said that Joe has shaped and directed not only a lot of young lives at Penn State, but school policy as well. Not many football coaches enjoy a full professorship with tenure. He cannot be fired. He is not looked upon as a Saturday-afternoon animal trainer, but as an educator who has something to say. Last June, he was awarded the distinction of being the first athletic coach ever chosen to be the university's commencement speaker.

He began the address by launching an immediate barb at an old nemesis, President Richard Nixon. "How could President Nixon have known so much about college football in 1969," Paterno asked the assemblage, "and so little about Watergate in 1972?"

This *was* in character—right back to the pop-off football coach who publicly told the President in 1969 that he had made a bad call when he awarded a "No. 1" plaque to Texas as the top team in the country. Penn State was undefeated as well and both teams were headed for bowl games; Paterno thought the award was arbitrary and premature, and he said so. When the President, in a conciliatory mood, offered to present Penn State with another plaque honoring its undefeated streak, longest in football history, Paterno declined it. "After all," he says, "it was only for something we already had undisputed possession of."

The commencement comment on Watergate revealed the depth of Paterno's resentment as well as his obsession. He wants to be Number 1—his way. The most convincing example of his commitment to his Grand Experiment occurred in December, 1972, when the National Football League's Boston Patriots offered him a reported $1.3 million to become their coach and general manager. It was the most any coach had ever been offered anywhere. Although Paterno had, in earlier years, refused pro offers from Pittsburgh and Green Bay, it looked like this time Penn State might indeed have to say goodbye to the man who had brought their Nittany Lions to perennial prominence.

With the decision weighing on his mind (and bumper stickers all over Pennsylvania saying, "Joe: Don't Go Pro!") Paterno took his 1972 team (10–1 in the regular season) to play Oklahoma in the Sugar Bowl. Some people say he was distracted; some say the Oklahoma defense was just too big and too fast. Whatever the reasons, Paterno suffered his first loss in five post-season games. He came back home humbled by defeat but still mulling the idea of becoming an instant millionaire. He says he was thinking primarily of how much more the pro contract would enable him to do for his family. His wife, Sue, is a Penn State alumna; they have five children under nine years old and his salary is estimated at about $30,000.

In January, after much soul-searching and consulting with family and close friends, he had decided to accept both the money and the challenge—but by 5 A.M. the next morning, after a sleepless night, he changed his mind, called Boston, and backed out of the deal. The love affair with Penn State was too deep. The quest for something yet unrealized was still too strong. Paterno said, "I've had a dream that Penn State could be the greatest in everything, whether it was a library or a soccer team. That challenge is what kept me. I just feel Penn State is too good a place to leave."

Suddenly, he was a man who could say no to a million dollars—in a time when society at large seemed to be on the take, such a man was too good to be true and the press said so. Paterno himself couldn't understand what all the fuss was about.

"First I was flattered by the offer, now I'm flattered by the reaction," he said. "But seriously, nobody in football is worth a million dollars! It's ridiculous!"

There are other coaches who look upon him as a heretic who should be expelled from the lodge. Although he holds a great personal admiration for the late Vince Lombardi, coach of the Green Bay Packers (and for General George S. Patton, for that matter), Paterno does not share their conviction that victory is everything in life.

"I resent this overriding thing about winning all the time," he says. "I think our whole country has been twisted a little bit because we don't know how to lose. This was basically our problem in Vietnam. Nobody had the courage to tell the American people, 'Look we got licked. Let's get out.' Because we weren't mature enough to do this, we lost many young lives that we needn't have lost.

"In that sense, by the way, I resent the values of professional football. It perpetuates the idea that winning is the only thing that counts."

Paterno's detractors insist that no one with such a philosophy could have succeeded in pro football anyway. They suggest that *that* is why he has consistently turned down professional offers.

"I'll tell you something," Joe says. "I saw myself winning the Super Bowl with the Patriots in three years. I wouldn't have even considered it if I didn't think I could do that and be the best."

It is this quality of supreme confidence which privately irks many of Paterno's peers in coaching. "Let's see how he feels about winning not being the most important thing after he has a 1–9 season," is the comment rivals are most likely to make.

Jim Tarman, Director of Athletic Public Relations at State and one of Joe's closest friends, says, "Even though he knows he's not going to win them all, a loss always comes as a shocking *surprise* to Joe." A great surgeon is like that when he loses a patient. It happens, but not to him.

Paterno's candor extends to questions about recruiting that most coaches always duck. "There's no question in my mind," he says, "that a football player playing for Penn State on a scholarship is not an amateur. Our football players are, in every sense of the word, professionals. But what's wrong with this if it is a means of getting a good education?" He adds that his football players consistently maintain higher grades than the average male student at the university.

"Any time a young man doesn't get this kind of an education to go along with his football," Paterno says, "we're exploiting him. If he doesn't graduate, he's being cheated out of the main reason for going to college—he's just been used as a grossly underpaid professional entertainer."

In his office, Paterno draws the shades, turns down the lights, and starts up a movie projector. Forward, back. Stop. Slow. Start again. He has done it for thousands of hours, days, nights, and weekends for 23 years. His concentration is intense. He knows every man—without the number on his shirt—by the way he moves. By the mistakes he makes. He knows which ones he will holler at tomorrow and which ones to leave alone. Which ones to shame with an epithet, which ones to spear with a glance.

He believes in authority, but he understands the dangers in authoritarianism. He can demonstrate a block to a 250-pound lineman, or he can argue the thesis of a philosophy book. But even though he was an English literature major and a would-be attorney; even though adoring friends say he should someday be Governor of Pennsylvania; even though he would sometimes rather talk about art or economics, football is still Joe Paterno's life. It is the only tool he has with which to create his Camelot—a place where winning will surely have its joys, but where defeat will not bring shame.

"Football really isn't as violent as they say," he remarks, looking away from the violence on the movie screen for a moment. "The pros did a big job of selling this violence thing to the public when the NFL thought that's what people wanted. They had all that NFL film with the sounds of bodies crashing into each other and the stirring background music. They were promoting violence, no doubt about it. But now they're changing. Pete Rozelle is reading the mood of the country. They're looking for ways to show that football has good social content.

"Sport is a product of human culture," Paterno goes on—it's one of his favorite themes. "America seems to need football at this stage of our social development. When you get 90 million people watching a single game on television it almost makes you wonder about our national mentality, but it shows that people need something to identify with.

"I don't know whether it's a sign of social ascendency or decline, but now that we've run out of frontier, we seem to need something like football. Some way to act it all out."

THE VIKINGS MINE THE 49ers

By Dwayne Netland

From the Minneapolis Tribune

If the Vikings go on to win the Central Division championship of the National Conference this season, they can look back to a frantic Sunday afternoon in Candlestick Park and a pivotal game in which they had every reason to lose but somehow managed to win.

The San Francisco 49ers yesterday threw everything they had at the Vikings, including an awesome 430 total net yards, a club record of 31 completions by quarterback Steve Spurrier, and a weird volleyball sequence of laterals on the final play of the game.

Yet the Vikings survived, 17–13, extending their unbeaten regular-season string to five and dropping the 49ers, now 2–3, three games behind the undefeated Los Angeles Rams in the West Division.

In a nail-biting finish before 56,359 customers on a beautiful day, the Vikings needed a couple of interceptions by free safety Paul Krause to hold off a San Francisco attack that performed with an almost fanatical determination. The 49ers, trailing only 14–13, were driving into position for a field goal when Krause made the first of his interceptions—a pass intended for Doug Cunningham—on the Minnesota 14-yard line with 6:31 remaining.

That could have drained the steam out of the 49ers, but it didn't, and Krause had to pick off another Spurrier pass, also intended for Cunningham, on his own 36 with 3:01 to play. Krause returned it 24 yards out of trouble. The Vikings capitalized on that by moving the ball deep enough into San Francisco territory to allow Fred Cox to kick a 22-yard field goal with 1.02 left, a play that took away any chance of a winning field goal for the 49ers and required them to go for a touchdown. They nearly did it, incredibly enough. Spurrier gunned a pass into the end zone for tight end Ted Kawalick, who wrestled defender Nate Wright to the ground and caught the ball out of bounds.

Penalized 15 yards for offensive interference back to the Minnesota 40, the 49ers gathered for one huddle with six seconds left and cooked up a pass play which ran like this: Kawalick made the reception and lateraled to Gene Washington, who lateraled to Forrest Blue, who tried to lateral to anyone wearing a red jersey. The ball caromed crazily across the field, Spurrier himself finally kicking it over the Viking bench in frustration.

"It should have worked," sighed Spurrier, a surprise starter for the venerable John Brodie. "I figured we had about three laterals left in our repertoire."

The Vikings although victorious, couldn't find much humor in the day. They were in deep trouble late in the fourth period, hanging on desperately as the 49ers, starting on their own 7-yard line, shredded the Minnesota pass defense with receptions to Kawalick, Gene Washington, and Danny Abramowicz. They sent running back Ken Willard crashing into the Minnesota defense on third-down situations five straight times, each one successfully, until they reached the Viking 13.

On a first-down play, the Vikings blitzed. Carl Eller tipped Spurrier's pass, and Krause picked it off on the 14.

"If Eller hadn't tipped the ball, Krause could never have gotten to it," said a dejected Dick Nolan, the 49ers coach. "On the second one Krause made a helluva play." That one also came on a blitz, by linebacker Wally Hilgenberg. "I didn't see Krause," said Spurrier. "I think he was laying back there and just snuck in ahead of Cunningham."

Krause, who now has had three interceptions in the last two games, was playing his man, Cunningham, on the blitz. "Cunningham turned the wrong way, away from the ball," said the Vikings' safety. "I caught it behind me, a little off balance. I didn't know how far I ran it back but there were a lot of bodies flying all around me."

The 49ers, acknowledging a superb play of Krause, indicated that they had been legislated out of a touchdown by the offensive interference call on Kawalick against Nate Wright in the Minnesota end zone. "That's not right," insisted Wright. "He threw me to the ground. Besides, when he caught the ball, he was out of bounds."

Vikings' coach Bud Grant agreed totally with Wright's analysis of that play, but contended that the 49ers did a pretty thorough job on the Minnesota secondary most of the afternoon.

"They did a good job of moving the ball through the air on us," Grant said. "And they had the best pass protection we've seen all year. It certainly wasn't our best game. We gave up a lot of yards."

The 49ers also cut off the Minnesota rushing game with their fleet, mobile defensive line that slid with the flow of the play and plugged the holes before they could materialize. This policy of containment forced the Vikings to go for the deep pass, a tactic they resorted to all the more after a knee injury in the first quarter immobilized Jimmy Johnson, San Francisco's best pass defender.

An example was the gamble by Tarkenton, on a third-and-two situation with the Vikings on their own 40 late in the second period. Tarkenton tried to hit John Gilliam with a bomb, but it fell incomplete and the 49ers were able to take over on their own 22 after Mike Eischeid's punt. They hurried downfield to set up a 41-yard field goal by Bruce Gossett on the final play of the half, a kick which reduced Minnesota's margin to 14–6.

"The 49ers had nine men lined up within a yard of the scrimmage line," explained Tarkenton. "I could have called a run, trying to get those two yards, and we might have lost four. I thought we could get behind them with a deep pass and get a quick touchdown, or a field goal.

"They played us tight all day, with the linebackers blitzing and the cornerbacks working the bump-and-run on our receivers. It was a gamble on their part, so we had to combat it as best we could. We didn't hit the deep pass, but another time we might. The 49ers are a good football team that played hard. They're chasing the Rams in their division and this was a big game for them. We knew they'd be tough, and they were."

The difference was in the turnovers. The Vikings lost the ball only once, on a pass interception in the first period by Bruce Taylor that bounced off Gilliam's chest. The Vikings, in addition to Krause's two interceptions, recovered three San Francisco fumbles.

The first one occurred on the opening series of plays. Jeff Siemon hit Vic Washington, popping the ball loose, and Eller covered it on the 49er 32. Three plays later, Tarkenton threw a 12-yard touchdown pass to Gilliam, a play on which the 49ers claimed the ball had been illegally tipped first by a Viking.

The officials ruled that defensive back Ralph McGill, in going for the interception, had tipped the ball instead, into Gilliam's hands. "I didn't touch it," insisted McGill, and linebacker Dave Wilcox, also in on the play, also denied contact with the ball.

Whatever, the Vikings later surrendered a 28-yard field goal by Gossett, who also missed kicks of 27 and 47 yards, the 47-yarder striking the right upright. After that one the Vikings moved 80 yards in 13 plays, Gilliam making three receptions and Chuck Foreman plunging over from the one for his first NFL touchdown by rushing.

In the third period the 49ers drove 80 yards for their only touchdown, the first touchdown the Vikings had allowed in the second half this season.

"I thought we played well enough to win," said Nolan, whose team had beaten the Vikings in their last three meetings. Spurrier, who attempted 48 passes without once being sacked, felt the same way. "I overthrew one touchdown pass out of the end zone," he said, "and I gummed up when I didn't see Krause on that second interception. But I wonder how the Vikings would have felt if we had pulled off that last play?"

The Vikings couldn't have cared less about what might have been. They had pulled out a gut-wrencher, the type they lost a year ago, and now have four straight home games in which to extend their two-game divisional lead over Green Bay.

THE HORRORS OF TRAINING CAMP

By Edwin Pope

From The Miami Herald

"You won't believe this," says Norm Evans, who is about the first professional football player you would believe, "but the hardest part of every training camp for me is starting to wear a helmet again. The first time I put it on, my head goes 'clunk!' over to one side."

The Dolphins' all-AFC offensive tackle will be thirty-one years old on September 28. He has been practicing football for 17 summers and his head still clunks.

"After a few days you get where you sort of draw your head down into your neck. Then there's a way you can tilt the face mask at a certain angle. Between the two they keep your helmet upright. But it's awful at first."

Of all Dolphins, Evans takes perhaps the most positive attitude toward training camp. Yet even he says, "The first two weeks you're just trying to survive out here. You don't really think about anything. Your whole body is in such agony you can't zero in on one place that hurts the most."

Manny Fernandez, all-AFC defensive tackle, nods dourly. This is Fernandez's sixth pro camp. "The hardest part is the first two weeks and the hardest part of the first two weeks is the first day, like last Wednesday," he says. "I dread the 12-minute run the most. If you've got short legs like me, with a 30-inch inseam, you have to take two strides to the other guys' one. It's torture."

After that, Fernandez says, "You just sort of stay numb for a couple weeks."

These are only two aspects of the little rectangle of hell that is the pair of practice fields at Biscayne College. They are purely physical manifestations of the overall horrors of training camp for a pro, even for a Super Bowl championship squad. They seem worlds removed from the dreams of recognition and riches, the floaty image of elegance that surrounds the aristocrats of the business.

This is a pro football training camp. Nothing else in sports is even close to it in harshness.

Twenty-six such enclaves of wallowing humanity dot America from Biscayne College in northwest Miami, to Thousand Oaks, California, where the Dallas Cowboys train, to Mankato, Minnesota, where the Minnesota Vikings sleep under blankets by night and sweat vatsful by day.

The pros practice from three to five hours a day in heat that would shrivel the hide of a Death Valley burro. Dolphin veterans' second afternoon workout was shortened by rain. That was the third time in four summers under Don Shula that a workout has been even partly rained out.

It is worse in Thousand Oaks. The Cowboys have had a total of a half inch of rain in eight summers there.

"If only you could remove your head," an old Minnesota Viking lineman named Larry Bowie mused, "and just send your body to training camp. . . ."

As agonizing as the physical strain is, mental pressure is worse.

"You'll do anything to break the routine," said Alex Karras, once the Detroit Lions' king of defensive tackles. "One night I sneaked out of camp at 1:30 A.M. and drove as fast as I could 17½ miles just to get one beer. One beer. A 34-mile round trip, speeding, breaking curfew, sneaking back into the dormitory. For one lousy beer. And I hate beer. But that's what training camp drives you to do."

The Dolphins are luckier than most in that many of their homes and wives and children are nearby for the two hours a day they are free, from about 9 P.M. until the 11 P.M. curfew.

The Houston Oilers base at Kerrville, Texas, and the New Orleans Saints camp at Hattiesburg, Mississippi, are examples of the in-the-middle-of-nowhereness obviously favored by pro coaches.

Heat and anxiety seem even less bearable when the camp is cut off from outside society.

"Camps are all hell because they're all hot," was the theme of Mel Branch, a charter Dolphin who retired before he could be cut in 1969.

Branch came into the American Football League at its clumsy birth. He was with the Dallas Texans, predecessors to the Kansas City Chiefs. The Texans trained at Roswell, New Mexico, where, Branch remembered, "it was 100 degrees, without any air-conditioning in the buildings, even screen windows."

The Texans were fed chili beans for their first meal. "Some guys quit the squad right in the middle of picture-taking in the first practice," Branch winced.

Don Maynard, a rare surviving founding member of the AFL, remembers with nauseous horror an early camp of the New York Titans (now Jets): "They left the mayonnaise right on the tables between meals—heat, flies, and all."

There is no relief from the withering heat and humidity of the Dolphin practice field. Nor will there be. The Dolphins play their home games under similar conditions. It gives them an edge going in. Shula knows it. So do other NFL coaches although they won't admit it because they don't want their men psyched out ahead of time.

But the players' domitory is comfortably air-conditioned, and so is the dining room, even if the cooling system in the chow hall is on the blink right now.

And the food is a treasured diversion. Dolphins' scorched palates are salved by the fare of Jack Kobrin, who studied under French chefs and graduated from the London Institute of Culinary Arts before whipping up dainties for patrons of the Palm Bay Club and Diplomat and Eden Roc hotels.

The 69 Dolphins now in camp daily consume 175 pounds of meat, 75 pounds of vegetables, 150 pounds of fruit, 15 gallons of liquids. Saturday night they ate filet mignon and lobster tails.

"It's a pleasure to see people enjoy your cooking so much," chef Kobrin says. He admits a tinge of dismay at seeing his best work downed in an average of 18 minutes per player, in their haste for naps, or when he prepares wine sauce and a player asks for "more gravy on the potatoes."

Still, a king's menu could not remove the overriding grimness of pro football camps in general.

The occasional prank is one with Nineveh and Tyre and pre-Shula, pre-George Allen days.

Offensive lineman Steve Wright became a former Washington Redskin a few seasons back when he loped onto the field for the opening practice waggling his little finger and joking, "I don't want to overdo it the first day." Allen made sure he didn't have many more chances, by cutting him.

Allen, Super Bowl VII loser to Shula, has replaced the hated wind-sprints ("grassers" or "striders" in most camps) at the end of a workout with "perfect-play execution." Shula sticks to the sprints with a vengeance. Even after one rookie quit, he asked him to run the sprints anyway, "so you can leave with a little dignity."

George Wilson, who coached the Dolphins their first four years, was renowned for his Easy Rider approach but even he took a dim view of practice-field nonchalance. As a rookie in 1968, safetyman Dick Anderson wandered to the sideline to chat with a writer during practice. "This isn't a baseball game, Anderson," Wilson snapped. "You don't sit down between innings."

It is much less of "a baseball game" under Shula.

"Have you noticed?" Anderson was wondering recently. "We haven't had any real card games in camp in about three years. Oh, there might be a few little ones, but not like there used to be when we trained at Boca Raton. Some of those went on until 2 A.M."

Linebacker Nick Buoniconti had an answer and it did not totally involve Shula. "The whole thing has changed," said Buoniconti, thirty-two, starting his 12th pro season. "When I was with Boston (from 1962 through 1968), some of us would even go to the race track between workouts. How many Dolphins do that, even with Calder a few minutes away?

"Back then, you'd see Boston players lined up 50 deep drinking beer at night. Now maybe eight or 10 Dolphins go out for beer. You do have time, you know, a couple hours at night. It's just that everybody is more serious about it. Most of the players are 'real' college graduates. They can see the opportunities pro football will open up for them if they make the grade. The entire atmosphere is more businesslike."

Management has seen too much of that. Until a half dozen years ago, facilities in some camps were almost laughable. Only three Dolphin players or coaches—Evans, receiver Howard Twilley, and assistant coach Tom Keane—remain from the makeshift first Dolphin camp at St. Petersburg in 1966.

Or look West, where the Oakland Raiders train at Santa Rosa, California, 45 miles north of the Bay Area. Center Jim Otto remembers when the base was at Santa Cruz.

"We stayed in a hotel about 120 years old," Otto says. "After one exhibition-game trip, we came back and they'd rented out our rooms. We slept in the lobby and even on tables in a pool hall nearby until they could get the people out of our rooms."

Now, at Santa Rosa, the Raiders have telephones and TV in each room (the Dolphins have TV but no phones) at the clean and modern El Rancho Motel. Their practice field is surrounded by 10-foot redwood fences.

Al Davis, Oakland's tough and secretive managing partner, has seen to the all-work-and-no-play surroundings of the Raiders.

Shula did it with the Dolphins. But now and then, uncharacteristically, Shula seems faintly wistful for other days. "They don't go out and sit around and have a few beers much anymore," Shula says. "They don't get as close to each other."

Another apparent victim of the big-money, big-success syndrome in pro football is the rookie-hazing. "I'd rather be on the phone tending to some business matters in my spare time," Buoniconti says, "than sitting around tormenting rookies like we used to. The things we did to them! Sending 'em out for sandwiches at 2 A.M. Making them wash cars and shine shoes."

Buoniconti has a theory about that too. "It's mostly the losing teams where they jump the rookies the worst. The veterans on a losing team feel they have something to prove. When you're a champion, you don't have anything to prove to a rookie."

In essence, there are not more superstars in training camp.

Larry Gardner was co-trainer for the Cowboys for eight years before succeeding Bob Lundy with the Dolphins this year. Gardner recalls quarterback Don Meredith "just walking into the dining hall and the whole squad coming to attention. Meredith would come down the steps and sing out, 'Show time! Dandy's here!' and they'd pop to."

Fear may not come jutting out to the training-camp visitor. But it is always there, just beneath the surface, for veterans as well as rookies.

Fear of missing huge play-off bonuses. Fear of something so ordinarily inconsequential as a slight muscle-pull. On a "set" squad like the Dolphins, there is little time to catch up for lost work.

A swimming pool sits 40 feet from the gate of the Dolphin practice field. The only swimmers are Biscayne College students. No Dolphin will risk a possible Super Bowl ring for a dip.

And Shula's $200 fine is the least terrifying prospect of missing curfew. No one wants to risk putting a strike on himself with Shula, although he is a reasonable man when it comes to cutting players.

Some coaches mix whimsy with tyranny in squad cuts. Almost every "rookie show," a series of skits in early August by whatever rookies are still around, lampoons the head coach. One NFL head coach dismissed the rookies who played the part of the coach *the day after* the rookie show.

Three years ago, during the veterans' strike, Kansas City coach Hank Stram had to fill in as a practice-field quarterback. He hit a first-year receiver with four perfect passes. All were dropped. When the rookie came through the cafeteria line at lunch, Stram asked lightly, "How can you carry that tray with all that cement under your fingernails?"

Trauma. And one less K.C. rookie.

Biscayne is a Catholic college but the Dolphin trainer becomes surrogate chaplain during camp. The sensitivity of Gardner's job is magnified when a poorly chosen word can send a veteran into a sulk or a rookie into a funk of fright.

"Kids just out of college don't realize what a pro coach can get out of them in a 90-minute workout," says Gardner, who at thirty-four has heard more players' lamentations than any coach ever will. "They lack confidence and they lack maturity. It's a delicate time for them both physically and mentally."

One of Gardner's original orders was for 4.31 miles of elastic and adhesive tape.

By the end of training camp, the week before the Dolphins open their regular season here, September 16, against San Francisco, that tape will be gone.

So will most rookies.

But not the memories of training camp, harshest of all professional sports exercises.

Basketball

"VERY BAD, VERY ROUGH, DAMN DIRTY BASKETBALL"

By Tony Kornheiser

From Newsday

By strictest definition, it had to be basketball. Five men on a side. Two referees. Each basket counted for two points. Television called its own time time-outs. And everyone who played wore short pants.

But if, in fact, it was basketball—it was very bad basketball. Very rough basketball. Damn dirty basketball.

Last night at Madison Square Garden, the American National Basketball Team went into overtime to defeat the Soviet National Basketball Team, 89–80, in a slaughter two blocks east of Tenth Avenue. A total of seven players fouled out as whistles blew so often it seemed the subway had been rerouted through the Garden. A crowd of 15,734—many of them the kinds of people who chase fire engines and go to automobile races to see crashes—booed everything dressed in red and cheered lustily as bodies slammed to the floor in heaps. Many of those in attendance would have liked nothing more than to have had the game continue out in the streets.

"Change the name to punchball, man," said Ron Behagen, one of the American forwards who did more than his share of pushing and punching. "That's not basketball. There's some real dirty stuff going on out there."

But the Russians weren't the only players acting dirty. Two teams made the last tango a boxing match last night. Swen Nater played the game like an uppercut looking for a jaw to land on. Tom Henderson's best defense was a short right hand to the ribs. Bobby Jones favored the blind-side block. It got so bad on both sides that the game looked like a roller derby. So bad that at one point in the final seconds of regulation time, the Russian coach, Vladimir Kandrashin, threatened to pull his team off the court to protest the officiating; or lack of it.

"It was ridiculous," said Len Elmore.

"That's the roughest basketball game I've ever been in," said Marvin Barnes.

"You just can't feel free to go to the basket," said Ernie DiGregorio, whose wonderful play in the last minutes of regulation time and throughout the overtime made him at last the hero. "It's not worth going to the basket for a deuce and breaking my legs. I'm thinking of me. I want to be around to collect some of my contract."

How rough? That rough.

And only in those final moments when DiGregorio took complete charge of the game did it look like a basketball game.

The Russians stayed close throughout the game by doing what they have done throughout the six-game series—establishing the physical tempo and making the Americans play that style. Though the Americans led for much of the game, they never took command. And with 5:52 left the Russians took a 62–61 lead. The teams traded baskets and leads for the next three minutes. But with 1:52 left the Russians held a 73–69 lead and looked like they would close out the game.

Then American coach Bob Cousy—who had been most noticed for his apparent lack of coaching from the bench—went to his fast team. Using DiGregorio, George Karl, and Jim Oxley as a ball-hawking trio, Cousy went to the desperation game plan. It worked. DiGregorio drove for a basket to make the score 73–71. Oxley and Karl combined for a steal—as the enraged Russians screamed for a foul call—and DiGregorio had another basket. With 21 seconds left, the game was tied. Kandrashin looked as if he wanted to commit a foul on the officials' faces, and threatened to pull his team off the court.

But the Russians stayed and played. And after DiGregorio missed a jumper with six seconds left, the game went into a five-minute overtime.

That overtime was the Russian Waterloo as Ernie D. ran the show like a Cousy. He dribbled the ball like a demon and combined with his Providence teammate, Marvin Barnes, for 12 of the 16 American points. Hurling his fists in the air after each basket, he brought the fans to their feet in hysterical fashion and gave his country a taste of revenge for its loss to Russia in the Munich Olympics.

"I love it," DiGregorio said again and again as the crowd pushed against him in the American locker room. "I love it." And the echo bounced against the walls and filled the room with smiles among the bruises.

THE GIANT AMONG THE CHAMPIONS

By Dick Lien

From The Peoria Journal-Star

Bill Walton was hopping toward the UCLA bench, only his right foot touching the floor, his left arm wrapped around Memphis State guard Larry Finch.

Walton, college basketball's best, was hurt. It was his left ankle that had been sprained with 2:51 to play in the NCAA championship game, and as he headed toward the bench he looked over his shoulder.

The scoreboard told it in everything but words. UCLA, with a 77–62 lead when Walton was injured, would win its seventh consecutive national title and its 75th consecutive game.

And when he saw the time and the score, Bill Walton smiled, shook hands with Larry Finch and sat down to watch his teammates clean up.

The final score was 87–66, the direct result of 44 points by the 6-foot-11 Walton, who made 21 of 22 shots in one of the most remarkable performances in basketball history.

"We were fortunate," said Bruin coach John Wooden outside his dressing room a few minutes later. "Suppose that injury had happened early."

If it had, Memphis State might well have become the first Missouri Valley Conference team to win the NCAA title since Cincinnati won two straight beginning in 1961.

"We probably didn't defense Bill Walton very well," said Memphis State coach Gene Bartow, "because when he only misses one shot. . . ."

The Tigers had tried to shove Walton away from the basket. They could not, and got Larry Kenon, Ronnie Robinson, and Wes Westfall in foul trouble trying to.

"Our game plan was to let him shoot," said Bartow, "but from 12 to 14 feet. We felt if we could dominate the boards—which we felt we could with Walton away from them—we had a chance."

But Walton, whose missed shot came on a high lob pass in the first half, had 13 rebounds to key 38–19 UCLA domination there.

He was named the tournament's Most Valuable Player and joined Kenon and Finch of Memphis State, Steve Downing of Indiana, and Ernie DiGregorio of Providence on the all-tournament team.

"I got hurt rebounding," Walton said beside the UCLA bench before award ceremonies were held. "I don't know how bad it is. I don't really want to talk right now."

He apparently did not want to talk much later, either.

"I'm splitting," he said as an unseemly gang of newspapermen lurched toward him when the locker room was opened later, and with that he did indeed split.

Other UCLA players, having finished a second consecutive 30–0 season and having won a 36th consecutive NCAA tournament game, had more to say.

"We knew it would be no runaway," said forward Larry Farmer, "and they proved that. Boy, they had a good team."

Memphis State was tied 39–39 at half time, despite having lost the 6-foot-9 Kenon for five minutes with 13 minutes to play when he acquired a third foul.

Two free throws by Finch to open the second half gave the Tigers their last lead, but it was not until a barrage of eight straight points seven and one half minutes later that UCLA was free.

Walton had all of these, which produced a 55–47 lead with 12:24 left, and would have had 10 straight points had not a scorer's error given Larry Hollyfield a basket his taller teammate had tipped in.

After that string, Memphis was at the Bruins' mercy and got no closer than six. UCLA flirted with 20-point leads beginning in the final four minutes.

Besides Walton, the only UCLA player in double figures was forward Keith Wilkes with 16 points. But as valuable was guard Greg Lee—once a scorer, now a passer.

Lee had 14 assists, including what may have been a world record number of high lobs to Walton under the basket.

"It was my best game since I came here," Lee said later, smiling.

"I used to score before I started playing the point in our offense, but that was in high school and we didn't win. Now we win. I like it."

Memphis State, which finished its season with a 24–6 record, got 29 points from Finch and 20 from Kenon.

"I thought we were in good shape at the start of the second half," said Finch, "but then we hit a cold streak, and when I looked up at the clock we were almost out of the game.

"With the time we had left, it had to turn into a rat race and when you do that either you blow a team out or get blown out."

It was UCLA which did the operating at that point, shooting 70 percent in the final 20 minutes and taking advantage of 37 percent by Memphis.

What Walton did before injuring his left ankle going up under the Memphis basket with the Tigers' Billy Buford was unreal from start to finish.

"He is so strong," said Bartow. "He bumps and he bumps and he keeps going at it. I've never seen a player dominate a game like he did tonight."

Wooden thought it was apparent from the outset that Walton would have his way offensively.

"When we're defensed as we were today, I'd say we'd be very foolish not to get the ball to Bill at every opportunity," he said.

Memphis' defense was fatal. In their man-to-man, the Tigers played behind Walton in an effort to force him out. They succeeded only in forcing the lob pass, and a zone worked little better.

Walton's 44 points broke the championship game record of 42 set in 1965 by UCLA's Gail Goodrich against Michigan. "Many of Bill's," said Wooden, "were absolute layups."

Walton had to survive potentially serious foul trouble. He acquired his third blocking a shot by Buford with 4:14 to play in the first half and was immediately replaced by Swen Nater.

After trailing twice by seven points and once by nine, Memphis caught fire with Walton's departure and tied the score with 2:27 to play on a jump shot by Robinson.

Walton was roundly booed by Memphis fans in the crowd of 19,301—second largest ever to see a title game—but Wooden defended him later.

"Bill's emotional," he said in response to a question about Walton's apparent questioning of fouls and two offensive interference calls against him. "He only disagrees with the calls that are wrong.

"He shows how he feels—he shakes his head, he nods it, but I don't think he blasts off or anything."

Walton's fourth foul came with 7:37 to play, but he remained in the game. "I didn't consider taking him out," Wooden said.

Not after what happened at the end of the first half.

NATE ARCHIBALD IS TEN FEET TALL

By Bob Greene

From Sport

A snowy day in Kansas City. The two people in the front seat of the new Grand Prix were both young, both black. The young woman turned to the young man at the wheel, who looked to be about sixteen years old. "The milkman told me it's early in the year to be getting so much snow," she said.

The driver said nothing. He was wearing a black leather hat pulled down hard on his head, and he was nodding in time to a slow rock song playing on the car's tape deck. The road was coated with ice, and the snow was blowing directly at the windshield, but it did not seem to be bothering the driver. He leaned forward, both arms resting on top of the steering wheel.

"I'd rather be in San Diego," the woman said. "I'd rather be driving in the rain than in this. Look, it's starting to hail."

Still nothing from the driver.

"Don't forget to stop at the bank," the woman said. "We've got to get that check cashed before we go downtown." The driver took a left, pulled into the parking lot of a suburban bank, and plowed his way through the slush, up to a side door of the bank. The woman walked inside. The driver got out of the car, pulled a snow brush from the trunk, and began to knock the ice from the back window. Short and frail, wearing a pair of brand-new, stiff-legged Levi flares, he looked like a kid who might be doing this for tips, on somebody else's pretty Grand Prix.

His name is Nate (Tiny) Archibald, and looking at him slipping and sliding in the deserted parking lot, it was hard to imagine that he was an athlete, even a high school athlete. The thought that he might be a professional athlete seemed simply ludicrous. A professional basketball player? In the NBA? Too silly to even consider. This little kid?

Tiny Archibald's wife Shirley was still in the bank. She was cashing a check that had been lying around the house, a check for $700. While Tiny (who at this moment was somehow, incredibly, leading the National Basketball Association in scoring *and* assists, who was becoming one of the most important names in professional sports) was living a fantasy known to every kid who was ever too short and too scrawny to let anyone else know of his basketball dreams.

The Kansas City Municipal Auditorium is a hopelessly dreary arena; it is much too dark and much too high, perfect for a rock band but not for basketball.

Which is unfortunate for a first-year franchise such as the Kansas City–Omaha Kings. The team had to move out of Cincinnati; no one was coming to see the Royals play anymore, and they figured that if they divided the team's home town between *two* midwestern cities, they might make it. They installed 40 bare light bulbs encased in steel reflecting covers, and hung them from the ceiling of the KC arena with long, skinny black wires, and that brought the candle-power just over the minimum level acceptable for television, meaning the minimum level acceptable for a professional sports franchise to live.

So the lights helped, but the thing that is really giving the Kings' franchise a chance to make it is the fact that Tiny Archibald shows up to play every game-night. Like tonight, with the Atlanta Hawks in town. It was camera night, with free film for everyone, courtesy of the Kansas City Area Photo-Mate Stores. At first the camera-carriers were all gathered around Pete Maravich. And then Tiny trotted out to warm up.

What an amazing sight. It's not just the size, although that is certainly part of it. The program lists him at 6-foot-1, 155 pounds, and those figures are a pair of lies. But everyone knows that, everyone has heard it a million times, and you are prepared for Archibald to be physically small.

But it is the face that is the truly amazing thing. Here are all these professional athletes on the floor, and the miles of basketball travel are chopped into their faces. The faces are tired, and hard, and set. And then there is Tiny. He has not shaved this day, but the beginnings of a beard only serve as a contrast with his face. It is a kid's face, open and young and almost puzzled. He is different. Even before the game starts, he is different from the rest of the players on the court. Tiny is twenty-four years old, and going into this game he was averaging 34.3 points and 11.9 assists every time he stepped onto the floor. But all of that is not what drew the people with the cameras to him. Instead, it was the unmistakable impression that, for some reason, a young man from the playgrounds was being allowed to try his stuff against the money players tonight. The illusion is transparent enough, but it's also about half true.

When the teams came out for the opening jump, Archibald could not stand still; he looked as if he did *not* think of this as a job he has to perform every night, that maybe he had forgotten about the realities of professional athletics for a moment. His mouth hung open, and he almost twitched, so eager was he for the shooting to start. The Kings have their names printed on the back of their shirts, but Tiny's back is so narrow that when he turns away from you, it looks as if his name is "RCHIBAL."

And when it started, he was incredible to watch. He missed an easy lay-up right away, but then he drove on Maravich and scored, and from that point on he did not stop. You could not look at him without a dumb, helpless grin coming onto your face; he is the kind of athlete who makes you smile whether you want to or not. There is just no other proper expression to be wearing while you are seeing him work.

Archibald waving teammate Dick Gibbs out of the way so he can take his own shot. Archibald passing behind his back while he looks in the opposite direction. Archibald being shoved aside, then shooting and making it anyway. Archibald driving on 6-foot-11 Walt Bellamy, and scoring. Archibald faking Maravich off balance. Archibald sneaking under the basket, among all the huge Hawks and Kings, to take a feed from Tom Van Arsdale and score again.

And shooting, shooting, shooting. Archibald loves to shoot, and the inevitable playground comparison comes back every time he does it. He looks almost apologetic, like a school kid who knows that he's better than the older players, and knows it's not cool to shoot so much, but also knows that the only way to prove just how good he is is to put the ball up there, time and again. Every time Archibald came downcourt with the ball, you could see it in his eyes: He was thinking about scoring, thinking hard about it. Every time.

During each time-out, while the rest of the players would sit on the bench and hock the phlegm out and gasp for air, Tiny would stay on his feet, pacing, looking back to the court. The game was never close, the Kings had it won from the start, but after every referee's whistle, Tiny would shoot anyway—and when it would go in, he would turn wide-eyed to the ref, hoping that somehow he'd be allowed two more points.

Four minutes left, the game won by a mile, and still he yelled "He stepped out! He stepped out right there!" whenever a Hawks player came near the side stripes. *"Archibald!"* the PA announcer would scream every time he scored, and the organ would sound. He was taken out with 3:49 to go, and he looked like his world was ending. He had scored 41 points.

He went to the end of the bench, but he could not sit still. He shouted and changed seats a dozen times, and kept stepping toward the court. The game was sealed up, and he had enjoyed a sensational night. But there was a game still being played, not 10 feet away from him, and he wanted to be in it, shooting a basketball. He looked very nervous and unhappy, pacing back and forth until the final buzzer went off.

The coach was in the practice gym early. He was shooting one-handed push shots from behind the key. A very large number of his shots were going clean through the net, without touching the backboard or the rim. The coach is not a young man anymore, and the gray is coming to his hair, the weight to his legs. He is still a stone-cold poet on a basketball court, though. The coach's name is Bob Cousy, and as the Kings came into the gym in their street clothes, he kept putting those push shots right into the center of the net.

"I'd like to take credit for Tiny, I'd like to say that there's a lot of me in him, but I can't." Cousy said. "He's all Nate Archibald. That's all there is to it. He's all his own."

The comparison is natural. There is so much in Archibald that is reminiscent of the young Cousy, starting, of course, with the idea of the very little man in a world of very big men. During a game, Cousy and Archibald do an instinctive eye-contact thing, Tiny on the court looking over at Cousy on the bench all the time. During the time-outs, Cousy is always reaching out to lay a hand on Tiny, even when Tiny is wandering around.

"He has so much ability," Cousy said. "So much speed, so much quickness. I've talked to him at great length about taking charge, becoming a leader. When we're running I want him to be the one out there who's on top of things. When we've gone up and down the court three or four times without scoring, I want Tiny to be the one to put the brakes on. He absorbs pretty well, he's just got to convince himself that he really is the leader out there.

"He's got a tendency to go schoolyard on you, though. He doesn't really discipline himself as much as he should. I was always fairly disciplined when I was playing—but then, I had nowhere near the ability to go to the basket that he does. He's so good at that, it tempts him to be a little bit loose."

Cousy started flipping hook shots toward the basket. Some people who had wandered into the gym stopped to stare. His movements were absolutely hypnotic.

"Sure, I feel good that Tiny is the kind of player he is," Cousy said. "He's a playmaker, and I like to see that. When he makes a great pass, I feel better than if it had been a great shot.

"I think I appreciate a good play more than the average guy," said Bob Cousy.

"We almost didn't make it back for the game last night," Tiny Archibald said. "We were in Baltimore the night before, and yesterday morning we went to the airport for a 10 o'clock flight back to Kansas City. But it was foggy, and we had to get out of there some way, so we got in a bus and then they finally got us to some airport somewhere, and we made it just in time for the game."

We were riding in Tiny's car, on the way to his home. At the moment, it was hot as a jungle inside the Grand Prix, because Tiny had just flipped the heater switch to full blast. He had already done this three or four times in the past 15 minutes. After the car steamed up, he would switch the heater back to "off," and it would become frigid inside the car. Then he would switch it back to full blast again. Apparently, the idea that there is a method of doing things halfway has not occurred to him.

Tiny is not much of a talker. Not that he is unfriendly; he is, in fact, gracious and polite and eager to make strangers feel comfortable. But talking is not what he's about; he is not very good at it, and he is almost pathologically shy, and he would simply rather not fill the air with words when there is no reason to.

This is not surprising; he came out of the boys' clubs and schoolyards of the South Bronx, New York, out of a broken home with no money, and it was not fancy talk that brought him to where he is right now. Tiny Archibald never bluffed or wheedled his way to anything. He was always the littlest person on the court, and he always kept his mouth shut and played better than anyone else. That is what he is interested in: Playing basketball.

Newsweek did a big story on him. I asked him what he had thought of it, and he evaded the question a little, and finally he admitted that he had not read it. "What did that story say?" Tiny asked. "I looked at the picture and said 'Yeah, that's me,' and then I put the magazine down. I never even read the sports pages after our games. You can get your head all swelled up if you start reading about yourself."

We pulled up to Tiny's home, a townhouse near Kansas City International Airport. Inside, a reporter and photographer from an Omaha paper were interviewing Shirley about what it is like to be married to the leading scorer in the NBA. Tiny came in, flopped into a double-width chair, and began flipping through a stack of records.

The Archibalds have four children, and they came in and started climbing all over him, pulling themselves up onto his lap, grabbing at the bottoms of his jeans. Tiny was wearing a T-shirt that said "Central Intelligence Agency" on the front, and the kids began to yank the shirt out of shape. Tiny didn't stop them. He selected a record called *The World Is a Ghetto,* by a group called War, and put it on the stereo. The Omaha photographer snapped away, and tried to make conversation. Tiny said "yeah" a couple of times, and concentrated on the record. "Your wife's so talkative, and you're so quiet," the Omaha reporter said. "Yeah, that's what people say," Tiny said.

Later, when the Omaha people had left, Shirley Archibald brought in tuna fish sandwiches for Tiny and me. Tiny said that if I wanted to do a formal question-and-answer thing, it was okay with him. He got up and turned the stereo down, and then came back to the plate of sandwiches.

It was strange. He was really trying, really making an effort to do the right thing. He wanted to be helpful. But all the ease and grace and relaxed confidence that he shows on the basketball court were gone. Now he was nervous and ill-at-ease, and there was no question about it: He would rather be anywhere but right here, being made to talk about himself. This just isn't what he *does,* it had nothing to do with him.

So we went through the motions as best we could. And Tiny responded to questions about his life.

On the idea of a poor black kid from the Bronx winding up as a wealthy superstar in the Midwest: "I don't mind being out here. I kind of like it. It's better for the kids, anyway, than the city. They can go outside and play, and we don't have to worry about one of them getting hit in the head."

On the current glamor being attached to ghetto street life in movies and songs: "I saw that *Super Fly*. I don't understand how any kid can believe in that stuff. I mean, they see the way it really is, right on their own block. You take 100 young black kids who are impressed by that movie. Maybe two of them are going to end up a big man on the corner, nice clothes, good cars, selling dope. The others are going to end up like Freddy, the junkie in the movie. And Freddy's dead, remember that. He ends up dead."

On his own experiences with dope: "I never did it. My friends were all gettin' high, but I just didn't indulge. It was kind of a struggle, going to school and making money for my family. I was fourteen years old when I became the man of the family. A lot of people doing drugs come down on you when you won't do it, but I was playing basketball and I just didn't do it. One of my younger brothers got messed up with it, and he's just getting over it now. I don't even drink beer. They have those little bottles of . . . what you call them, those little bottles on the airplane? I don't even take them."

On his recognition of his own ability: "I didn't even realize I was any good until last year, in the NBA. In elementary school I was just one of the crowd, trying to play. I had a lot of problems even making the team in high school. They didn't even let me play a complete season until I was a senior. And then in college, at the University of Texas at El Paso, we weren't a high-scoring team, so I didn't really know. Last year, when I started scoring big against everyone, it hit me that I was really making it."

On going back to the Bronx: "Some guys I used to play ball with are still standing on the same street corner they were on when I left. A lot of them are taking a lot of dope. Just standing around. After a while, I stop talking to them so much. There's nothing you can tell them. A lot of them ask me for money, and you know what they're going to use it for. I can't tell them about dope, they know all about it, they know what they're doing. I can't tell them."

When we were done, Tiny had to go run an errand.

"Tiny, you'd better wear a coat," Shirley called to him.

"I've been wearing a coat," Archibald said.

"I mean a heavy coat," she said. "You know how you get when it's cold out."

So Archibald went back to the closet and picked out a heavier coat. Then he walked to the front door of the townhouse, and on his way he did something that any twelve-year-old who has ever fantasized about being a professional basketball player would recognize instantly. Tiny Archibald, the leading score in the National Basketball Association, took a little jump into the air, and tapped his hand against the top of the doorframe.

The Paterson Housing Project, on Morris Avenue in the South Bronx, is part of a world that knows a lot more about junkies and prostitutes and strongarm criminals than it does about inspirational success stories. Tiny Archibald grew up in the Paterson Project. His mother, Mrs. Julia Archibald, still lives there.

"The basketball headlines haven't changed my Tiny," Mrs. Archibald told Sam Goldaper of *The New York Times* recently. "He doesn't forget his family. He comes back here all the time, visiting family and friends and playing basketball in the same playgrounds and centers where he grew up. He loves the game almost like life itself. He makes me proud. He has never forgotten who he is and where he comes from."

That sounds like standard proud-mother-giving-predictable-quotes stuff. But in the South Bronx, it means more. For every boy on the street who carries a basketball under his arm and hangs around the playground, Tiny Archibald represents the only hope, the only sign that there *is* a way out. They talk about him in the hallways of DeWitt Clinton High School, and they feel that they are a part of him, that they can somehow identify with the good things that have happened to him. It's not going to happen to many of them; maybe it will not even happen to one of them. But the fact that Tiny came up the same way they are coming up, and that he is making it as big as an athlete can make it in America, gives them a little something to reach out for, and that counts for something in the South Bronx.

They all know Tiny's official biographical data: One of seven children; DeWitt Clinton High School, Arizona Wesleyan Junior College, UTEP; second draft choice of the Cincinnati Royals; starter in rookie year; passed over for the NBA All-Star game last year, after which he went on a scoring binge that stunned the league; brightest star in the NBA this year.

But that isn't why Tiny is so big in his old neighborhood. The reason they love him is because he has not turned his back on them. When he was a young boy, a man named Floyd Layne convinced him that basketball could get him out of there, could give him a better life than the street. Archibald knows that if Layne hadn't been there, urging him to play, he might be on the corner with so many of the other South Bronx twenty-four-year-olds. So he goes back. He coaches. He advises. He sits and talks. He makes a point of just *being there,* an example of what can happen if things fall right.

One day last summer, Tiny and Shirley drove nine hours straight to get to New York from the Midwest. Tiny went directly to the Wager Center in East Harlem, where a team he helps was practicing. He worked them for four hours straight, and got to his mother's home at 2:30 A.M. The next morning he got up early and drove to Newark, New Jersey, where he gave a clinic for young boys, and talked with them afterward. Then he drove to Temple University to appear in an exhibition game. He scored 52 points.

There are all kinds of stories around the South Bronx about fine young playground basketball players who end up in jail, or nodding out in some doorway every day, or dead. Some of the players have collapsed right on the schoolyard courts, the heroin getting to their systems even as they are doing the one thing that might get them away from it. So if Mrs. Julia Archibald sounds corny when she says, "It's a big day around here when my son comes home," forgive her. In a place where there aren't a whole lot of big days, she knows what she's talking about.

John Green is thirty-nine years old. He has been playing basketball as a professional for 14 years, which is a long time to pick up the paper every morning and see yourself referred to as "Jumpin' Johnny." He was a college star when Tiny Archibald was seven years old, and now the two are teammates, and Tiny is the star. On this day Green was sitting in the field house of Rockhurst College in Kansas City, waiting to get his official team portrait taken. The Kansas City Municipal Auditorium was being used today, so after the pictures were taken the Kings would practice here.

"It'll be about five minutes, sorry," one of the jeans-and-flannel-and-hair photography crew called to Green. He went and sat down on a bench. We struck up a conversation, and I told him I was in town to do a story on Tiny.

"Boy, he sure got hot all of a sudden," Green said. "He's a real superstar, man. But he's so quiet. That's good. Some guys who get all the attention all of a sudden let it mess them up. Tiny's so shy, he'll be okay. He's really going to be big."

Just then, Archibald came into the gym from the parking lot. No matter how many times you have seen him, the impression is always the same each time he rejoins his teammates: This can't be the leading scorer in the NBA, this must be the team's equipment kid. He was wearing that leather hat, and a pair of blue-and-red platform shoes, but the added height did nothing but make him look like a teen-ager trying to appear taller by wearing a hat and stacked shoes.

Everyone was shouting and making jokes during the picture taking. Everyone except Tiny. He paced the perimeter of the gym, his blue shorts ballooning over his skinny legs, waiting for all this to be over so he could play basketball. Finally he took a ball and went off to shoot by himself, at the far end of the court. When they called him back for his individual picture, he sat uncomfortably in the chair, turning his head when they told him to turn, smiling politely at the photographers' gags, offering nothing of his own. As soon as they were done, he ran to a ball, dribbled downcourt, and was shooting again.

When practice started, Tiny and Cousy teamed up to bring the ball downcourt. It was something to see. They were, of course, the littlest men on the court, and Cousy by all rights should not even have been competing with these present-day athletes. But here they were, Cousy looking far into the distance as he dribbled, Tiny cutting under the basket, lost among the giants except for his hand sticking up, yelling "Whoooo!" as he broke into the clear for a moment, grabbing a hard underhand pass, putting it in.

The Kings would rotate, some of them taking the court while the other ones watched from the bench. But Tiny never went to the bench. When he was told to stay out of the scrimmage, he would stand just behind the half-court line and watch. He would bend over, his hands on his knees, and follow the play with his eyes. He would talk under his breath, and sometimes he would giggle a little when someone made a silly mistake. He would move, too; he would mimic the play, even though he was not in it. He would move as if he were the guard with the ball. Sometimes he would go in the same direction as the man who really was in control of the ball; but often he would look another direction, see another man open under the basket, and even though it was only practice, a pained look would come to his face. He had seen his opening, and he couldn't take advantage of it.

Late in the practice, three men came into the gym. Two of them were wearing jerseys that said "WHB." They were local disk jockeys. The third man was in a suit. He was the disk jockey's promotion man.

Their radio station basketball team would be playing an exhibition game during the half time of a Kings' game the next week. The disk jockeys', Johnny Dolan and Phil Jay, had come to practice to have some promotional photographs taken with the Kings, and to cut some tapes for their shows.

The WHB promotion man went into a coach's office and placed a telephone call to the station. He had an engineer get a tape ready. Then, one by one, he led the Kings' stars into the office, handed them a script, and told them to repeat their lines twice.

It went smoothly enough at first. The disk jockeys were turned on to be in the presence of the professional athletes, and were full of hip, happy patter.

It was a good enough way to get away from the practice grind for a few minutes, and the Kings were more than willing to hang around the coach's office and talk with the disk jockeys. When it seemed to be all done, the WHB promotion man said "Wait a minute. We're missing somebody."

Tiny Archibald was out on the court. He was still shooting. He had not come into the office to do the radio spots. When he saw the disk jockeys and the promotion man coming after him, he began to dribble quickly away from them. But they called to him: "Come on, Tiny, we just need you for a minute."

He took the ball inside the office with him. Johnny Dolan and Phil Jay were talking at him, and the promotion man was shoving the script into his hand. Archibald seemed almost scared. His eyes were darting from one man to the other, and he tucked the ball tightly under his arm.

"Nate, if you'll just read it twice, that's all we need," the promotion man said.

Tiny looked at the script. "Over and over again?" he said. He was almost whispering.

"That's right," the promotion man said, "Easy as that." He handed the phone to Archibald.

The line that Tiny was supposed to say was: "This is Nate Archibald of the Kansas City Kings, and even if Johnny Dolan was smaller, I don't see how he could be any big advantage for the WHB Basketbawlers."

Archibald looked at it for another moment. "Any time you're ready," the promotion man said.

Tiny started to talk. It was awful. His voice was still a whisper, and he hurried through it, in a nervous little monotone. The disk jockeys and the promotion man looked at each other.

"Let's give it another try," the promotion man said.

Archibald held the basketball even tighter. He read the line again. It was just as bad as the first time. He was out of place. It was not right for him to be here, doing this.

"I've got an idea," said Johnny Dolan. "Why don't you just say, 'This is Nate Archibald of the Kings, and Johnny Dolan . . . forget it.' "

Tiny looked at the telephone receiver. "This is Nate Archibald of the Kings, and Johnny Dolan . . . forget it," he said. The line was so short that Archibald's uncomfortable giddiness sounded like tough-guy cockiness, which was fine for the WHB spot.

"Beautiful!" the promotion man said. "That was better than the first bit anyway. . . ."

But Tiny was already running out of the office, toward the sound of basketballs pounding on the court. When he got there, though, the Kings were gone. Practice had ended, and a physical-education class from the college had come into the gym and taken over the court.

So Archibald went into the locker room. The rest of the Kings were naked, heading for the showers or talking to the trainer. Archibald went to his locker, turned the combination, opened it. He sat on the bench and started to unlace his shoe. Then he stopped.

He laced the shoe back up again, and walked down the hallway of the locker room. He headed back out toward the court. The boys in the gym class were running a lay-up drill.

Tiny picked up a ball. He dribbled a little bit, standing out of bounds. Then he began to shoot.

At first, the gym-class players didn't pay any attention to him. They knew that the Kings used the fieldhouse to practice; but practice was over, and this new kid on the court was smaller than most of them, anyway.

Then the shots started to go in. One. Two. Three. Four. Five. Six. Little by little, everyone in the phys-ed class stopped shooting, and turned to look at Tiny Archibald.

Some of the Kings, in street clothes, were already walking out toward their cars. All action on the court had halted, except for Archibald. He drove toward the basket, he twisted in the air, he flipped shots from behind his shoulder. He picked up the ball, dribbled back toward the half-court line, wheeled, jumped high, arched a shot off toward the distant hoop. It went right in. "WHOOOOO!" yelled Tiny Archibald. He looked around him. All the phys-ed players were gaping in amazement. Tiny grabbed the ball and drove for the net again, a huge grin on his face. He looked very happy. He looked like a man who was doing exactly what he was meant to be doing.

THE KNICKS UPSET THE FORM CHARTS

By Dwain Esper

From the Pasadena Star-News

After a one-year marriage with the NBA championship, the Los Angeles Lakers became bridesmaids once again.

The upstart New York Knickerbockers threw up a barrier against the fast break and executed the passing offense to perfection, claiming a 102–93 verdict before a capacity throng of 17,505 at the Forum and a national television audience.

Thus, the Knicks, who finished second in the Atlantic Division, won the championship in five games, which hardly matches the form charts.

Hobbled with hamstring pulls in both legs, Laker superstar Jerry West may have played his final professional game. He was able to perform for only 33 minutes, hitting five of 17 shots for 12 points.

"I don't want to make any comment on the reported offer from CBS [to do color on NBA games next year]," West declared. "But it is possible that I won't be back. I think it's bad for a player to continue to play when he isn't helping his club."

Laker coach Bill Sharman gave the Knicks plenty of credit for their victory, but he didn't hesitate to point how the injury to West hurt his team, which won the NBA championship in five games over the Knicks last year.

"He does so many things for our club," said Sharman. "With Jerry healthy, I'm sure it would have been a different story."

Sharman elected to get more offense from Wilt Chamberlain in a desperate effort to pull the game out of the fire. Chamberlain took 16 shots, converting nine for 23 points. He also played tough defense and hauled in 21 rebounds.

"He's a big man out there," said New York's Willis Reed, who was named most valuable player in the series. "We had to do a lot of things to try and neutralize him."

Chamberlain got Reed in foul trouble with his offensive maneuvers. But Knick coach Red Holzman was able to employ Jerry Lucas as a backup, which helped nullify Sharman's strategy.

"I don't think I've worked harder in a game this year," said the massive Chamberlain. "But I tried to do what was necessary to win. I was hoping that my offensive moves would spring open some of our other players, but it didn't work out that way."

Gail Goodrich led the Lakers with 28 points, 10 in the last quarter when they rallied from a 14-point deficit to make it interesting.

But the balanced Knick attack proved far too productive on this night. Earl Monroe scored 23 points, Dave DeBusschere 20, Walt Frazier and Reed 18 apiece.

"We moved the ball," said Frazier. "That's what you have to do to get open shots."

But the Knicks also did a magnificent job putting the brakes on the Laker fast break.

"We got back on defense," explained Holzman. "We try to have one of our guys go to the board so that it won't be easy for them to clear the ball out. Then we get back. If one man is late, then another fills in for him."

Jim McMillian, who pumped in 19 points for the Lakers, admitted that being denied the fast break hurt.

"But we have the kind of team that can adjust to the slowdown," he said. "But we didn't do it."

Although the Knicks shot out to a 20–12 lead on a barrage of baskets by the hard-working Bradley, the Lakers came back in a sensational second quarter to take the lead 41–39 at half time.

But they went salty in the third period when the Knicks did all the right things, especially on defense. The brilliant Frazier was instrumental in most of the 12 Laker turnovers as the Knicks breezed to a 71–59 lead entering the fourth quarter.

"Going for an interception is a gamble," said Frazier. "But I know how the court is set up. If I miss, I know we have a man in recovery position."

The Knicks kept up the pressure, increasing their lead to 79–65 when DeBusschere suffered a severe sprain on his right ankle. He was assisted to the dressing room as the Laker fans gave him a standing ovation.

Suddenly the Lakers came alive with Goodrich hitting from outside. Soon they had closed the gap to 84–80.

Said Goodrich: "We fell too far behind. Then we had to play catch-up. It took too much out of us to get back in it."

The critical play of the night then took place. Laker forward Bill Bridges barreled to the board to put in a follow of a West miss. But he was called for charging—his sixth personal foul.

Said Bridges: "I thought I got position for the play. But the official didn't agree. It's one of those things."

Said Sharman: "That's what was happening to us throughout the series. We never seemed to get the breaks."

Monroe's three-point play with 2:15 remaining made it 91–82 and put the Lakers away for keeps.

So the Lakers put their gear away for another season. It's an old story for them—runner-up in the NBA championship race.

THE RECRUITING OF KENT BENSON

By Dave Kindred

From The Louisville Courier-Journal

This is a story about college basketball recruiting. It deals with Kent Benson, a 6-foot-10 redhead who may become an All-America. He's a freshman at Indiana University. To say that the University of Kentucky wanted him is to understate the case. Read on.

During Benson's senior year at New Castle, Indiana, he shut off any contact with college recruiters. This didn't stop the Committee of 101, a UK boosters club. Maybe 50 of the members drove the 250 miles from Lexington to New Castle to watch Benson play. They wore their UK blue blazers.

The Bensons had their telephone unlisted. UK loyalists organized a letter-writing campaign. Kentucky's U.S. Senators Walter (Dee) Huddleston and Marlow Cook dashed off telegrams. Why? "Because UK asked us to," said an aide in Cook's office.

When the high school season ended, UK rolled out its big guns. The university president, Dr. Otis Singletary, went to New Castle to chat with Benson. Dan Issel, a UK grad and now a Kentucky Colonels star, took Benson to dinner.

On April 8, last spring, Benson came to Lexington for a visit, making the trip in a UK alumnus' plane. The Committee of 101, as always, was ready.

As Benson stepped off the plane at Bluegrass Field, an estimated 2,000 people were there to greet him.

"It was a beautiful sight," said Ray Alcorn, then the 101 president. "We had people carrying signs, we had pictures of his face blown up into posters. The airport manager has a red carpet we roll out when a boy comes to town. And all the while everybody was screaming, 'We want you!' "

Some of the signs read, "KENT-ucky wants you." Such a reception, the sort of thing you'd expect for a visiting head of state, is not given to every UK prospect. "It depends on whether the coaching staff thinks a player is receptive to this," Alcorn said.

Benson said he was stunned. "It was something like I'd never thought of before," he said, smiling at the memory. "Cars were lined up, people were standing out there. It was a windy, gloomy, gray day—and all those people out there. It was really something unreal."

From the airport Benson was whisked by limousine in a motorcade to a reception put on by the UK coaches. That evening, Alcorn said, coaches, former UK players, and 101 club members attended a dinner for the high school senior.

During the visit, Benson was escorted at times by UK coeds recruited by the athletic department and called "Kittens." The player and his father, Robert, were taken on a tour of some horse farms, and they were guests of honor at a luncheon at Keeneland Race Course.

When it was time to go back to New Castle, the Lexington airport was fogged in. So UK's basketball coach, Joe Hall, drove the Bensons home himself.

"And when we got there," Kent Benson said, "I think Digger Phelps was waiting on the telephone and Fred Schaus was sitting in the living room." Phelps coaches basketball at Notre Dame, Schaus at Purdue.

Did Benson enjoy the UK visit?

"I'd heard a lot about Kentucky hysteria," he said. "It really impressed me."

Two days after Hall drove Benson home, Benson signed a letter-of-intent to attend Indiana University. This was not the final, irrevocable step. It only committed Benson to IU—if he chose a Big Ten school. The last signature, on a national letter-of-intent, would come May 4.

So, Joe Hall didn't give up.

Instead, he went to Germany.

Benson was to play in the Albert Schweitzer Junior Basketball Tournament in Heidelberg and Mannheim, Germany.

"We were in the Chicago airport," Benson said, "and who do I see? Coach Hall."

Surprised? "No, not really. He asked if I would mind if he came to Germany to watch me play. I told him I was going mainly for some peace and quiet, so I could decide what I wanted to do.

"Coach Hall said he wouldn't bother me. He just wanted to show me that Kentucky was interested in me. And that's all he did. I think he watched four games. After the games, he'd come by and we'd talk.

"He never put any pressure on me, and I really appreciated it. I really respect the man."

Hall said, "We just wanted to demonstrate our interest, and that we needed him and had a place for him."

Even in these high-pressure recruiting times, Hall's trip to Germany was extraordinary. The UK Athletics Association financial report showed that UK spent $17,958.50 on basketball recruiting in fiscal 1973. How much did the trip to Germany cost? Or did someone give Hall a free ride?

"I went commercial," the coach said.

The cost?

"A couple hundred dollars."

Hall must have found a rare bargain. Pan American airlines says a round trip, economy class ticket from Louisville to Munich—the airlines couldn't figure Lexington to Heidelberg—costs $682.00. "Maybe Joe swam over," said an Indiana newspaperman.

Hall didn't agree with the financial report figures. They showed UK's recruiting costs went up from $7,228.60 in fiscal '72—Adolph Rupp's last year as coach—to the $17,000 figure.

"They went up from $13,500 to $15,000," Hall said. "I can't imagine how those other figures got in there."

Scouting costs, often lumped in with recruiting because a coach does both on the same trip, went up for UK from $4,420.81 in '72 to $10,132.70. The total for scouting-recruiting, then, rose from $11,649.41 to $28,091.20, according to the university's figures.

"George Raveling [the basketball coach at Washington State] spent $150,000 recruiting last year," Hall said. "The average in the Atlantic Coast Conference is $37,000."

In any case, Kent Benson chose Indiana. He signed within a week of his return from Germany. "The Kentucky visit was the most fun I had—but I wasn't looking for fun," Benson said. "I've got nothing against Kentucky. I just felt Indiana was the school I wanted. I'm very happy."

Hall said, "I don't think we've ever recruited a player harder." He paused. "Maybe we tried too hard." Pause again. "But IU needed a big man, and there was that home-state pressure."

If there was pressure on Kent Benson, Indiana coach Bobby Knight said he had nothing to do with it. Knight is vehement in denouncing the sort of recruiting practices used by Kentucky in the Benson affair.

"Make it clear that I'm not knocking Kentucky," Knight said. "Joe and I are really good friends. I've told Joe the same thing—that this stuff hurts us all in recruiting. We don't put up any signs for kids coming to Bloomington, 'Welcome Home, Kent Benson.'

"Damn, there's no way that has anything to do with recruiting. When I have to do that, they can get somebody else for this job."

Knight said the extent of his wining-and-dining of Benson amounted to "a pot of Sloppy Joes that my wife made up before Kent went to a movie one night."

Knight said friends helped him. Dick Van Arsdale, an IU grad now with the pro Phoenix Suns, called Benson. So did John Havlicek of the Boston Celtics, once Knight's teammate at Ohio State. Indiana's recruiting-scouting cost last year, Knight said, was $8,200—almost $20,000 less than Kentucky's.

"We don't tell a kid he's going to be a starter right now," Knight said. "We don't tell him he's going to be all-conference or All-America. We don't talk about winning a national championship. I tell a kid to come to Indiana because nobody is going to work harder to be certain you get a good education, and nobody is going to work harder to develop you as a basketball player."

Indiana's relatively low recruiting costs, Knight said, come because he doesn't believe in recruiting gimmicks. "We don't send a mother orchids for her birthday," he said.

"Scott May's mother was in the hospital," Knight said, naming IU's sophomore forward. "We sent her a 65-cent card, signed by all of us. It was right there next to a $75 floral arrangement sent by another school recruiting Scott."

Knight didn't follow Benson to Germany. "I told him, 'There's no way I'll go to Germany to see you or anybody else play,' " the coach said. "He knew we were interested in him. And I liked what he said when he came back. Somebody asked him about me not going over there.

"Kent said, 'Coach Knight was back at home helping Steve Downing sign a pro contract.' "

Knight thinks recruiting can stand a solid dose of reality. "Every time Kent Benson goes home for the weekend, we're not going to have Holiday Inn put up a sign saying 'Welcome Back.' So why do it in the first place?

"I tell you what I'd do. If Walter Byers (executive director of the NCAA) called me and said I was in charge of rewriting the recruiting rules, I'd nail all these guys.

"I'd limit a kid to four visits. He'd make all those visits from April 1 to April 30. He'd have May 1 to 10 to make up his mind. If he hadn't signed by then, he loses a year of eligibility.

". . . Look, what do you do? A player comes up to you and says, 'Coach, you gotta get me an extra $50 a month.' After you've done all these other things, what's one more?

"We've created a monster."

Golf

TOMMY AARON IS FINALLY NO. 1

By Phil Taylor

From The Seattle Post-Intelligencer

The pro from Avis finally got to be No. 1.

Much-maligned Tommy Aaron, old self-destructing Tommy, the nice guy who finishes second, didn't. He whipped the whole world yesterday, removing in the process the unwelcome albatross that has been his personal burden for too many years, by winning the 37th Masters title with a five-under-par score of 283.

In conquering this illustrious field—and the stubborn lady known as Augusta National—Aaron put together rounds of 68–73–74–68, squirming before the television screen in one of the nearby cabins as he sweated out the final three holes of his closest pursuer before victory was assured.

That man, in the final accounting, turned out to be J. C. Snead, the long-hitting, slow-talking nephew of Sam, whose last chance died on the 72nd hole when an 18-foot downhill birdie try curled left of the hole. His task had been magnified as early as the 12th hole when the quiet waters of Rae's Creek snatched an errant seven-iron shot and flung a double-bogey back in his face.

J.C. came up one shot short, his four-day work totaling 284 on a 70–72–73–70.

Peter Oosterhuis, the surprising Briton who took a three-shot lead into yesterday's play but is perhaps not yet ready to withstand the pressure of this kind of competition, slid back into a three-way tangle for third at 285. His companions were tubby Jim Jamieson, who played as well here as he does poorly elsewhere, and Jack Nicklaus, whose final-round 66 made only plausible a task that was simply impossible.

Oosterhuis bent to a two-over 74 and Jamieson made a mild run with a 71.

But it was Aaron's day and no victory could be more popular with citizens in this section of the universe. The thirty-six-year-old veteran of 12 years on the tour hails from Gainsville, Georgia, down the road a piece, and his friends and family have suffered, even as he has, through the years of torment and suspicion that he couldn't win this frustrating business.

Off the tour much of this year because of his wife's serious illness, he rejoined the group recently, only when her return to health was assured. A consistent big-money winner through the years, he had bagged but $10,221 thus far. Yesterday's check for $30,000 should provide at least a down payment on a couple of sides of beef.

It has been his unhappy experience in the past to fritter away the wealth of early hot rounds. Yesterday, he came from off the pace. Yesterday, the field backed up to him.

Starting the day four large shots behind Oosterhuis, Aaron had a piece of the lead as early as the eighth hole and was in sole possession of it at the turn on the strength of a four-under 32.

Aaron lost ground momentarily with bogeys on the 10th and 11th holes and the crowd began to suspect the Georgian was about to disappear again.

Not so.

He reached the 475-yard 13th hole in two shots and two putted for a birdie. Then, at about the same time Snead was gazing unhappily at his ball sinking beneath the waters at the 12th, Aaron birdied the long 15th from four feet to take the lead for good.

Three careful pars on the final strides left him five-under and set up the agonizing moments to follow as he watched every Snead struggle to get something, anything, going over the same final strides.

Snead, who had gone out in 33 and regained the lead following Aaron's bogey-bogey start on the back nine, died as so many have before him on the 12th-hole bend of Amen Corner.

Changing his mind on club selection, the seven-iron choice proved to be a monumental blunder. The ball hit at the top of the bank in front of the green on the 155-yard hole, then trickled slowly down the slope and into the water. It cost him a double-bogey and eventually the tournament. He did follow with a birdie at 13, but there was nothing left the rest of the way.

Oosterhuis did not go quite as spectacularly, only in short gasps. Two over at the end of nine holes, he had lost his advantage and a one-over 37 on the journey home was simply not enough to regain the ground.

Nicklaus attacked with all the ferocity of a man desperate to make up eight shots. It was a valiant effort, fashioned on eight birdies, but troubled by a pair of bogeys.

In the final analysis, Nicklaus did not forfeit a fifth green coat because he failed here yesterday. He threw it all away a day earlier when he pumped two balls into the water on the 520-yard 15th, taking a back-breaking triple-bogey eight on a hole considered easy birdie territory for the game's premier player.

Kermit Zarley bounced back from yesterday's 77 with a strong one-under 71 to finish at 293 and earned a return trip to this event next season by finishing in the top 24. Kermit had four birdies and three bogeys. Rod Funseth couldn't match that, the ex-Spokanite using up 76 strokes for 298, missing the 295 cutoff point.

Something always happens at the Masters, they say. Jack Nicklaus does not always win.

And Tommy Aaron does not always lose.

WEISKOPF CONQUERS HIMSELF

By Bob Addie

From The Washington Post

They used to say about Tom Weiskopf that he had the disposition of an ingrown toenail. Tall, erect, with the carriage of a British Army sergeant major, Weiskopf has long been his own devil's advocate—putting his psyche up on a public dartboard and throwing the darts himself.

Now, however, he is the tour's hottest golfer, a winner of three straight tournaments earlier this summer, a contender at the PGA here and in almost every other tournament he has entered since the Masters, a man who thinks he has at last overcome himself.

The legends about Weiskopf are legion. He was born in the football-oriented city of Massillon, Ohio, on November 9, 1942, the first child of Eva and Tom Weiskopf, a railroad man. Weiskopf grew up in Bedford, a Cleveland suburb about 10 miles from the Canterbury Country Club. His mother and a fifteen-year-old brother, Danny, still live there, on Bexley Street.

With his Massillon background, Weiskopf has always been a football fan. Massillon is the city that spawned Paul Brown and shared the distinction with Canton of being the cradle of pro football. So it was natural that Weiskopf dreamed of being a football player, but he never made it.

He turned to golf because of "environmental influences," he said. Weiskopf's father was a scratch amateur golfer and his mother, Eva Weiskopf, was well-known herself. She was the first woman to play on the Wooster (Ohio) College men's golf team and she was Akron women's champion eight times.

Kaye Kessler, sports editor of the *Columbus Citizen,* knew the

Weiskopf family well. "Tom Weiskopf, the father, wasn't quite what one would expect," says Kessler. "That is, he wasn't the 'stage mother' type with young Tommy. The father was a tall, spare man and young Tom is built just like him (6-foot-3, 185 pounds). Tom senior always was in the background when he followed his boy around junior tournaments. He didn't always watch his son play and if the father did show up he was hard to find—even in as small a group as that which follows these kids."

The father knew early that his son was a brilliant golfer. "Tommy could make something out of the game," the elder Weiskopf once confided to Kessler, "if he could only get his head on straight. He's got to learn to control his temper."

There is evidence that father and son did not have the close relationship, according to Kessler, that existed between Jack Nicklaus and his father, Charlie. There are some striking parallels in the careers of Nicklaus and Weiskopf—if a few legends can be brushed away.

First, both golfers went to Ohio State University. "There is a legend that Tom caddied for me," Nicklaus said. "That's not true. It doesn't make any difference but it just sets the record straight. We never played on the same golf team at Ohio State. He was a freshman and I was a senior and we both played under coach Bob Kepler. But that's as far as the similarity went."

Nicklaus dropped out of school lacking only a few credits for his degree because he had become involved in golf. He started his major in pharmacy—his father was a successful pharmacist—and then switched to business. Although he never graduated, he did receive an honorary degree from his alma mater—something Weiskopf has yet to attain.

Weiskopf attended Benedictine High in Bedford and then went to Ohio State, where he stayed two years. He credits much of his development to Kepler, who didn't quite have that same influence over Nicklaus.

"Golf probably came easier to me than to 98 percent of the other guys," he said. "Maybe that's what made me lazy and took the edge off my dedication. I never had to work too hard on my game."

Golf came easily to Nicklaus, too. He won his first major pro title, the U.S. Open, at twenty-two. When Charlie Nicklaus died, the golfer did his own soul-searching. Nicklaus told the story once.

"Maybe things had come too easily," he said. "My dad always

thought I had to work at my game and not get complacent. I think I was complacent until he died in 1970. I decided then I owed it to him to really try. I dedicated myself to getting really serious about my game."

Nicklaus did get serious. He won the British Open in 1970, the PGA in 1971, and the U.S. Open and Masters in 1972—all, of course, in addition to some 12 other tournaments.

Similarly, it was the death of the elder Weiskopf in March that brought the same self-analysis and maturity to his son. Weiskopf played the Masters after his father's death and finished an undistinguished 34th. Then he started to move.

Weiskopf admits that the memory of his father was a spur to his ambition after the Masters. He won the Colonial, Kemper, and Philadelphia Classic in consecutive weeks and then finished second in the Atlanta Classic. He was really hot when he hit the U.S. Open at Oakmont in June, but he finished third behind Johnny Miller.

But Weiskopf had his temper under control in the Open. "I don't expect to win every week," he said at the time. But he was disappointed—although Nicklaus and Arnold Palmer publicly lauded him for his "new attitude."

There is the inference from Weiskopf that he never really was close to his father and didn't appreciate the elder Weiskopf's counsel.

"At times I think of how my father thought I was neglecting my talents," Weiskopf said after winning his three straight tournaments. "He wanted me to control my temper and mature. I wouldn't listen then. I wish now he could have shared some of this success."

Weiskopf was a Cleveland junior champion and a two-time public links champion as well as the winner of the Western Amateur. That was his only big title before turning pro in 1964. He joined the tour a year later.

"Tom's trouble always was that he was not finely honed in amateur competition," said Nicklaus. "He never really started to realize that golf demands a strong attitude until he joined the tour. You could say he has had on-the-job training."

Weiskopf agreed. "Take Ben Grenshaw," he said. "Ben has played more amateur golf than the average pro plays on a tour.

"He's tournament-sharp, something I never was until I hit the tour.

"But I will never consider myself even a good golfer until I win a major tournament—one of the Big Four, like the Masters, the U.S. Open, the British Open, and the PGA," Weiskopf once said. "You start rolling. You don't want to lose the momentum. I feel confident I have conquered myself—and that has always been my biggest trouble. I don't get mad at anybody but myself."

But a crack in Weiskopf's new armor of control came only a week after the U.S. Open in the American Golf Classic in Akron. In retrospect, it was not his fault, and even a saint might have gone up like a volcano.

Weiskopf was behind a tree and turned his club to take a left-handed shot so he could get out on the fairway and get a shot to the green. Just as he was on his downswing, a photographer leapt out from the crowd to take a picture. The ball caromed off the tree and hit the cameraman. Thoroughly upset, Weiskopf took a triple-bogey seven on the hole and eventually finished tied for fifth.

But he went on to win the British Open and at last had his first major title. He followed that up with the Canadian Open—a lucrative victory, although it is considered merely another tour stop.

Then came the Westchester Classic in Harrison, N.Y., last week. On the last round (they played two 18-hole rounds Sunday because of a rain postponement), Weiskopf took an eight on the par-four fourth hole and missed a play-off by one stroke. Again, it was an amateur photographer who bothered Weiskopf.

"It was on the ninth hole the day before," Weiskopf noted, "that this same guy snapped my picture. I lost my concentration and took a bogey six on what is considered an easy birdie hole."

The same man haunted Weiskopf the next day on the fourth hole of that final round. Weiskopf was on the backswing of his tee shot when the photographer clicked his camera again. That led to the eight.

Weiskopf complained so bitterly to the marshal Sunday after the camera incident, that the photographer was escorted off the hole and presumably off the course. But Weiskopf sees it now as another milestone in his struggle to control his temper.

Weiskopf, who has won $220,777 this year, second to Bruce Crampton's $245,141, already is trying to get away from it all. He is married to a stunning girl, Jeanne Ruth, who was a runner-up in the Miss Minnesota beauty contest a few years ago. The Weiskopf's have two children, a girl, Heidi, two, and a boy, Eric Thomas, six months.

This week the family is staying with Eva Weiskopf in her Bedford home. Tom's pals, Bert Yancey and Tony Jacklin, like to drop by for some of Mrs. Weiskopf's spaghetti, her specialty. The mother is a slight woman who gave her son his sandy, curly hair. She says she always thought Tom's success inevitable but she admits she wasn't quite prepared for the overwhelming publicity.

She has kept a scrapbook ever since her son started to play golf and she is surrounded with dozens of his trophies.

"Tommy always had the shots," she said with the expert's observation, "but he is putting exceptionally well now. He is a very shy person but everybody is pulling for him and following him because he is winning. It's a great feeling to have the fans on your side. I've always felt that helped."

"I've still got to get used to realizing those galleries are following me," said Weiskopf. "I try not to let anything interfere with my game plan. I know I need patience and I'm determined to maintain a good attitude. After all, that's the sign of a pro—keeping your cool. Look at those pro quarterbacks. They don't get flustered when they're behind with two minutes to go. They just take their time and let things happen."

Eva Weiskopf and young Danny have been following Weiskopf through every hole of the Canterbury course. Tom Weiskopf looks back at the gallery often to spot his mother and brother—but now he doesn't look back in anger.

A $500,000 TOURNAMENT . . . AND WHO CARES?

By Hubert Mizell

From Golf Digest

Back in 1952, Dwight Eisenhower was winning the Presidency. Gary Cooper was winning an Oscar for *High Noon,* the Brooklyn Dodgers were winning the National League. That same year, America's touring golf pros were playing their entire 32-tournament circuit for a measly $498,016. Meanwhile, little Jack Nicklaus was back in Columbus struggling with seventh-grade math.

Just 21 years . . . so much has changed. Ike is gone, so is Coop. The Dodgers long since deserted Brooklyn for a richer existence in California. But perhaps the most shocking evolution of them all has been in professional golf. Today's better-heeled, better-dressed tour troupe is about to play a single event for $500,000 . . . more than the entire tour was worth in 1952!

In the intervening 21 years Nicklaus has gone from a puffy kid with a 75-cent allowance to a trim, handsome, one-man sports conglomerate with personal income in the $1-million-a-year bracket. His tour earnings alone are regularly in the $300,000 league. In 1952 the leading money winner was Julius Boros at $37,032.

Nicklaus earns so much, in fact, that he doesn't become excited about even a $500,000 tournament, the unique 144-hole World Open scheduled November 9–18 in the North Carolina golfing capital of Pinehurst. Actually, few of golf's leading players have shown much excitement about the event. Money isn't always their prime motivator any longer.

"I hate to pass up a chance at the $100,000 first prize in the World Open," Nicklaus said recently. "But I don't want to play in front of 10 people, either. I can't imagine them drawing a gallery in Pinehurst at that time of year." He also showed dislike for the elongated format, twice the length of a normal event.

Nicklaus plans to spend that time hunting elk in the mountains of northern New Mexico. And he hopes Tom Weiskopf goes along with him. Weiskopf became the tour's dominant figure during the past summer when he won five of eight tournaments, including the British Open, and almost $200,000, in a two-month stretch. At a suddenly-more-mature thirty, he established himself as one of the game's half dozen superstars. Weiskopf would be a major gallery attraction at Pinehurst, but apparently only the New Mexican elks will be seeing him and Nicklaus during the World Open.

Lee Trevino has continually maintained that he wouldn't show up. "I can't stand to spend two weeks any place," he said, "not even for a half million dollars. I'm going home to El Paso and rest." Yep, this is the same poor Mexican-American boy who didn't have nickels to rub together six years ago. He now commands an empire that nets him over $500,000 a year.

Arnold Palmer, too, took his time when considering the World Open for his schedule. It is clear in Palmer's case that a competitive drive to win another golf tournament would be his motive . . . not simply a big check in the largest tour payoff ever. Palmer is still the money-making king of golf, and a close associate says his income is "somewhere between $1.5 and $2 million."

Gary Player's appearance depends on his physical well-being. The South African hero has had one of his poorest years after undergoing surgery in the off-season.

Bruce Crampton, who plans to play at Pinehurst, can become the first foreign golfer since Player in 1961 to lead the American tour in prize money. A victory by Crampton, indeed, would smash Nicklaus' one-year record of $320,542 set in 1972 with perhaps more than $50,000 to spare. The top check of $100,000 could even catapult a Lanny Wadkins into contention for the money title with only a handful of tour stops remaining after they close the bank at Pinehurst.

"For most of us," says Frank Beard, "a quick $100,000 can be a season." The largest single payoff heretofore has been the $60,000 claimed by Bobby Nichols in the Dow Jones, a $300,000 extravaganza which folded after a single staging in 1970. After the Dow's demise the $52,000 paid to the winner of the Jackie Gleason-Inverray Classic became the largest bankroll available.

Perhaps it's the lofty tax bracket of the few superstars that allows them to be so blasé over the World Open's huge jackpot. They're all so financially loaded that most of the dollars by this stage of the year are going into Uncle Sam's pockets. This elite little pack also shares a belief that there is no extraordinary prestige to winning the $500,-000 event.

Golfers of extreme stature are seldom moved by purse sizes any-more. They usually make playing plans around the Big Four cham-pionships. The name of the game is prestige . . . the money takes care of itself. A fellow like Nicklaus will play the Masters, U.S. and British Opens, and PGA. He'll play a couple of tournaments tuning up for each of those. He'll also play events he personally enjoys, such as the Bing Crosby Pro-Am. After that, it comes down to either participating in tournaments for some commercial reason or simply attempting to play in some cities at least every three or four years to keep the local sponsors moderately happy.

It's unrealistic to compare the outlook of Nicklaus or Palmer or Trevino with the more active heroes of the past such as Ben Hogan, Byron Nelson, Walter Hagen, or the venerable Sam Snead. The money prospects have changed so drastically since their heydays that golfers now ranking between Nos. 25 and 30 on the tour cash list are much better off financially than some of the leading money winners of two or three decades ago, even considering America's unchecked inflation spiral.

If you're disappointed at the prospect of seeing the richest tourna-ment in history with a Class B field, think about the men responsible for putting up the 500 grand. Bill Maurer, president of the sponsor-ing Diamondhead Corporation, is predictably unhappy over an-nouncements that some of golf's mightiest names won't be in the fold. "If those people do that, who do they really hurt?" he asks. "They hurt golf. In the future, every time a group with the financial means talks about creating a tournament like this one, they'll re-member what happened to us. It will make it more difficult to get truly big money events in the future. If this happens, tour golf can blame itself."

Diamondhead, which owns both the town and resort of Pinehurst, says its break-even figure for the tournament is $900,000. It would seem the company's chances are good of dropping well over a half million on an event designed to glorify the game of golf and, of course, hype its land sales and resort trade around golf-crazy Pinehurst. Maurer indicates that a colossal flop probably won't cause the World Open to go the way of the Dow Jones. "I project three or four years to make it work out so that it won't cost us anything. But I wouldn't be doing it now if I didn't think it was going to be a good investment. You know it's going to cost us money. Only a fool would put on a tournament like this and think he was going to break even."

Like any sponsor, whether he's putting up $100,000 or $500,000, the Diamondhead boss knows that a "great field" must include heavy representation from the Nicklaus-Palmer-Travino-Weiskopf-Player-Crampton bunch. It appears he won't get it. "The name players have taken a lot out of golf," he says. "I would think they would want to support the tournament. I think the attitude expressed by some of these people is very shallow and also very self-centered. Maybe there are a few fat cats out there on tour with endorsements and money running out of their ears. They can afford to go home in September and not play. But there are a whole bunch of guys who try to make a living on the tour. And if a tournament like this fails, it hurts everybody."

It's not unusual in modern golf to hear a sponsor, disturbed at his tournament field, tearing into the superstars for not showing up at his event. But times really have changed, changed to the point where a top earner can come closer to living an average home life while still raking in big dough from the tour. Almost without fail, the top names have excused themselves to spend more time with their families . . . to pursue some sort of relaxation . . . to live a life far from the carnival-like existence of a touring pro. It's not too unlike the search by professionals from almost any field. They feel a need to "get away."

Sam Snead is a living example of the change. He was leading money winner in 1950 with $35,758. Twenty-two years later, at age sixty, Snead piled up $35,462 . . . and was ranked 71st on the 1972 tour money list. "If the money had been like it is today throughout my career," Sam says, "I might've won $4 million. But I'm not complaining. I got my share of the money."

Snead, with a record 84 PGA tournament victories since going on tour in 1937, has won barely $600,000 in official earnings. Nicklaus, born as Snead began his fourth year on the tour in 1940, is at age thirty-three some $1.4 million ahead of Sam.

Although there was a steady growth in purses after World War

II, the significant money explosion didn't arrive until the flamboyant Palmer began winning tournaments in the late 1950s. He captured the attention of a sporting nation. Galleries ballooned. Television became seriously interested in golf. Cities, medium and large alike, developed a thirst for a spot on the tour headlined by this charismatic figure from Pennsylvania.

From 32 tournaments worth an aggregate of $820,360 in 1957, the total went over $1 million in 1958, hit $2 million five years later, and was over $3.7 million by 1966. Nicklaus was firmly in the superstar picture by then. So were the diminutive Gary Player and colorful attractions such as Doug Sanders and the late Tony Lema. In 1968 the tour offered a whopping $5 million for 45 events and two years later it reached $6.7 million for 55 tournaments, including a budding "second tour" for less-accomplished golfers.

The same sport that had offered average purses of $10,000 two decades earlier was suddenly moving beyond the reach of any city not able to post at least $100,000. The 1973 schedule had 47 tournaments classified as "major" by the Tournament Players Division of the Professional Golfers Association. Their combined worth was almost $8 million, averaging an amazing $168,830. Fourteen events paid $200,000 or over, and 34 of the 47 hit at least $150,000.

Compare the $168,830 average to 1962 when it was only $36,537. Snead can tell you about 1938, his second tour season, when the average purse was a paltry $4,160. The winner often got only $800.

In comparison, the $500,000 World Open at Pinehurst will pay $800 apiece to 170 golfers who fail to make the 72-hole cut in the 144-hole marathon that covers eight days. Following a winner's check of $100,000 there will be a $44,175 payday for second place, $27,513 for third, and even $10,462 for ninth.

It became a highly publicized accomplishment in 1963 when Palmer and Nicklaus became the first golfers to top $100,000 for a single year. But, with the available money increasing by a ton every year, there were suddenly 17 men above the $100,000 plateau in 1970. It's possible that you've even forgotten some of the guys who have won 100 grand. Do you recall, for instance, that Dick Lotz was in that bracket in 1970 and Dave Eichelberger attained the distinction a year later?

You have to wonder where all the purse money comes from. How can they afford to pay $100,000 at Columbus, Georgia, $210,000 at Greensboro, North Carolina, or $125,000 at Robinson, Illinois? Not only must these communities cough up the huge purses, but they must gather an average of over $125,000 in additional income to cover tournament expenses. They also must recruit a battalion of volunteer workers to do everything from driving courtesy cars to managing caddies to creating sophisticated communications setups that allow spectators to know who's leading the tournament. It's not uncommon to have bank vice-presidents parking automobiles on dusty fields and millionaires' wives pumping Cokes.

In some cases corporate aid makes the tournament possible. Large companies such as Eastern Airlines, Kemper Insurance, Monsanto, United States Industries, and Mutual of New York contribute checks for $50,000 and up with an eye toward enhancing their images and building business.

In most cities, however, it's community muscle that insures the success of a $175,000 tournament. It's usually a devoted few workers who light the fuse under the local hordes. Sales forces are established to push high-priced ticket package plans. Expensive spots in pro-amateur events are peddled at four figures.

It's highly in vogue to have an entertainment celebrity attached to a golf tournament. It helps sales when you can say, "Sammy Davis and I invite you to take part (financially, of course) in the Greater Hartford Open." Bing Crosby and Bob Hope long have hosted their star-spangled golf picnics in Pebble Beach and Palm Springs, but now we have Glen Campbell tied into the Los Angeles Open, Andy Williams is the man in San Diego, Dean Martin took Tucson, Jackie Gleason carries the banner at Inverray, near Fort Lauderdale, and Danny Thomas does his bit in Memphis.

When Dean Martin holds a pro-am, he naturally tries to get Frank Sinatra, Sammy Davis, Glen Campbell, and friends to participate. It helps in prying money from local benefactors.

About 30 percent of a tournament's gross income is usually derived from the pro-am prelude. About 45 percent comes from ticket sales, a heavy number of them included in sponsor packages that go for as much as $1,000.

Most tournaments, according to a *Golf Digest* survey, make about 10 percent of their money from television-radio rights, three percent from program sales, two percent from parking fees, five percent from concessions, and five percent from miscellaneous projects. Television networks pay healthy sums for rights, but well below the amounts shelled out to televise football, baseball, basketball, and hockey.

Yet over and above these income sources, many of the tournaments are heavily subsidized by big business. If the participating major corporations decided to pull out, most tournaments would be forced to reduce their purses, perhaps by as much as $75,000. Some events might fold up altogether.

John Montgomery, a one-time Duke University football star and now the professional tournament director for a dozen tour events, is delighted to have corporate dollars easing the financial burden on cities but he worries about becoming too dependent on industry. "Suppose we hit bad times on Wall Street, maybe a recession," says Montgomery. "I'm afraid that when big companies begin cutting back, the first budgets to be sliced will be in public relations. Golf tournaments usually fall into that category. A bad recession could cause a major pullout and the tour would be tremendously shaken."

For that reason Montgomery enjoys seeing communities handling tour events on their own. "Locally run, locally financed tournaments are the backbone of the tour," he says.

Montgomery would like to see tour purses stabilized at a reasonable maximum. "The big-name pros don't make their schedules according to money any longer," he says. "There was a time when Arnold Palmer might play one tournament because it was worth $15,000 or $20,000 more. I doubt that he even looks at the tournament's money figure before entering today. He knows that any place you play, it'll be for big money."

In a way, Montgomery is owned by Jack Nicklaus. Jack holds 25 percent of the stock in Executive Sports, Inc., the Montgomery group. He talked Eastern Airlines into purchasing 50 percent and loaned John the money to buy the rest. Montgomery, however, controls 51 percent of the stock.

It's just another section of the Nicklaus business combine, now headquartered in offices across Lake Worth from Jack's beautiful home in North Palm Beach, Florida. Nicklaus also is heavily into golf course construction and designing as well as being involved with a battery of companies for personal endorsements of items such as Pontiac autos, Hart, Schaffner and Marx clothes, and MacGregor sports equipment. MacGregor even created a Jack Nicklaus Division as part of a 10-year deal involving millions. Nicklaus may even wind up promoting fishing gear, bowling balls, pool tables, and outboard motors for Brunswick-MacGregor. It's all a part of the financial fun of being one of golf's superstars. Somehow you have to believe that

Nicklaus' goal is to out-Palmer old Arnold in golf-created income. He's not there yet, but he's gaining and he's 10½ years younger than the man from Latrobe.

But these aren't the only ones making big golf money. Corporate giants Nicklaus, Palmer, and Trevino are joined in the tour's Million Dollar Club by Crampton and Billy Casper. There are a handful of others rattling the gate. In '74 the club may include Player, Gene Littler, Weiskopf, Julius Boros, and Frank Beard. "It's ridiculous not already to include me as a million-dollar winner," says Player. "For instance, I've won the World Series of Golf three times at $50,000 a crack. But they don't count that. It's funny, that money spends just like the other I've won."

Even for golfers who float around the middle of the top 50 money winners on tour, there is a handsome existence. In addition to averaging close to $100,000 a year, they have scads of opportunities to play in side events. Pro-ams, many in cities too small to host a tour tournament, often guarantee a golfer $2,000 to show up for an 18-hole or 36-hole affair. Many businesses use touring pros to help entertain customers and prospective customers. A pro can pick up $1,000 and more for a day of golf, drinks, and food with corporate guests.

"It helps to fatten a pro's income, especially a younger fellow who's trying to get established," says Forrest Fezler, who became a large breadwinner on this year's tour.

The top 50 or 60 golfers also get shots at great playing vacations. A tournament in Japan offers a $300,000 purse each October and pays the full expenses of about 50 American tour players, including a first class air trip to the Orient. Billy Casper ramrods a similar fall junket to Morocco, where he's the king's personal pro. It includes expenses and a chance at a $100,000 purse.

Equipment companies, clothing manufacturers, and shoe companies make nice deals with dozens of tour players, not just the super players. "I always figure that my published tour income should be my taxable income," says forty-two-year-old Dan Sikes, a man who gave up a budding law career in 1960 to play pro golf. "In other words, I usually make enough on a few outside deals to cover all my tour expenses, which can be around $25,000." Sikes is not at all a rarity. He isn't a superstar, he has no super contracts. But anyone with mild golf-tour accomplishments can live only a shade below millionaire standards. Sikes' official tour earnings are well over $700,000.

Being a failure on the golf tour is still one of the toughest existences in the sports world. You get no salary, no guarantee, and must pay your own expenses. You can start with $15,000 and go home broke in eight months. But if you can play a winning game, you may rival John Paul Getty . . . or John William Nicklaus.

WHERE'S KEN VENTURI?

By Phil Jackman

From The Baltimore Evening Sun

Ken Venturi should be here.

Ken Venturi should be at every U.S. Open as long as they play the thing.

Just as Brooks Robinson was the World Series of 1970 and Bill Walton was the NCAA of a few months ago, Venturi has been the Open for going on a decade.

Our story starts one sultry evening in Baltimore nine years ago. The Boston Red Sox, on their way to an accustomed eighth-place finish in the American League, had just beaten the Orioles and the teams weren't due to play again until the following night.

What to do, what to do, a pair of visitors kept asking themselves as they conducted a glass-emptying contest in the bar of the old Sheraton-Belvedere Hotel.

The golf fanatic mentioned that the last two rounds of the Open were being conducted at Congressional Country Club outside Washington, and the other guy said what a smashing idea. But aren't they all at one o'clock in the morning and after a few brews?

It was not such a good idea at six when the wake-up call came. And it was worse yet when the bus to Washington dropped them off downtown, miles from the course.

Up to a red light rolled a complimentary car taking Chi-Chi Rodriguez to Congressional. Better than the lift were the extra participants' passes Chi-Chi had. The wanderers had the run of the joint.

The heat was already oppressive before the sun burned through the haze and Arnold Palmer and Tommy Jacobs, the leaders, weren't due to tee off for 16 minutes. Off at the moment were Venturi and his playing partner, young Ray Floyd.

"This guy's quite a story," Clif said, mentioning the operations Venturi had had on his hands for some mysterious malady. "Let's tag along a few holes and see how he does."

Venturi, six off the lead at 142, hit the first green in regulation and was putting for a birdie from nine feet. About 10 people were watching what Ken later described as "a heartening sign."

The putt rolled up, hung on the lip for the longest time, then plopped in. Clif said, "That's it, we're going with this guy." Venturi and Floyd were to get to know two baseball writers nearly as well as their caddies by day's end.

"With that putt as a start," recalls Venturi, "I said to myself, 'What the heck, let it fly.' " And did it. Ken made the turn in 30 (3–3–4, 3–3–4, 3–3–4), matching the all-time Open record for nine holes. His birdie at 13 put him six under for the round and in the thick of it.

But all week he had been weak, dehydrated, and somebody said the temperature reached 115 degrees in the valleys of Congressional by mid-morning. And the field had an afternoon round to go, the Open closing with a double round on Saturday in those days.

"I don't know why," said Ken, "but I'll never forget the 15th hole. My whole body began to shake and tremble. By the time we got to 17, I was so dizzy I was seeing three cups on the green. Putted for the middle one on each of the last two holes and missed for bogeys."

Still, he had a 66 for 208 and was just two back of Jacobs.

It was during lunch that touring pro Paul Harney expressed the opinion Venturi wouldn't be able to come out for the afternoon round: "We played a practice round the day he got here (Monday) and could go only 12 holes."

Harney excused himself, went to check his buddy, and came back shaking his head: "He's white as a ghost in there. He's already had a dozen salt tablets and the doc keeps pumping more in him."

Meanwhile, Floyd was consoling Venturi's wife, Conni, as Dr. John Everett was saying to Ken, "I'd suggest that you forget about trying to play again. If you go out there again in that heat in your condition it could actually be fatal."

But Venturi wasn't about to let this chance slip by no matter what it might cost him. Remember, this was the guy who a dozen years before, and as an amateur, had blown the Masters with a closing 80.

Choker, they called him; he hadn't won a tournament in four years and it wasn't certain the operation on his hands had been a success: "I had feeling in them, I recall, but the back of my left hand seemed to go out, although that was the least of my problems . . . my eyes just wouldn't focus properly."

The rumors floating around during the lunch break ran the gamut: Venturi was unconscious . . . Venturi was on his way to the hospital . . . Venturi was packed in ice.

"Actually," he said, "I was laying on the cool locker-room floor with my feet up on the bench drinking glass after glass of iced tea and gulping down salt tablets."

He was there five minutes early for his afternoon tee time, complete with medical staff. Dr. Everett explained if his body temperature went any higher he might go into convulsions, so he was going along with a hypodermic needle ready in case Ken collapsed in the heat.

Conni Venturi kissed her husband goodbye and he shuffled out and knocked the course dead. He looked like Ben Hogan moving along, not only because of the semilimp, but the way he was playing the game—dead to the pin on every shot.

By the 13th hole, it was over. Venturi had made up seven shots and led by five. At No. 18, he rolled in a 12-footer to the delight of 25,000 people and the putter dropped from his hands. "My God, I've won the Open," he said. Floyd was bawling.

Ken was a delight at the press conference: "Last time I talked to some of you fellows was at Augusta in 1960 when Palmer made those birdies on the last two holes. Somebody walked in and yelled, 'Plague,' and you all ran out and I was sitting there twiddling my thumbs and drinking a soft drink."

Thinking back on the eve of this year's chase and the anniversary date of his super achievement, Venturi said, "Another thing I'll never forget is the beginning of the press conference that day.

"Sports writers are a breed apart because to them victory and defeat are everyday business matters. So I was particularly touched when they rose to their feet en masse and let out with a thunderous ovation as I walked in."

It was late now, the ball game was due to start in Baltimore in about an hour, and most of the crowd had left. Venturi, in the parking lot and headed for his motel, stopped a couple of guys, shook their hands and said, "You two did all 36 holes with me today, didn't you? Thanks, but you gotta be nuts."

The hitchhike back to Baltimore was slow, so there was no time to hit the hotel for a quick cleanup. It was straight to the ball park, tired, dirty, sore, sunburned, and famished.

"You two look awful," somebody in the press box said. "What did you do today? Shoulda stuck around, we had a pretty good card game going this afternoon."

"Oh, we didn't do nothing much," answered Clif, slumping into a chair to get caught up in the ball game. "Took a little bus ride, that's all."

Yes, Ken Venturi, who failed to qualify, should be here, no doubt.

GOLF PARALYSIS . . . FORM ANALYSIS

By Ted Green

From the Los Angeles Times

I can hit a golf ball as far as many professionals. There's only one difference. It's called out of bounds.

This flaw—inability to hit straight—has me frustratingly short of golfing greatness. I can't seem to get out of the 80s.

Thus, when a story involving golf lessons was proposed, I was a logical, if not entirely willing, candidate.

The assignment: to present my problem to four pros with varied backgrounds, to see how professional advice varies. It was recognized that there is no one best way to correct a flaw, and that a single lesson is not likely to effect a cure.

I chose pros who teach in diverse settings—a country club, driving range, city course, and county course.

To test the value of the lessons, I played a round beforehand and shot 84, about my norm, for comparison with a post-test round.

The scene was a plush country club in Los Angeles. The pro, a casual-looking man in his early forties, was once "golf teacher of the year" in L.A. I could tell how enthused he was as soon as I hit the first warm-up shot.

"Your grip is absolutely horrendous!

"You do watch TV, don't you? I bet you've never seen a pro hold the club the way you do."

"But I shoot in the 80s."

"That doesn't matter," he said. "You're making other compensations, like shifting your weight well so you can power the ball around. But you've reached a plateau. You'll never get any better."

He said my misfirings were a result of my unlocked grip. He demonstrated the proper grip.

"If you don't learn the interlock [right pinky locked with left forefinger] you can forget about playing good golf."

So I tried it his way. The next 25 swings with a seven iron resulted in 25 pitiful ground balls.

"Don't worry about a thing," he assured me. "It took you more than a half an hour to get this way. Let's not be impatient."

Roughly 50 grounders later (at least I used to hit them in the air) the 30 minutes were nearly gone and there still were a few balls left in the bucket.

"I've got another lesson now," he said. "Do you think you could speed this up a little?"

Hesitantly, I asked if there was any way to remedy this newest affliction—groundballitis.

"Practice, lots of practice," he answered. "And I'm gonna give you a real good tip. When your new grip causes you to swing in an outside-in arc like you're doing now, stand up to a sprinkler and swing inside it. You know, barely miss it."

"Barely miss it? I'm having enough trouble barely hitting it."

"Don't worry about the ball so much," he said. "Just remember the sprinkler."

For $9.25, I had learned more about gardening than hitting the ball straight. He had decided the only way to solve my dilemma was to totally alter my grip. Possibly sound advice, but not practical without months of steady practice.

The next stop: a driving range in Orange County, where a tall pro in his fifties, a crony of Sam Snead who has taught pros Bob Goalby, Charlie Sifford, and Dave Hill, presided.

He led me to a shack adjacent to the range. Inside, one wall was covered by a long mirror, and two others were plastered with autographed pictures from Bob Hope and Dean Martin and dozens of magazine cutouts depicting Palmer, Nicklaus, et al, in perfect form.

The fourth wall was covered with a heavy canvas mat. In the middle of the room stood a portable tee, the rubber kind common to driving ranges.

He said study of canvas shots is the best way to teach.

"What seems to be the problem?" he asked.

"I can't hit straight as often as I'd like."

"Hmm," he replied, readying one of the many singsong catch phrases he'd offer in the 45 minutes.

"Let me first say I don't believe in paralysis from analysis." He chuckled appreciatively. "Why don't you hit a few?"

Using my old grip, I thudded three balls into the canvas mat.

"You can't do a thing if you don't use your spring," he said.

I smiled back, but must have looked bewildered.

"What I mean is you have to control the right leg. Yours points out. The energy and accuracy of every swing (for right-handers) comes from the inside of the right leg. If your left hip is pointing toward 12 o'clock (the target), that right foot has to point at 3 o'clock (a right angle), not 4, 5, or even 3:05. It can be a little earlier than 3, but not one second later. Keep checking it in the mirror."

"And my grip. It's OK?"

"The overlap, interlock, or unlocked grip are all acceptable," he said. "Whichever one lets you control the club is the one to use."

I vigorously bombarded the canvas.

"That's good, that's good. Fine rhythm and balance," he said.

I emptied the bucket of balls, cautiously eyeing my 3 o'clock foot before each swing. The pro nodded approvingly after each thud.

"Remember, leg control," he said later as we walked from the shack. "Leg control."

For $10, I'd have to go out on my own to see if he was right. So I bought another bucket and took it to an outside tee.

The result: not quite as much distance, erratic as ever.

"Geez, you're all fouled up. No wonder you can't hit straight."

The words came from a former pro champion, about fifty, who teaches at a city course in Los Angeles.

Firmly, but in a soft voice, he continued his analysis after watching me swat a few more.

"First," he said, "you don't grip the club correctly. It's loose in your left hand. Second, your feet are too narrow. You have to stand much wider because you're off balance when you swing. Third, there's entirely too much superfluous movement. Your whole body is involved in your swing. Way too much herky-jerky motion.

"Here, give me the club. This is how to do it."

Effortlessly, he hit a perfect drive with a picture swing.

"It isn't a hard game," he said. "People make it hard. They think they're supposed to hit the ball, but they're not. The club hits the ball. All you have to do is control the club, talk to it, make it do what you want.

"Take control."

I took control. For 20 minutes I tried to tighten my grip, widen my stance, and eliminate the herky-jerkies.

"I'm going on vacation for a few weeks," he said afterward. "If you're still having trouble, give me a call. This one's on the house."

At first glance, the last pro seemed least likely to help. A short man with a weather-beaten face in his late fifties, he has taught for years at a county course. And he was the cheapest—$6—for a half-hour lesson that ran over an hour.

He watched the old me (I had no trouble reverting to my original form) and said nothing for quite a while. Finally he spoke.

"Every golfer's swing is molded around his physical characteristics. You can't change someone's swing who's been playing for 10 years," he said. "A pro's job is to find what a golfer does best and then work within the confines of his ability.

"Guys like you who hit hard but cockeyed usually have trouble in the hands.

"There are many ways to hold clubs," he said, "just as there are many people with different physical makeups. You have to find the style that fits your personality, one that lets you hit the ball good. There's no set way to do it."

Allowing me the comfort of an unlocked grip (known as the baseball grip), he made minor changes in hand position on the club until I began hitting the ball better than I had all day.

The results were encouraging—still solid contact and a bit more on target.

The day had been enlightening, if not overly helpful. I left the final lesson convinced that more often than not, a pro is off base when he suggests drastic changes in the swing of someone who's played for years.

It's fine to create a swing for new players, but for me the most helpful advice came from the pro who concentrated on minor modifications.

Extra lessons seemed called for from the country-club pro and ex-champ, considering the changes they proposed. And although he didn't suggest any major alterations, the driving-range pro implied that a return visit would be beneficial.

To complete the experiment, I headed back to the course where I had scored 84 earlier, imperfect swing and all.

Walking to the first tee I thought about the sprinkler. I remembered the 3 o'clock foot. I fought off the herky-jerkies. I adjusted my hand position. And I shot 60—for nine holes.

Not only did my errant missiles find trees, fences, and gravel roads, like the prelesson round, but sand, rocks, water ditches, the driving range next to the first tee, and a petunia patch in someone's backyard off No. 7.

Clearly, I was the victim of an acute case of paralysis from analysis.

Boxing

IT TOOK HIM 4 MINUTES 35 SECONDS

By Eddie Muller

From the San Francisco Examiner

Bombs in the sturdy, black fists of George Foreman struck like streaks of lightning. And, when the thunder subsided, a badly battered, disjointed, and disillusioned Joe Frazier was led on shaky legs back to his corner.

At one minute and 35 seconds of the second round—with a swearing, milling mob pushing its way into the ring—the twenty-four-year-old Bay Area boxer from Hayward was declared the new world's heavyweight champion.

They came out last night to see the battle of the unbeatens, two former Olympic Games gold medalists. And they didn't leave until an hour after the abbreviated destruction ended.

It was a glorious night for the man who once waved a tiny American flag following his victory in the Olympics at Mexico City in 1968.

Now, five years later, this big, muscular, talented, and personable fellow heard the shouts of victory by thousands who paid tribute to one of the greatest and most dramatic endings in a championship fight.

To Big George it was, in his own words, "just another fight." He repeated that often in pre-fight statements.

Those who sat in on this title match, first ever offered in Jamaica, will long remember it for a number of reasons. To them it wasn't just another fight. It was a spectacle.

An upset, if you will. And dramatized in such a way that millions seeing it around the world on closed circuit TV and home television will probably forget Muhammad Ali, the ex-champion who still insists the crown belongs to him.

Six times the bearded Frazier, who said nobody could knock him out, visited the blue-colored ring canvas. In the first round, one many thought would find Foreman freezing, the champion was decked three times.

The powerful, perfectly thrown Foreman blows smashed Joe's features and dug into his body as he staggered about the enclosure until referee Arthur Mercante mercifully halted what now was a slaughter. Frazier was also down three times in the second.

Startled handlers, including manager Yank Durham, worked feverishly on their man when they finally got him on a corner stool. It must have been as least three minutes before the dazed Frazier realized he was no longer the man who could proudly boast that he was the world's heavyweight champion.

Undaunted by Frazier's reputation of being a bruising, crowding body smasher, the cool Foreman met his foe in mid-ring in the opening session. He was first to lead, with a right to the body. And, right there, some at ringside said he was amateurish and was committing a cardinal sin by leading with his right.

Frazier probably thought likewise. He shuffled in, disdain written on his features. Moving quickly on his strong underpinnings, Foreman reached Frazier's jaw with a left and then for the first time the power in Big George's right, which had 217 pounds behind it, cracked home. Down went Frazier. And every one of the 36,000 howling fans, who paid $412,000, stood as one. Here was a champion floored, even before many had been seated. Nine seconds were tolled while Frazier was near his corner, staring at referee Mercante.

With the same kind of a deadpan look that Joe Louis wore, Foreman bided his time. He didn't become overanxious. He knew what he had to do. And he kept Frazier off with pushes with his long left and then crashed in a right uppercut. There was the champion down for a second time.

Later, Frazier said the reason he got up from all but the first knock-down without taking a full count was that he was in full control of his faculties.

To get to Foreman's body, close in on him, and rough him up seemed uppermost now in the champ's mind. Foreman's moves thwarted whatever attack Frazier tried. Jabs, stiff and straight, caught Frazier in the face.

He tried unsuccessfully to come in from one side, instead of a straight line, the way he did in piling up his 29 straight victories as a pro.

In front of him he had a thinking man who had come a long way on a rocky road, a former juvenile delinquent who was determined to win the biggest prize in boxing.

Those who said Foreman couldn't win because he threw punches in round-house fashion now saw how wrong they were. A well-timed hook and a follow-up right had Frazier down again. Instinctively, he climbed up. He shook from head to toe. Luckily the bell rang, ending the round. Frazier's second scrambled through the ropes to get him back to the corner.

He needed more than that one-minute reprieve, however. If he had gotten more it wouldn't have been of any help. In the opposite corner, waiting anxiously to tear back into action, was this determined youngster who knew it was only a matter of time before he would end it all.

Later, a demoralized Frazier was to say, "I know I should have come out for the second and boxed him. I just couldn't. I'm a fighter and I like to charge."

Frazier admitted he made a mistake. But Foreman didn't make any. Could Frazier, who stood up under tremendous punishment in his 15-rounder two years ago with Muhammad Ali, shake off the effects of the first round and bulldog his younger foe?

He and his followers got the answer in a hurry.

Two rights, thrown with uppercut motion, careened through the humid night air and found their mark on Frazier's bearded jaw. Quickly, Foreman sent a chopping right to the side of the head and Frazier went down for the fourth time.

You could see the look on Frazier's kisser. His eyes were rolling somewhat. Nobody in Foreman's corner had to shout instructions. The long preparation for this all-important battle found Foreman with all the answers. Coolly, he planted a left hook on Frazier's chin. The down-up routine was repeated.

After a brief exchange, Mercante brought boos from the crowd when he warned Foreman for what he said was shoving.

It was then the last of the thunder and lightning struck. Backed to the ropes, a position in which he usually places his opponents,

Frazier was a target for a volley of head shots. There were no less than eight that thundered off the chin that was supposed to be indestructible. Only the hemp, it seemed, kept the now badly battered champion on his feet.

To get solid punching range, Foreman took a half step backward. Then he fired two hooks to the head. Then a power-paced right sent the well-whipped Frazier floundering along the ropes near George's corner.

Joe sagged to one knee. Back in a neutral corner, George stood waiting. Was there to be more? If so, he was ready.

When Frazier stumbled away across the ring, Mercante wrapped his arms around the beaten champion, signaling that it was all over.

"I gave him every opportunity to continue," said the referee. "I looked at his eyes and they were glassy. His legs were gone."

A deep cut inside the lower lip was one of several Frazier wounds.

There had been reports Frazier took this fight over manager Yank Durham's objections. Despite last night's bad beating, Joe said he didn't plan to retire.

Apologizing for his performance, the former champ said, "It wasn't the Ali fight that did it."

Muhammad has insisted ever since their 1971 battle that although he lost the title, the terrible beating he administered ended the effective career of Frazier, as indicated by Joe's long stay in the hospital.

"I was in good shape," said Frazier last night, "but Foreman's left hooks to the body and the right uppercuts to my head took it out of me."

Strangely subdued for a man who had just won the heavyweight championship, Foreman said in his dressing room he had won because he had "prayed hard, worked hard, and made sacrifices."

Foreman told the former champion he had more respect for him than any other fighter.

"What did he say?" writers asked.

"He said, 'Right on, George, right on.' "

Foreman isn't going to defend his title in a hurry. He said he will visit a number of Job Corps camps around the country instead.

"I want to talk to those kids," said the man who started his boxing career at Camp Parks Job Corps center in Pleasanton, California.

Dick Sadler, Foreman's always-confident manager, seemed to take it all in stride.

"We knew this would happen," he said. "Sure, we're happy. Now we'll just rest for a while. We came a long way, hurdled a lot of obstacles, and through the help of a number of people, got this chance. George took care of everything in great style."

The victory was Foreman's 38th, the knockout his 35th. The second round seems to be his lucky one. It was the 13th time he has scored a KO in that session.

Bob Aru of Top Rank Inc., which handles Ali's TV deals, said a Muhammad-Foreman fight "would do millions."

Aru promised to try to make the match for Houston in June. But he'll have to do some tall dickering with Sadler before negotiations can be completed. It's an open secret Dick doesn't lean too kindly toward such a fight this year.

"He [Ali] kept us waiting," said the hustling, dynamic Hayward manager. "I guess we can make him wait, too."

It had been said that this fight was Frazier's big gamble. It was costly, all right. He lost his crown and the Ali rematch, which could have netted him $3 million.

Now the young man who became the third heavyweight champion developed in the San Francisco Bay Area stands to make a fortune. Like James J. Corbett and Max Baer, Foreman deserves it.

And the gamble he took by joining Sadler in a fighter-manager partnership will make one of boxing's most readable stories.

THE GREATEST IS NOW THE TIREDEST

By Dave Anderson

From The New York Times

In other years, after other fights, Muhammad Ali liked to touch his face and preen.

"Look at this face, ain't a mark on it," he would shout. "No other fighter ever looked this way, I am The Greatest."

But now he's The Tiredest, his eyes weary, his voice a whisper. And his body is betraying him. Two years ago, after he lost the unanimous decision to Joe Frazier, the right side of his jaw appeared to have a balloon inside it. Instead of preening and shouting, he hurried to a hospital for X-rays, which showed no fracture. Last year, in an eighth-round knockout of Bob Foster, he bled for his money for the first time, from a long slit on his left eyelid. Six months ago, in losing a split decision to Ken Norton, the left side of his jaw was fractured.

And last night, after a dramatic flourish in the final round for a split-decision victory over Norton in their rematch, Muhammad Ali wobbled into his dressing room and slumped on a brown leather couch. He shook his head and flexed his right hand, which Dr. Ferdie Pacheco was inspecting.

"It ain't broke, is it?" Ali asked.

"It doesn't feel like it," Pacheco said.

"It hurts in the wrist," Ali said.

"You jammed the bones of the hand into the wrist, that's all," the doctor said. "I don't think anything's broken."

"What's it hurt for then?" Ali asked.

"It's a fighter's hand." Pacheco said.

Indeed it is. In his struggle in recent years, Muhammad Ali has shown himself to be a fighter, not merely a boxer. Years ago, when he was Cassius Clay, his courage was suspect, mostly because of his confused fright when he was momentarily blinded by a salve on Sonny Liston's face in their first bout.

"I can't see," he told Angelo Dundee, his trainer, in the corner. "Cut the gloves off."

"This is for the title," Dundee said. "It'll clear. Run until it does. Run, run, run."

Dundee pushed him into the ring for the next round. Soon the title was his. But for years after, some boxing critics scorned his courage. No longer. When he was knocked down by Joe Frazier, he got up as quickly as a man can. When he had his jaw broken by Ken Norton, he could have quit but he didn't. When he knew he needed the 12th round last night to assure a victory, he responded.

"This is it, we got to have this round," Dundee exhorted him in the corner. "Go out and do your thing."

Ali did, dancing as he had in the early rounds, dancing as he had years ago, flicking his jab in Norton's face, convincing the referee and the two judges that he deserved the round. By winning it on all three scorecards, he earned a split decision. Had he lost the round, he would have lost the decision.

"I knew if I closed the show," Ali was saying now, "I'd stand a better chance of winning."

He was still slumped on the leather couch, still wearing his long white satin robe, an ice bag in his right hand, holding a paper cup of Coke in his left hand.

"I thought it was your most courageous fight," somebody said.

"Did you think so?" Ali asked. "From where you were, were the people satisfied?"

"They loved it," somebody else said.

"Norton's better than I thought he was. The times I fought Liston, if I fought like I did then, Norton would have beaten me. But my experience got me through this."

"Who's next?"

"I got that trip to Jakarta to fight Rudy Lubbers," he said. "Then we'll see what's happenin'."

"What about a title bout with George Foreman?" he was asked.

"Foreman will be much easier than Norton was," Ali replied.

Not really. For a few rounds, Ali might be able to escape Foreman's sledgehammer strength. But not for 15 rounds. Sooner or later, the new heavyweight champion will land one of his sledgehammer punches. For the first time in his career, Muhammad Ali will be counted out. In his prime, Ali might have eluded Foreman, frustrated him and won a decision. But not now. More and more, it appears that Ali and Frazier destroyed each other, physically and emotionally, in their brutal epic. Their bodies haven't been the same since. And their spirits never again will soar, as they did before their $20-million extravaganza. Now, sadly, there is talk of an Ali-Frazier rematch.

"I want Joe Frazier," Ali said softly. "I got to get my revenge."

Outside his dressing room, dozens of people were waiting. Outside the entrance to The Forum, hundreds more waited. He has advertised himself as "The Peoples Champ" and the people were waiting, but in his weariness, he shook his head.

"I think I'll stay here a couple hours," The Tiredest said. "I think I'll duck the people.

THE SQUARE WHO BECAME CHAMPION

By Will Grimsley

From The Associated Press

George Foreman was shooting pool in a dingy billiard hall in Houston in 1966 when he happened to hear a radio commercial extolling the benefits of the Job Corps.

The speaker was Johnny Unitas, the quarterback.

"That's for me," Foreman said.

On Monday night—four and a half years later—this one-time junior high school dropout, delinquent and bane of the Houston cops, smashed Joe Frazier to the floor six times in the space of four minutes, 35 seconds, and became the heavyweight champion of the world.

Carried to the dressing room on the shoulders of joyous fans, Foreman called his manager, Dick Sadler, and a half dozen other associates around a rubbing table and said:

"Let's pray."

It was a moving moment.

"It really sounds corny, but this is a genuine man," said Sargent Shriver, former head of the government's Office of Economic Opportunity, which envelops the Job Corps, and 1972 Democratic vice-presidential candidate.

"He sounds like a square but he is for real. I have known him since he entered the Job Corps. He is not stupid. He is not dull and uninteresting. There's nothing fake about him."

Shriver's sentiments were echoed by one of Foreman's closest friends, Leroy Jackson of Glendale, California, former counselor of the Job Corps and business adviser to the No. 1 fighter in the world, who is on the threshold of millions.

"This is a great man," said Jackson as the ring world gradually returned to its sensibilities after one of boxing's most astonishing upsets.

"He doesn't drink. He doesn't smoke. He doesn't cheat on his wife. He is such a straight guy, you wouldn't believe it. They don't make his kind much anymore."

Foreman, a 6-foot-3, 217-pound giant with arms like the trunk of an oak, is a big bear with a marshmallow heart.

There is no air of arrogance or pomposity about him—even now that he is king of all the heavyweights. He is modest, mild-mannered, retiring in nature.

When he speaks, the words are so soft and low that they are almost inaudible. He constantly has to be asked to repeat them.

He talks of love, understanding, duty, and patriotism.

Before Monday night, Americans remembered him best as the nineteen-year-old black fighter who, after winning the Olympic gold medal at Mexico City in 1968, had circled the ring waving an American flag.

Somebody asked Foreman Tuesday how it felt to wake up as the heavyweight champion of the world.

"I thought it would be different," he replied. "But I felt like the same old George Foreman."

The new heavyweight champion is not surrounded by a court. He has no palace guard telling him where to go and what to say. He steers himself.

Not even peppery little Dick Sadler, the manager who has brought him along so adroitly, is allowed to dominate his life. Foreman is his own man, and apparently intends to stay that way.

Interviewers sought, in the post-fight interview, to get him to say that Frazier was a farce or out of shape.

"You would think I fought a little girl," George said, with one of his rare displays of impatience. "This man beats everybody. He went right down the line of heavyweights. He beat up on his sparring partners. He was 100 percent fit."

Foreman said the first thing he did after returning to his Skyline Hotel headquarters near midnight was to call his wife, Adrienne, and ask about his seventeen-day-old daughter, Mich. They are in Minneapolis.

"I want to go home and be with my wife and daughter," the champion said. "But I realize I can't take it easy long. Boxing is my livelihood." George was up early Tuesday morning and had breakfast with three friends in the main hotel dining room. Nobody bothered him.

Later, still wearing a red sweat shirt and tan slacks, he gave a poolside interview. Shriver was there. So were Dick Sadler, Leroy Jackson, and others who have had an impact on his life.

It was Shriver who recalled the pool hall incident in Houston. Shriver also remembered that, after joining the Job Corps, Foreman was almost kicked out because of his behavior.

"One of the officials reported that George was causing a ruckus and was a disruptive influence," Shriver related. "It was then that Doc Broadus, the camp's vocational guidance director, stepped in.

"Broadus said, 'Wait a minute—this is what the program is for. Let me have him and I will let him fight to his heart's content.' "

Foreman was inserted into the boxing program at the Parks Job Corps Center in Pleasanton, California, some 40 miles east of Oakland, much against his will, and it was Broadus who tied on his first boxing gloves and taught him to fight.

Foreman insisted that Broadus be in his corner for the Frazier fight.

"That gives an idea of what sort of fellow this guy is," Shriver said. "He is intensely loyal to friends."

Foreman, who became something of an idol to Jamaicans, promised an early return to this tropical island.

"People gave me love and support," he said. "I appreciate it very much."

Meanwhile, boxing men analytically examined the game's new Wonder Boy.

"There is no telling how great he is," said Angelo Dundee of Miami, trainer for Muhammad Ali. "Certainly he was greatly underrated, but I knew any man who won as many fights as he had—37 before Monday night—had to have something. He had a winning habit."

Dundee, who predicted a Foreman victory, said a Foreman-Ali bout, matching two superb athletes with power and finesse, should make a great match.

Ali's man Friday, Drew "Bundini" Brown, also said he was not surprised.

"You might say it was the 17th round," he said, referring to the

15 rounds Ali fought with Frazier. "When a man gets his brains scrambled the way Ali scrambled Joe's, the brains are like jelly.

"But I don't think George is going to fight us soon. He's gonna sit and let us grow old."

Horse Racing

THE SAGA OF SECRETARIAT LIGHTS UP AGAIN

By Nelson Fisher

From The San Diego Union

Light up again the saga of Secretariat. Bury the hoodoo against sons of Bold Ruler winning a Kentucky Derby. Bold Ruler himself failed, so did Bold Lad.

Erase time records for the Derby and revive the bold thought of a ninth Triple Crown champion, the first since Citation in 1948.

This and more was the story blazed by the flying hoofs of the Meadow Stable's Secretariat, a stunner for looks and performance, before a record crowd of 134,476 on a beautiful day at Churchill Downs.

Rolling so easily not even jockey Ron Turcotte dreamed he was record-bound, Secretariat curled California's Sham straightening in the long homestretch and continued on to defeat Sham two and a half lengths. It was a record 1:59 2-5 for the mile and one quarter. Sham also bettered the Derby record.

Secretariat, whose red chestnut coat reflects gold in the sun, smashed three-fifths of a second from Northern Dancer's 2:00 flat, set in 1964.

Later at the stable, trainer Frank (Pancho) Martin revealed that Sham suffered a cut mouth and the loss of two teeth, apparently injuring himself at the break of the starting gate.

Martin's shirt was bloody from treating the horse. He did not claim the mishap as an excuse for defeat in view of the record performances of both horses, only pointed out that Sham did not have an assistant starter at the time.

Secretariat, the son of Bold Ruler and a Princequillo broodmare, Something Royal, unleashed a phenomenal last quarter of a shade better than the :23 1-5 shown on the chart.

Colonel Ed Bradley, who won three Derbies three decades ago, used to say, "Give me a horse that can run the last quarter in :24 and I'll win the Derby."

Since he was looming up on Sham's hindquarters passing the quarter-mile pole, Secretariat could claim :23 for that last quarter. It was almost three ticks faster than Shecky Greene scooted the first quarter. Shecky hit 1:11 4-5 for the first six furlongs and Sham got the mile in 1:36 1-5. Whirlaway ran the previously fastest last quarter of 24 seconds in 1941.

Our Native, the consistent winner of some part of the purses in major stakes this year, came along to be the remote third finisher, eight lengths back of Sham. He held half a length over Forego, a horse so huge he has had trouble leaving the starting gate.

The redemption of Secretariat, a disappointing third behind Angle Light, his running mate, and Sham in the Wood Memorial two weeks ago, was worth $5, $3.20, and $3 to those who made him the 3-to-2 favorite in the field of 11 betting choices.

Sham, second favorite at 5-to-2, saved $3.20 to place, $3 to show, and Our Native $4.20 for third.

To owner Mrs. John Tweedy, daughter of the late Christopher T. Chenery, master of the Meadow Stable, Secretariat brought a record $155,050 first money from the richest gross purse in Kentucky Derby history, $198,800.

An exacta wasn't conducted here on the Derby, but in the New York OTB Secretariat and Sham paid $21.60 on a $3 exacta. A $3 quiniela there returned $17.70 and the $2 OTB mutuels on straight and place pools only were $5.80 to win and $6.20 to place for Secretariat and $4.80 to place for Sham.

For owner Sigmond Sommer, New York construction magnate, Santa Anita Derby champion Sham earned $25,000 for second place.

It was no surprise that Shecky Greene was shot into the lead from his No. 11 post position, but it was a surprise that he lasted as far as he did, finishing sixth.

Behind him were Florida Derby champion Royal and Regal (eighth), the disappointing Blue Grass winner, My Gallant (ninth), Wood Memorial champion Angle Light (10th), and Warbucks, the 13th and last finisher. Some sort of an injury report might be expected on Warbucks today.

California's Gold Bag, a 68–1 chance, flashed brief early speed and came in 11th, ahead of Twice A Prince and Warbucks.

Mrs. Tweedy, trainer Lucien Laurin, relieved from a week of pressure in a war of nerves with Frank (Pancho) Martin, Sham's conditioner, and jockey Ron Turcotte enjoyed still another record.

It was the first time since the Derby began in 1875 that the same owner, trainer, and jockey have made it two years straight in the Derby. Their Riva Ridge did it last year, fell from grace when fourth as a relative unknown named Bee Bee Bee won the Preakness and came back to take the Belmont, third jewel of the Triple Crown.

The magnetism of Secretariat, voted Horse of the Year for 1972 as a two-year-old, in this chance to wipe out his horrible afternoon in the Wood Memorial stimulated the record throng into wagering a Derby record of $7,627,975 for the day. That's nearly half a million more than the previous high of $7,164,717 set last year.

The Wood, in which Secretariat misfired in running third, four lengths behind Sham, now becomes something unreal, something unexplainable except for the old saw, that, after all, "Horses aren't machines." Even machines are faulty in our era of automobile emission controls.

Jockey Turcotte's ride was flawless. Secretariat was last going by the grandstand the first time, but Turcotte sat cool.

Earlier in the week, trainer Laurin said that the handsome colt doesn't care to be handled and Turcotte let him make his own decisions.

Relaxed, Secretariat slipped inside two or three wide runners around the first turn but headed to an outside lane curving into the backstretch.

Laffit Pincay, meanwhile, had placed Sham in third position, took after Shecky Greene from the half-mile pole and steadily closed the gap while still in hand.

Secretariat, given his head, moved cadence with Sham. When Turcotte stung him briefly with the whip, the rangy red colt ate up the ground in one swoop, caught Sham and drew clear under a hand ride.

Pincay was whipping furiously through the last furlong, but to no avail. Sham had used too much speed too early to tag Shecky Greene.

Asked how many times he batted Secretariat, Turcotte said, "Two times." He also said that he believed Sham was running easily, inferring that he thought Laffit also might not have realized they were crumbling a two-year-old track record.

In two weeks, on May 19, Secretariat will go for the second leg of the Triple Crown in the Preakness at Pimlico. Three weeks after that, June 9, comes the Belmont Stakes and the elusive finish of the defiant Triple Crown for American three-year-olds.

1,001 SURE FIRE WAYS TO LOSE A RACE

By Mark Shrager

From Turf & Sport Digest

The Del Mar nightcap was producing no surprises this hot August afternoon—Admiral Lazarem was the favorite, and Admiral Lazarem was winning. At least that's the way it appeared, as the Admiral, having led from the start, moved into a commanding three-length lead at the head of the short stretch. With little more than a furlong of turf still to be covered, nothing in the field was close enough to mount a serious challenge, and none of the supposed come-from-behinders seemed to be coming. In short, the race was won; it belonged to The Admiral. As those who held tickets on him began edging toward the cashiers' cages, the remainder of the bettors started the long trek back to the parking lots.

The Admiral, however, had other ideas. Del Mar's turf course is bordered on the inside by a thick hedge, and with one quick burst of speed Admiral Lazarem shot through the hedge and into the infield. In the process he lost his rider, who wisely bailed out just before The Admiral, still running at full speed, crashed head-on into the eighth pole, leveling both the pole and The Admiral in one jarring thud. When finally caught by the grinning outriders, Admiral Lazarem was slightly bruised but otherwise uninjured, although the curses of his frustrated backers undoubtedly would have weighed more heavily upon a human head.

Admiral Lazarem's trip that day was unusual, perhaps even unique, in the obvious sense that Thoroughbreds do not daily leave race courses to attack eighth poles; yet in a broader sense The Admiral's race *was* typical. One of the more respected maxims of a sport fraught with hoarty truisms is that "there are a thousand ways to lose a horse race, but only one way to win one." Admiral Lazarem had, possibly, discovered a thousand-and-first way to lose, but certainly this didn't render him immortal—it merely made him another loser, although a rather more spectacular loser than most.

All of which simply points up the amazing variety of ways a horse can find to lose a horse race. Of course, this is hardly something to be wondered at, for considering the nature of the sport—in which large groups of big, rather stupid, and characteristically spooky animals ridden by tiny men who cannot possibly have full control of them, must attempt to negotiate distances of ground at high speed without getting in the way of the other members of their company—the fact that one-third of all betting favorites actually do win is really quite phenomenal. Consider: in the normal course of any horse race, even the best of horses can lose by being boxed in, fanned out, or trapped in the middle of the pack. He may be beaten by a premature move, by moving too late, or because, for some perverse reason of his own, he decides to make no move at all. He may be beaten by a poor break, or he may start beautifully, only to be bothered by another horse's poor start. He might even lose because he's become too smart—some horses discover after racing for a while that running slowly is much less tiring than running fast, and besides, after being soundly beaten there isn't that bothersome business of being photographed in the winner's circle. Literally anything can cause a horse to lose a race—this is one reason most successful betting systems emphasize eliminating likely losers rather than picking winners.

This unpredictability must forever be the bane of the handicapper, who is forced to go at his work knowing that some mishap not only may, but probably will, defeat him in his labors. On the other hand, this multiplicity of losing possibilities is, in all likelihood, what makes the sport so unthinkably exciting. Every race is supremely uncertain, and since luck is likely to play an important role in the eventual outcome, each and every horse, even the "hopeless" 99–1 shot that everyone eliminates from his computations without a second thought, is potentially a winner, or at least a danger to the choice of the selector. Thus, at least in terms of unpredictability, and therefore excitement, the fifth race at Cahokia Downs is every bit as enticing as the Kentucky Derby, if one has a financial stake in the outcome, or even just a personal favorite in the race. If the fifth at Cahokia fails to measure up to the Derby in terms of impact, this is because the horses entered in the Derby are so good (and so inexperienced), and because they have only one chance to win this best-known of all horse races. Lose the fifth at Cahokia today, and you can come back next week against the same field. Lose the Kentucky Derby of your year once, and you'll never win it. Both races, however, are affected equally by the "Thousand-Ways-To-Lose" syndrome.

It is probably quite significant for the human race that, despite Man's supposed superiority over the rest of the animal kingdom in terms of intelligence and creativity, the horse always seems to be one jump ahead of the horseman when it comes to discovering the means to foil his winning strategies. Put blinkers on your charger, for example, and he'll probably ignore the surge of another horse going by until it is too late to catch him, losing all chance of winning. Remove the blinkers, however, and one of two things will happen—either the horse will lug in, terrified at the sight of the multitudes of onlookers, and tire both himself and his jockey, or he'll become so totally entranced at the sight of the crowd that he'll forget to run fast enough to beat the other horses. Fast Fellow, a fine sprinter on the West Coast, once lost an important handicap in just this way—at midstretch his lead appeared secure enough, but by the finish his nose was one of three on the wire. The first two were pointed directly ahead, but Fast Fellow's, the third one, was turned at a 90-degree angle to the others as he stared into the crowd. On the way back to the barn, Fast Fellow may well have turned his head toward the stands again, this time to watch his frustrated backers as they tore up their win and place tickets.

A similar such instrument of self-torture designed by horsemen is the shadow roll, which is basically nothing more than a roll of cloth placed around a horse's nose to prevent him from seeing the track. Ideally, a shadow roll will prevent a nervous horse from being bothered by such distractions as shadows and windblown scraps of paper on the track; thus it can be very useful on certain high-strung animals. Unfortunately, though, some horses will sulk and become unmanageable if their vision is so impaired, and so on these horses a shadow roll cannot be used. Take a shadow roll off of a horse, however, especially after he has become used to one, and he becomes odds-on to do exactly what Neurologo did in the 1970 Hollywood Gold Cup—blow the race by jumping over shadows until he's thoroughly exhausted.

The blinker, the shadow roll, and other such pieces of light equipment are, however, but puny insignificant weapons in Man's never-ending battle to find ever-more complicated, ever-more frustrating ways of losing horse races. As any nervous Thoroughbred who has ever been contronted by one would gladly tell you if he could, the ultimate such instrument of despair for the horse—and therefore for the horseman as well—must undeniably be the starting gate.

The starting gate. So fiendishly innocent, so maniacally simple, its inventor must rank with Edgar Allen Poe and the Marquis de Sade as history's most demoniacal creators of the implements of torture.

The starting gate was invented originally to make more equal the chances of all horses starting in a race, since in the old days of standing starts a very quick horse could have an unfair advantage. In essence, the gate is a row of small stalls on wheels, with back doors that lock shut and front doors that open simultaneously when the starter pushes a button. The starter's button also activates a loud bell located within the apparatus—when the doors spring open the bell sounds, and the horses, adrenalin spurting, fly from the gate. Or at least that's the way it's supposed to happen.

Thoroughbreds, of course, are suspicious creatures, so before a horse can be broken out of the gate he must first be persuaded somehow to get into it. Every young race horse, then, goes through a period of schooling, in which it becomes somewhat accustomed to the gate, is allowed to walk through it, and gradually becomes used to its everyday presence. After some weeks of slowly learning to accept the gate as something other than a mortal enemy, the young horse will be broken from the gate at full racing speed, an event that usually marks the end of the schooling period. When the horse has demonstrated some proficiency in full-speed starts, it is deemed ready to race.

Unfortunately, the first actual race in which a horse participates will quite probably cure him forever of any growing fondness he might be developing for starting gates. To begin with, the young horse will definitely not be allowed to enter the gate at his own cautious speed, but will probably be moved in hastily and physically by the gatemen, who, after all, have a horse race to get started. The break, too, rather than being rewarded by a lump of sugar or a friendly pat on the nose, will in all likelihood be quickly followed by the sting of the whip, to assure that the young horse understands he's running for keeps this time. Very early in a horse's career, then, he learns to associate the start of a race with confusion and pain, and thus learns to fear starting. This, of course, means that the horse is likely to begin hating the starting gate with the total passion of one who has suddenly been betrayed by an old friend.

Inevitably, then, many horses develop neuroses in response to the starting gate. Such animals are a common sight at all racetracks, breaking into a lather at the sight of the gate, throwing tantrums, and generally doing all they can to lose the race before it's ever run, as they're led (or frequently, shoved) into the proper enclosure. Probably nothing at any track is more pathetic—or more likely to finish far down the track—than the neurotic gate horse that has had the totally bad luck to draw post position No. 1. Walked slowly toward his rail stall like a condemned man approaching the gallows, he may reluctantly allow himself to be led in. Then he must stand there, traumatized, in his tiny enclosure, possibly for as long as two minutes or more, while the other neurotic animals are inserted into their respective claustrophobic boxes, offering resistance of various types and quantities along the way. By the time the gate is sprung, the chances of our No. 1 horse are virtually nil, and the same can frequently be said of Nos. 2, 3, 4, and 5, unless they are exceptionally placid and well-adjusted beasts. ". . . The race," one might paraphrase Ecclesiastes, "is not always to the swift, but to the runner so totally dense as to be unmoved by the prospect of entering a starting gate."

A classic case of starting-gate neurosis was viewed recently, undoubtedly with a certain amount of shock, by tens of millions of television viewers across the country in this year's Kentucky Derby. This, of course, was Twice a Prince, who appeared to come very close to breaking a leg as he twisted and thrashed in the gate. Twice a Prince's panic-stricken reaction to the gate was completely typical of horses suffering from this neurosis, although the tense Derby atmosphere probably magnified considerably the colt's actions. As is also typical, Twice a Prince's response to the gate totally destroyed whatever opportunity it might have had of actually winning the race. Of course, it must be admitted that even a calm Twice a Prince, in perfect condition and excellent trim, might very well have been buried by the stretch charge of Secretariat that day. Nevertheless, what meager chances Twice a Prince did have when it entered the gate, it no longer had when the gate opened.

Twice a Prince, however, even though its neurosis vis-a-vis starting gates is both pronounced and highly well-defined, is still merely a neurotic gate horse, lacking the necessary credentials to be accorded the title of true psychotic. The psychotics, a much rarer breed than the ordinary, everyday neurotics, are also infinitely more effective when it comes to losing races. For while the neurotic Thoroughbred, after much trouble for both himself and his handlers, loses the race because he's either too exhausted from his struggles, or too terrified to race well, the psychotic loses because it never runs at all. Such a horse was, at one time, Indulto.

The story of Indulto is a fairly well-known one. After a year or so of trying to adjust to the idea of starting from a gate, he finally determined that staying in was considerably safer than coming out, so that before long he had accumulated on his record a depressingly large number of comments like "Refused." Indulto's performances, or rather his lack of performances, ultimately led to his being barred from racing at many of the East Coast's tracks, whose management, quite correctly, felt that amid the usual insecurities of betting on a horse race, this particular one shouldn't have to be shouldered by their patrons. For a while it was feared that, although he was obviously a horse of some talent, Indulto might never again be able to set foot on a racetrack.

As will be obvious to any lay racing psychologist, Indulto was a "starting-gate schizophrenic," a horse whose personality was split where starting gates were concerned—he didn't want to go in, but once in he wanted no part whatsoever of coming out. Fortunately for his career, Indulto was cured of his psychosis and became a highly useful horse indeed, earning nearly $500,000 in his many years on the track.

A horse named Skalkaho, racing on the West Coast several years ago, managed to go Indulto a step or two better. After going through a series of typically neurotic gyrations on the way to and inside of the starting gate, Skalkaho would first refuse to break with his company, and then, after the field had gotten safely out of his reach, would dump his jockey, circle behind the gate, and run back to the stable area as fast as he could. Finally, however, he attempted this maneuver once too often, forgetting the location of the stables and taking off in the wrong direction on the racetrack itself. Skalkaho, one of Fleet Nasrullah's quickest sons, was easily capable of shading 1.09 for six furlongs if given the opportunity, so it was most fortunate that an outrider with an alert stable pony was able to run him down before he met up with the rest of the field. As you can well imagine, the last thing a thundering collection of Thoroughbreds needs is an added peer flying directly at it as fast as Skalkaho was capable of running; therefore the horse was retired, much to the relief of jockeys and owners alike, before he could attempt that particular undertaking a second time.

The starting gate, at any rate, is to date unmatched as a means for inducing otherwise well-meaning Thoroughbreds to lose horse races. Mankind, however, constantly on the lookout for ever better ways to accomplish its ends, seems now to have come upon a new and particularly effective deterrent to winning. In fact, this new method has proven so good that, thus far at least, it has been reserved for special occasions only.

I refer, of course, to the practice of having an ultra-loud band or orchestra in the stands play blaring music before especially important races. Having observed loud music-playing in connection with only a few events (i.e., before the Kentucky Derbies, Preaknesses, and Belmont Stakes of the past few years), I, nonetheless, have never failed to be highly impressed by its seemingly infallible ability to pick out the nervous animal that is looking for an excuse to make a major nuisance of itself, and in the process blow an important horse race.

Undoubtedly the current all-time champion among music-hating Thoroughbreds must be Naskra, whose Triple Crown races in 1970 were run in accompaniment to the themes of "My Old Kentucky Home," "Maryland, My Maryland," and "The Sidewalks of New York," approximately half an hour prior to the events in which he was scheduled to participate. Naskra's reaction to the traditional music of the Kentucky Derby was particularly instructive—never before had he raced in front of nearly so many people, never before had he seen *anyone* in an infield (much less an infield like that of Churchill Downs, which on Derby Day is literally thick with humanity), and never before had he had occasion to feel that brand of tension that is peculiar to Louisville, Kentucky, on the first Saturday of every May, because at no other time or place is quite this same tension produced. Add to this a band playing "My Old Kentucky Home" loudly enough to be heard blocks away from the racetrack, and Naskra broke into a cold sweat as soon as he reached the track. Of course, Naskra was an atypically timorous animal, so acutely sensitive to his surroundings that it was frequently necessary to saddle him far away from the other runners.

The loud band, however, will probably continue to be of only limited utility as a means of confounding form. Most tracks, after all, can hardly afford to have a loud band playing cacophanous music before each race, and anyway, the horses soon would become accustomed to the noise. Still, the traditional means for creating losing probabilities will remain available, both to the horseman and his horses, and should continue to be effective for as long as a man is willing to lose his $2 on a horse race.

Generally speaking, then, while winning is what makes it all worthwhile for the bettor, losing is, in fact, what "makes" horse racing. Racing, after all, owes its very survival to losers—both the losing fans, whose dollars ultimately finance the Sport of Kings, and the losing horses, the unsound platers who make up the majority of races at nearly all tracks. In fact, while it is totally impossible to imagine a field of any size at all finishing in an all-comers dead-heat (although a few triple dead-heats have been recorded), it is quite easy to envision a race in which all entrants lose, and each loses in a unique manner. Racing, after all, provides only one way for a Thoroughbred to win a race, but offers to the loser any number of opportunities to demonstrate its unfitness to win. This is the way it must be, of course, for while it is quite truly said that everybody loves a winner, in order to have winners there must inevitably be losers. And in the end, therefore, mustn't it be true that losing, rather than winning, is really what racing is all about?

THE GREATEST HORSE RACE IN HISTORY?

By Neil Milbert

From the Chicago Tribune

Late this hot and humid afternoon at Belmont Park, a three-year-old thoroughbred named Secretariat ran what may have been the greatest horse race in history.

There can be no doubt that this was the greatest performance in the 105 runnings of the Belmont Stakes.

The clock and the camera proved that beyond any shadow of doubt;

. . . the clock tells you that Secretariat ran the mile and one-half in 2:24, obliterating the track and race record of 2:26 3-5 established by the great Gallant Man in 1957 at the old Belmont;

. . . the camera shows you that Secretariat crossed the finish line with 31 lengths partitioning him from his nearest pursuer, burying the classic's previous record margin of 25 lengths which the immortal Count Fleet inscribed in the record book in 1943.

After the way he won it seemed almost anticlimactic that Secretariat had just become the ninth thoroughbred in American racing annals to win the Triple Crown and the first in a quarter of a century.

A crowd of 69,138—second largest in Belmont history—saw it come to pass.

The New York racing zealots—said to be the most sophisticated in the world—knew a Superhorse when they saw one, and sent off the commanding winner of the Kentucky Derby and Preakness as the overwhelming 1–9 favorite.

But nobody—not even trainer Lucien Laurin—expected Secretariat to win in this awesome manner.

"No, not that big," admitted Laurin with a sigh. "Naturally, not that big!"

Secretariat's four pursuers might as well have been hobby horses for all the competition they offered.

Lightyears is the best description of the chasm that separated the chestnut son of Bold Ruler—Something Royal, by Princequillo from longshot runner-up Twice A Prince.

Then came My Gallant (son of Gallant Man), trailing Twice A Prince by one-half length.

Pvt. Smiles was fourth—so far out of it that he might as well have been in Chicago—and last was Sham, the runner-up in the Derby and Preakness. Sham stopped as if he had been struck by a bolt of lightning after fighting Secretariat for the lead for three-quarters of a mile.

Then, there existed the optical illusion that this was some kind of contest.

Breaking from the gate, Secretariat and Sham went for the lead and it seesawed.

By the time they hit the backstretch, the three other contestants were lagging far behind, just as Sham's trainer, Frank Martin, had predicted. Thereafter, Martin proved to be a false prophet.

With Ron Turcotte in the saddle calling the shots, Secretariat kept pouring on the speed. Sham couldn't keep up and as Secretariat shot further ahead, Martin's colt suddenly screamed "Uncle." Secretariat had yet to bid adieu to the backstretch when it became obvious that he was going to be the first Triple Crown winner since Citation—barring disaster.

"The horse we had to kill, we did," Laurin said, looking back on Sham's demise. "This was the easiest race of his life."

Never once did Turcotte wield the whip, but he implored the magnificent physical specimen with the striking three white stockings to pour it on in the stretch, knowing they had a chance for the record.

Secretariat did not let Turcotte down. The record time and margin were his response to the resolute hand ride.

Secretariat's fractions were :23 3-5; :46 1-5; 1:09 4-5; 1:34 1-5; and 1:59 flat.

"He can do anything he wants to do whenever he wants to," marveled Angel Cordero, My Gallant's rider. "He's just like a car."

Not only did Secretariat set a Belmont record, he established an

American standard for a mile and a half on the dirt. The old mark was 2:26 1-5 by Going Abroad at Aqueduct on October 12, 1964.

However, still standing following the onslaught is the one and one-half mile grass record of 2:23 set by Fiddle Isle at Santa Anita on February 23, 1970.

Foaled at the sprawling Virginia farm of his owner Mrs. Helen (Penny) Tweedy, Secretariat will retire in November and stand at stud at Claiborne Farm in Kentucky. His syndication price—based on his potential to become a Triple Crown winner—was $6,080,000.

This afternoon's victory was the 12th of Secretariat's 15-race career. Only once has Secretariat run out of the money—in his debut last July 4, he was jarred viciously at the gate and finished fourth.

In last year's Champagne Stakes here, he was disqualified from first to second and in the April 21 Wood Memorial he ran third, but the victory went to his stablemate, Angle Light, so for the bettors it didn't make any difference.

Because of the short field, there was no show betting today. Ironically, Secretariat paid $2.40 to place and only $2.20 to win.

Martin scratched Knightly Dawn, who was scheduled to go as an entry with Sham, reducing the gross value of the race to $150,200. Secretariat's $90,120 winner's share brought his career bankroll to $895,242.

Knightly Dawn is a speed horse and a handful of people thought beforehand his presence might pose problems for Secretariat.

No way. After what transpired today it seems as inconceivable as Babe Ruth striking out after calling his shot or Mark Spitz drowning in quest of his seventh gold medal.

Auto Racing

WHAT PRICE INDY GLORY

By Bob Feeney

From the Buffalo Evening News

What price glory in automobile racing?

It was mighty high—in life, race cars, and payoffs—here Wednesday in the rain-shortened 332-mile Indianapolis 500 won by Gordon Johncock at 6:33 P.M. Buffalo time.

The greatest moment in the life of this 5-foot-7, 150-pound former Michigan farmboy obviously was marred by what happened to two members of his three-car STP Offenhauser team.

In a day ranging from his winning $150 in a mid-morning blackjack game to getting 40 percent of a $220,000 victory paycheck, this thirty-six-year-old father of five children sadly said:

"I almost quit right then and there when the race was red-flagged (stopped on the 58th lap) because of a fiery crash. A. J. Foyt told me, 'It's Swede, go back to your car. Don't go near there.'

"I didn't find out until after I won that Armando, a crewman for our other team car (driven by Graham McRae), had been killed by a safety-patrol fire truck running the wrong way up pit road to get to Swede."

Swede is David Earl Savage Jr., a husky twenty-six-year-old expectant father from San Bernardino, California.

A survivor of a March 28, 1971 head-thumping crash, in California's Questor Grand Prix that supposedly ended his racing career, he drove the No. 40 flame-red Andy Granatelli STP rear-engined Offy.

Johncock was in the 1,620-pound No. 2 methanol turbo-charger, while McRae, the New Zealander who was named Indy Rookie of the Year, piloted the No. 60, also owned by Pat Patrick and Granatelli.

It was McRae's crewman, handling the lap-board out on the outer pit wall, who was struck down from behind, as he rushed toward the scene of Swede's crash.

Swede today is in critical condition but stable in Indianapolis' Methodist Hospital. He has burns on his face, both arms, and right hand, as well as compound fractures of both legs.

The crewman who arrived DOA (dead on arrival) at the same hospital at 5:23 P.M. Buffalo time, was Armando Teran, twenty-three of Culver City, California.

An STP crewman since 1972, Teran suffered a basal skull fracture and broken arms. He was catapulted 50 feet when struck by a fire truck driven by Jerry Blake of Indy.

It happened thusly:

The 500, after a five-hour 11-minute delay Wednesday, because rain had washed out two 33-car flying start attempts Monday and Tuesday, finally got under way at 3:11 P.M. Buffalo time, making it a three-day race.

Turned loose at 100 miles per hour by a front-wheel drive Cadillac pace car, Bobby Unser, the 1968 Indy winner from Albuquerque, New Mexico, took the lead from pole-sitter Johnny Rutherford. He's the Texan who set 1-and-4-lap time trial qualifying records of 199.021 mph and 198.413 mph.

Bobby led the first 39 laps. He set race completion records of 182.223 mph in eight minutes, 13.26 seconds for the first 10 laps, or 25 miles, after a first-lap mark of 177.620 mph.

The pace slowed with seven minutes of yellow slow-down lights for laps 17–21 when Indy hometown hero Bob Harkey spun his rear-engined Ford—one of six against 26 Offys and a stock block Chevy—on the 3300-foot backstretch of the soggy 2.5-mile oval.

The slow-down fouled the sparkplugs of Bobby U's red-hot Offy. Johncock took over the lead for two of the 68 laps he eventually was to front-run right to victory lane.

Then Savage winged his way to the lead for laps 42–54.

On the 55th lap, the ill-fated Californian pitted for the first of what was to be four mandatory pit stops for 500 miles.

His six-man pit crew needed only 21 seconds to fill both of his side-saddle rubber fuel-celled tanks with 75 gallons of methanol. Unwittingly, this pit stop set him up to be a flaming torch, reclining in the bathtublike fiberglass cockpit.

Nearing the end of lap 59, and closing in on leader Al Unser, Bobby's younger brother and the 1970–71 Indy winner, Savage's flame-red STP Offy veered left out of the groove entering the fourth turn. His five-foot rear wing came loose at its left edge.

Running not too much slower than his then-record 196.582 mph second-row qualifying speed, Savage's flaming 1,350-foot slide brought the late-arriving crowd of more than 100,000 screaming to its feet.

The fuel-laden red No. 40 headed straight for the inner retaining wall off the fourth turn. At the last instant, Swede right-turned his racer.

It slammed fuel-tank first sideways against the inner wall. The 500-pound rear Offy engine flew off the racer over the wall. The two left-side wheels, 14 and 10 inches wide, sheared off.

The magnesium wheels exploded, igniting the highly inflammable 37 gallons of fuel in the left tank. A 40-foot high ball of fire mushroomed across the track.

The racer spun, twisting off its two remaining nitrogen-filled tires. Then the bathtub frame with Savage securely strapped in it, slid wheel-less and slammed the right fuel tank against the outer wall.

There was another blinding explosion. Securely strapped in the bathtub, Swede's new $750 foam-spray fire-protective suit already was drowning his body and face with a nitrogen-charged spray.

An ambulance rushed the still-conscious Savage to the Speedway's infield hospital, then by helicopter to Methodist Hospital.

The same hospital where Dave (Salt) Walther, twenty-five, still lies with critical burns.

He's the Dayton driver of the flipping Offy that pinwheeled off the front chute wall during last Monday's seven-second, 400-yard 10-car demo derby of an ill-fated 11-row 33-car flying start.

As Savage's car came back up pit row, with its engine and debris in a tarpaulin, its badly charred wheels in another pickup truck, and the mangled, flame-scarred bathtub body in a third truck, Johncock shook his head and said:

"If Swede lives, it'll be the new foam fire suit that saved him. Gary Bettenhausen and Mel Kenyon wore them, too, but I didn't put mine on because the outer uniform needed cleaning.

"USAC [governing United States Auto Club] insists we must wear a clean uniform to start the Indy 500."

Despite the one-hour, 15-minute delay on Swede's fiery crash and nine yellow slow-down flags, the former sprint-car world's record-holder, had an Indy 500 speed record within reach.

What cost him was a three-lap (73–75) 80 mph run under the amber light electro-pacer as a result of Jimmy Carruthers running over debris from Savage's fourth-turn thriller.

In a masterful slow-down from 180 mph, Carruthers careened down the 3,300-foot front chute with his right front tire shredding. The flapping rubber slapped his front suspension silly.

Johncock, who pitted only twice for fuel and right-side tires, in 21 and 27 seconds on the 42nd and 100th laps, had a 27.5 second lead on the gold No. 2 Offy piloted by Bill Vukovich Jr., twenty-nine. Vuky was closing in on his father, Bill Sr., who won the 1953–54 Indys, but was killed leading the 1955 race.

Suddenly the rain began on lap 130. The 11 race cars still left from the flying start of 32 slowed down and held position under the 80 mph pacer lights around the oval.

Before the 134th lap was completed, Harlan Fengler, the seventy-year-old red-headed chief steward, told flagman Pat Vidan to "red-flag it. Rain is making the track unsafe and it's already an official race because we ran more than 50 percent of 200 laps."

From a record speed of 163 mph at 130 laps, Johncock fell off to 159.014 mph for 133 laps. That made 332 miles in two hours, five minutes, 27.56 seconds. This compares to last year's 200-lap record speed of 162.962 mph by Mark Donohue. Before his engine soured, Donohue was up front.

Thus, after trying since Monday, this 57th Indy 500 was both the longest and the shortest of them all.

SPEED, SEX AND HEROES

By William McIlwain

From The Atlantic Monthly

It is nearly midnight, hurting-cold, bonfires streaking the darkness for two and a half miles, and farm pickup trucks, U-Haul vans, family automobiles, wreckers, growling jacked-up street racers, converted school buses, motorcycles, and a magnificent black hearse pour through the tunnel into the infield of the Daytona International Speedway, jamming side by side to park in the grass. Rock music, raunchy and joyous, covers the night, louder than the country laments ("Sugar, don't never leave me again") coming from the pickup trucks. In the back of a EZ Haul truck, two stereo speakers are set up near the tailgate and eight teen-agers are dancing, a red-haired boy and a striking dark-haired girl driving their hips at each other, the crowd of kids on the ground shouting, and older men, admiring or leching, perhaps both, move nearer the truck, a few of them trying to pick up the beat, staggering with their beer and whooping, "Ooooeeee! oooooooeeeeee!" And the cars and trucks arrive all night long.

Where are the sociologists and the psychiatrists when we need them? I can give you only the straightforward facts: It is dark and cold, still 13 hours before the start of the Daytona 500, the biggest stock-car race in the world. It will be attended by 103,800 persons and it offers $236,325 in prize money. The qualifying record, set three years ago by Cale Yarborough in a Mercury, is 194 mph, which will suggest that these "stock" cars are not precisely like *your* stock car. The speedway occupies 455 acres, with parking for 75,000 automobiles, and has a 2.5-mile asphalt track. On this track, 40 drivers will attempt to race 500 miles tomorrow. The majority of them will not finish: their garishly decaled $20,000 to $30,000 automobiles will fail them.

What's happening here? The liquor-drinking, God-fearing, coon-hunting, short-haired, fried-chicken-eating redneck stock-car fan and his honey, pointy-breasted, fixed-up *special* for the race . . . they are going to lie down in this infield like lambs with these atheist, long-haired, bushy-bearded kids with their free-love girls wearing blue jeans and no brassieres. The old-time stock-car fan is being subjected to pressures of change. They come not only from the world in general but from his own heroes. Hell, can't he walk over by the garage and find Richard Petty standing next to his Dodge, No. 43, with sideburns down his jawbones and a big new moustache? And you don't win 148 Grand National races, boy, being no freak. The hair ain't hurt Richard. And Cale Yarborough, as good an old boy as you ever want to see from Timmonsville, South Carolina—Cale don't look half bad when you get used to it, that cornsilk hair covering *both* his ears.

As for the kids turning out in great numbers, it is far more likely to happen at this track than, say, Bristol, Tennessee, or North Wilkesboro, North Carolina. The natives here are more understanding and the Atlantic Ocean, a diversion, is four miles east. But the biggest reason is that Daytona is a long-running spectacle, offering races of various types for three weeks before the big Daytona 500. It is an "occasion," a reason for going somewhere, taking along tape decks, speakers, a few friends, beer, and maybe a little pot to smoke. Sort of a rock festival with 500-horsepower engines.

Certainly for many fans—both young and old—the race itself is incidental. On Race Day some sunbathe on the tops of trucks; some fall asleep; some drink beer or bourbon all day and forget to watch. But for whatever reasons, more and more fans come each year—to Daytona and to big and small tracks all across the country. During 1973, more spectators in the United States will watch automobile racing than professional football or baseball or basketball. Only horse racing, with its lure of pari-mutuel betting, will have greater attendance.

Why does automobile racing, oftentimes a monotonous sport, draw such big crowds? There are a number of heavy cerebral theories, but for the moment consider that it offers speed, sex, heroes, alcohol, and adulation.

Here is what a visitor finds during the week of the Daytona 500.

On Atlantic Avenue, a gaudy north-south strip that runs beside the Atlantic Ocean, motel signs read, WELCOME RACE FANS . . . WELCOME STP . . . WELCOME ABC SPORTS . . . WELCOME UNION 76. At the Silver Beach Inn, a pair of huge racing tires stand together in the lobby. Along the strip, topless dancers shake and an all-girl rock band rocks, but two of the places drawing the best crowds offer shows featuring interviews with racing drivers. A radio commercial says, "If you're not as avid a race fan as your husband, pick up some needlework at Charley's to pass away the time. Make a pit stop at Charley's." A white Cadillac "pimpmobile," down from New York, perhaps, or Atlanta, cruises the strip at 3 A.M. The movie *43—The Petty Story* is showing at the New Daytona, drawing crowds. It is a wholesome movie, with Richard Petty playing himself, but an ad shows a girl saying, "Racing is a man-size game. Mister! You play it with busted bones and miles of scar tissue to get your RPM up!" At Mac's Famous Bar, a girl in a pink miniskirt pushes through a tough-looking crowd with trays of beer. A bed sheet hangs against the side wall and films of past 500-mile races are being projected onto it. "Petty's got him!" hollers a man. "Nah!" says another.

I should pause right here and put down some rudimentary information about stock-car racing, in case you're ever in Mac's and want to strike up a conversation. First, stock cars are not to be confused with the Indianapolis 500 cars, the low, exotic, wide-wheeled racers with open cockpits. In appearance, stock cars are like the Fords, Chevrolets, Mercurys, Dodges, and Plymouths that you see everywhere. There are minor differences—no headlights or taillights, no glass in the windows; the doors are welded shut, and the interior has a single bucket seat for the driver and an elaborate crisscross of padded steel bars that keep the car from crushing him if it should hit a wall or flip over. But the lines are the same as the car you can buy from a dealer. The magnificent engines, of course, are not.

Stock-car racing started in the South, and in the early days some of the top performers also dealt in moonshine whiskey. They drove the souped-up, jacked-up 1940 and 1950 Fords that screamed out of the hills at night running 100 miles an hour, sometimes without lights, carrying their whiskey to the cities. It was natural, then, that with their great skills they took these fine automobiles to quarter-mile and half-mile dirt tracks and raced for money. As stock-car racing has become "respectable"—a multimillion-dollar business—

these whiskey cars are often referred to now as the "family cars" of the early racers.

The National Association for Stock Car Auto Racing (always called NASCAR) was formed 25 years ago, and it has spread across much of the United States as a sanctioning body for races. There are several divisions of NASCAR. The tops is the Winston Cup Grand National Division, the major leagues of stock-car racing. After the race here on Sunday, the second of the season, there will be 29 more Winston Cup races this year, nearly every Sunday, extending as far as Michigan and California, winding up on November 4 with a 500-mile race in College Station, Texas.

There are good drivers who have raced for years and have never won a Grand National race. That gives you an idea of the fantastic dominance of the sport by folk hero Richard Petty, a hard, lean North Carolinian with a pearly grin who has won 148. For comparison, here are the figures for some other "big-name" drivers: Bobby Allison, 43; Bobby Isaac, 41; Cale Yarborough, 14; Buddy Baker, 7. David Pearson, a tough thirty-eight-year-old driver from Spartanburg, South Carolina, is closest to Petty; he has won 67 races. (And Pearson has been picked by a panel of "expert" writers to win Sunday's race here.)

The money in Grand National racing can be big. Bobby Allison was the top money winner last year with $274,995; Petty was second with $240,515. In the 15 years that he has been racing, Petty, who is thirty-five, has won $1,378,648—an average of nearly $92,000 a season.

On the other hand, a run-of-the-mill driver may make $20,000 to $30,000 a year in prize money. And out of that must come expenses—the upkeep of his car, all of his travel costs, and the wages of mechanics, if he can afford any.

The aim, always, is to attract a high-rolling sponsor. Drivers and sponsors won't talk specifics, but it is reported that Coca-Cola is putting up $100,000 this year for Bobby Allison to go racing in a 1973 Chevrolet with COCA-COLA emblazoned on its sides. And Petty has a hefty backer in Andy Granatelli and his oil additive, STP. But a lesser driver has to settle for a small-time sponsor, if he can find one at all. Then, by doing most of his own work and holding expenses down, he may break even for a year's hard work.

The tracks on which Grand National races are run vary in length from approximately a half mile at Martinsville, Virginia, to 2.66

miles at Talladega, Alabama. Generally speaking, the longer the track, the greater the speed of the cars. In 1969–70, the days of the so-called "winged cars"—those with high stabilizers on the rear end—speeds were approaching 200 miles an hour on the "super tracks" such as Daytona and Talladega. But for several reasons, including the vain hope that lesser drivers would have a better chance, NASCAR deliberately cut the speed of the cars. This was done by requiring restrictor plates on the carburetors, with different size openings for different style engines, thus limiting the amount of fuel and air the engine can receive. For that reason, the speeds Sunday will be in the 180s, rather than the 190s.

Tuesday

It is a warm, cloudless afternoon. In the vast field at the western end of the speedway, campers sunbathe, cook, work on motorcycles, and visit each other. It is much like driving into a national park and seeing license plates from all over North America and sleeping accommodations that range from two-person tents to expensive trailers.

A middle-aged couple sit under a canvas awning, warming tomato soup on a Coleman stove. Further on, nine young men from Ohio cluster about an old white school bus and a red van, drinking beer and working on their motorcycles. "We put in $40 apiece," their leader says, "and that paid for a new engine for the bus and 15 cases of beer. All the beer's gone but we only have to put in $15 more for the whole trip—gas and more beer and all."

Their leader, who weighs 270 pounds and appears to be about twenty-four, says he likes it here because it is a friendly place. "He got in some trouble at Indy," one of the group says. "That was an accident," the leader says. "I like a quiet time. You want a beer?" What happened at Indianapolis, he explains, was that a man pushed him; he hit the man; two cops hit him; he hit the two cops; six cops put him in a straitjacket. "It was all an accident," he says. He opens another beer. "Are you going to the parties in the infield?" he asks. "Some girls told us there'll be some good ones."

At the racetrack itself fans stream in and out of the grandstands, even though there is no racing today. Drivers are on the track running practice laps, trying to wring out another mile or two of speed. Coming down the asphalt ramp from the high stands is a blonde, wearing a red jersey playsuit cut like a tank bathing suit. In her left hand she carries an almost empty bottle of Beefeater gin and an almost empty bottle of Seagram's; in her right she carries a glass of gin. She is barefoot, burned pink by the sun, and walking well. A few steps behind her, not walking as well, is a barefoot man in shorts, with just the beginning of a pot belly. He is saying something to her that sounds like "Shoog."

The spectators are of all shapes, ages, and manner. Why are they here? Why will 103,800 persons sit for hours in the cold on Sunday? Says Dr. Jeremy Nahum, a Boston psychiatrist with faculty appointments at Harvard and Tufts and a broad knowledge of automobile racing, "There's a mystique about stock-car racing. It evolved from something illicit (driving bootleg whiskey cars) into a popular sport. A man who was clever enough to evade the law, which was seen as an unreasonable power, would be viewed as a folk hero. The retaliatory pleasure in making a fool of a seemingly more powerful, forbidding figure had immense appeal.

"To the men at the races, the car is the personification of virility. The women are not primarily interested in machines the way the men are. It doesn't have as strong an appeal for the female psyche. The women are there more ornamentally . . . more in a decorative sense."

Dr. Richard Proctor is a psychiatrist who works right in the heart of stock-car country as chairman of the department of psychiatry at Bowman Gray School of Medicine, Winston-Salem, North Carolina. He says, "In our culture there are very few socially acceptable ways that we can ventilate our feelings of aggression and hostility. That's why someday I'm going to write a learned treatise on the therapeutic value of umpires and referees to our society. You should have seen me at the basketball tournament last week—I was a mess, hollering at the referees. People probably said, 'Look at that crazy psychiatrist!' But it's good for us.

"In an automated society, there's little that a man can do to vent his hostilities. What can he do—kick the machine? Stock-car fans feel that they have little control over what's happening to them. They want to identify with Richard Petty, who has *complete* control. Look at Richard out there in his Dodge, controlling it, passing cars at 180 miles an hour. . . . The fan puts himself in Richard Petty's place and it makes him feel like a man.

Wednesday

Most of the drivers have been here for a week or ten days, working with their crews on their automobiles and running practice laps on the track. In mid-morning it is sunny, in the low 70s, and drivers are walking about the garage area, some still in street clothes, others in fireproof racing suits. A. J. Foyt, who has won the Indianapolis 500 three times and who won this race last year, stands beside his gold and red Chevrolet, joking with a mechanic who is firing a water pistol at another mechanic. Foyt races in only a few big-money stock-car events; most of the season he drives an Indianapolis-type car, racing on another circuit. "This is a brand-new car," Foyt says, "and it's taking a while to get it right."

Richard Petty, who is wearing navy blue pants with a slight flair, black cowboy boots, and a print shirt, has a tiny pocket knife in his right hand. He picks at a thin white line that separates the red and blue of his 1973 Dodge. "The car's not handling good," he says. "Can't tell what's wrong. But we're working on it."

Small white letters on the left rear of Petty's car read, MADE IN LEVEL CROSS, an inscription that, however brief, would be understood by any southern stock-car fan. His car has been put together, piece by piece, body and engine, in Petty's pinewoods manufacturing plant, adjacent to his home in Level Cross, North Carolina. Thirty men work there, building "stock" racing cars, and one of them is Duck Holder, a mechanic who learned to make moonshine whiskey when he was fourteen. Duck is proud of the new car, which he values at $30,000. "It's the best car we ever built."

Benny Parsons of Ellerbe, North Carolina, a good driver who is not nearly so well established as Foyt and Petty, has been running practice laps on the big track and he pulls his red No. 72 into the garage stall. It is booming and snorting and blasting, as all these cars do, making it seem impossible that drivers and mechanics could make themselves understood. But they can. Travis Carter, Benny's twenty-three-year-old chief mechanic, who would like to be a driver himself, sticks his red head into the car, close to Benny's face. He goes to the engine, does something, and Benny signals that he's ready to go out again.

"It's getting better," Travis says, "but we got to get more speed. Benny's running 178—you got to run at least 180 here."

In the parlance of stock-car racing, Parsons is neither a "hot dog" nor a "stroker." The "hot dogs" win most of the races, driving the finest, best-maintained cars, almost always with heavy financial backing. They ride the "high groove" (the upper part) of the banked track, dueling each other; a flagman mounted on a stand will wave at slower cars to move down nearer the track's apron to let the "hot dogs" whistle by.

The "strokers," on the other hand, drive onto the track knowing they have no chance of winning. They plug away, not extending their engines too much, and hope to finish the race. They usually pick up a little prize money each time. The etymology of "stroker" is uncertain. One mechanic explains, perhaps whimsically, that a stroker races so slowly that he can sit back comfortably, maybe in 17th place, and masturbate. Another mechanic says, "Well, you know, he just sits back there and strokes. Maybe it comes from piston strokes. He ain't trying to race hard, he's just stroking."

A great racing driver has to have many qualities: magnificent reflexes (at 180 mph the car directly in front of him spins), an uncanny "feel" for his car (how hard can he push it? is anything starting to go wrong?), nerve, judgment, and tremendous stamina (the temperature inside the car reaches 135 degrees on southern tracks in mid-summer). You will hear drivers say, "I passed him and he was sitting low in the seat," meaning the man had wilted.

No racing driver can be timid, but some are known to be bolder than others. Cale Yarborough is one. "He drives a car hard," Travis Carter explains. "He'll take a chance." A member of Petty's crew concurs: "Cale tears up a lot of sheet metal out there. But you give him a car that'll run 200 and Cale will drive it 200."

Wearing a cowboy hat, dungaree pants, and sharp-toed cowboy boots, Cale Yarborough is standing beside his new Chevrolet. He is a friendly man who speaks quietly. Asked about his boldness, or courage, he says, "Oh, I don't know. I don't know whether I have any more than anybody else . . . but you won't win without it. I never set out to do anything but win in my life. I never got in a car thinking I'd finish second."

The man who owns Cale's Chevrolet, Junior Johnson, used to race exactly that way himself. Junior, who quit racing seven years ago, grew up in Wilkes County, North Carolina, which at the time produced more moonshine whiskey than any other county in the United States—and some of the finest drivers. Junior won the Daytona 500 in 1960 and he perfected a technique that has been used ever since on the long tracks—"drafting" and "sling-shoting." He found that a slower car can keep up with a fast car by getting directly behind it, almost touching it, thus escaping wind resistance. That's "drafting." At 180 to 190 mph. The object is for the slower car, at the last possible moment, to "sling-shot" past the leader and win the race.

Junior and Cale understand each other. On Sunday, Cale will be driving Junior's car hard. Or, as some of the stock-car people like to say, "flat out, belly to the ground."

Drivers speak matter-of-factly about things that would scare you or me to death. Of a terrifying skid, they say, "I got sideways." David Pearson, talking about the weather says, "Well, yes, it would be good if the wind dropped a little. It moves you around out there." Benny Parsons, discussing this track, concedes that it is a tough one to drive. "It feels as if you slam into each turn." He gestures, angling his hand. "It's as if you're running on a flat surface, then suddenly bang in at 31 degrees."

At 3:45 in the afternoon, Richard Petty comes in from running and his car goes up on four jacks. Dale Inman, his first cousin and crew chief, slides under the rear end and begins making adjustments on the suspension. "I'm trying to free it up a little," he says.

Free it up a little?

"Yeah," Dale says. "You know."

Imagine never having played bridge and looking over someone's shoulder, trying to figure out what the game is about. That's how you feel much of the time in the garage area, pondering the intricacies of stock-car racing. The noise is constant, the explanations almost always esoteric and short but offered as if they were self-evident truths.

Free it up a little?

Petty, who has pulled his lanky body head first through the window of the car, stretches and grins, which he does often. "Sure," he says. "You got to walk tippy-toe. You don't want it too much this way and you don't want it too much that way."

He then explains, as best he can to an outsider, how crucial it is for a car to be "set up" right—each wheel putting the proper amount of weight on the track. It determines how well the car handles at high speeds, particularly on the sharply banked turns. Drivers and mechanics talk constantly of this delicate balance, trying to strike it precisely, using expressions that are, of course, self-evident: "It's loose . . . It's pushing . . . It needs wedge . . . It's hanging out."

Petty's car, then, is handling poorly. That fact will be known by all drivers and some fans. But there are still three days until Sunday, and Petty and his crew will be working hard. Trying, you understand, to make sure that by race time the car is not *pushing* or *hanging out.*

Thursday

It is warm, with scattered clouds. A crowd of 50,350 comes out to watch a pair of 125-mile qualifying races. Buddy Baker wins the first; Coo Coo Marlin wins the second.

What is the significance? Fans will argue about what it foretells of Sunday's 500-mile race.

Coo Coo, forty-one, a cattle rancher from Carter's Creek, Tennessee, has never won a big race in his life. His car is fast but it may not be durable, and Coo Coo will not be regarded as a serious contender.

Baker, on the other hand, will be. He is a 6-foot-5 North Carolinian who has been racing for 14 years and has won seven Grand National events. At the moment, even the other drivers agree that Baker's 1972 Dodge is the fastest car here. Earlier in the week he ran an official qualifying lap of 185.662 mph—more than two miles per hour faster than anyone else—and there are suspicions that he can run still faster.

In today's race, it appears that Baker is hard pressed by Cale Yarborough, but Junior Johnson says ruefully, "Nah, Baker's just playing with us. He can run faster than that."

Baker denies it: "I run just as wide open as a barn door all day."

And there are other big-name drivers to consider: David Pearson, picked by the experts to win Sunday, finished ninth today in the race won by Coo Coo Marlin. A. J. Foyt finished third in the same race. Richard Petty finished fourth in the race won by Baker.

In the next two days, while drivers and mechanics struggle for more speed, fans will drink beer and predict.

Friday

The temperature has dropped 30 degrees, portable heaters burn beside the race cars, and a young woman in turquoise hot pants and high heels stands behind the chain-link fence that keeps fans out of the garage area. She must be cold. Wearing a yellow shawl and a sloppy yellow hat, she has been there at least 45 minutes, peering at the drivers, or perhaps at one particular driver. Ten yards down the fence is a woman, a bit older, wearing black pants and a gold coat. She has been standing there even longer.

There are men, women, and children all along the fence, but some of the women stand out because you see them there every day—and most likely would see them next Sunday at the race in Richmond, Virginia, or the following race in Bristol, Tennessee. "Pit lizards," "camp followers," or "dedicated racing fans," whatever you choose to call them, they are part of the scene and their presence is pleasing to racing men. "Sweets, you do look *good!*" a pit-crew member will say as he passes the fence, pulling a red wagon bearing racing gasoline.

What is the lure that draws these women to racing? Dr. Nahum says, "The woman's interest is usually not what is of interest to the man. She comes in the service of furthering her relationship with the man who is so obviously involved here." Deep down, psychiatrically speaking, deeper down than most of us think, that may be true, but laymen see it another way. "I'm gonna get me some of that," a mechanic says, nodding toward a woman beside the fence. And a college girl, who knows a fair amount about racing although she dosn't especially like it, says, "Why, you know women see those drivers as virile studs." Another mechanic supports this: "Sure, they go for the drivers. When they find out you aren't a driver, you have a harder time getting a woman."

A young woman of twenty-five, looking even younger, her dark hair in pigtails, nose peeling, has been here since Saturday and will leave Sunday night after the race, driving 20 hours to get back to her job in Michigan. It is her sixth straight year at Daytona and she travels to many other races, too. "I won't make Richmond," she says. "Maybe Bristol. I'm certainly going to Darlington." She speaks enviously of a woman her age who has taken a year off work to travel the circuit. "That's the way to do it."

What is her deep interest in racing?

"Well, I first got interested because I was going with a guy who drove down here in '68. He finished 13th in a Chevy. We broke up about four years ago."

Do you go with any of the drivers now?

"No. I'm just good friends with them. I love the competition and I like the guys. They're just good, down-to-earth guys who like to race. It's in their blood. I know most of the drivers and mechanics and if I want to know something I can ask about it and they'll explain it to me. They don't treat me like I was some dumb broad asking a question."

In the garage stalls, which are open, enabling the fans to see the comings and goings of their heroes, the drivers and mechanics are hard at work. Maurice Petty, Richard's younger brother, who builds the engines for all of the Petty automobiles, is unhappy with the car. He has been all week. "Terrible," he says. "Terrible."

Richard says the same thing: "Terrible. It's still not handling good. But we've changed a whole lot of things and now we have to see if they're right."

In response to calls from his fans, Richard walks to the fence, goes through the guarded gate, and begins signing autographs. Two teen-age girls ask if he will have his picture taken with them. Looking a little fatherly, he nevertheless puts his arms around them both and flashes his great pearly grin. "Thank you, Richard! Thank you, Richard!"

For about 20 minutes, he stands outside the fence signing autographs and talking. I asked him later about spending so much time doing this.

"When you got the time, you ought to do it," he explains. "When you got a lull like this. Because sometimes when you're working on the car you've got to walk by somebody like they aren't there. So when you got the time, you take it."

Saturday

Miss Permatex of California is standing in the grass between the pits and the racetrack, turning from side to side for the photographers who have formed a ring about her. She has on a rabbit-fur cape, which is open to display her body; it is cold but she never stops smiling. A short, gnarled man with "Valvoline" on his jacket steps forward, tentatively at first, stands beside her, and a buddy snaps their picture. Miss Permatex smiles. Then another man comes forward. And another. She is smiling all the while.

Using women as billboards seems to be an inevitable part of stock-car racing. Even on a half-mile track in a small town, you might find a lone country girl, a bit chunky in the thighs, doing her best, waving kisses to 4,000 persons. Here, Miss Permatex has company. Union 76, which spends an estimated $1 million a year on racing, has four of its "racestoppers," all professional models, waving and smiling. The Winston cigarette girls, in red and white, are here. And Miss Speed Weeks is reigning and beaming. And coming around the track on top of a station wagon, Miss Red Cap Ale from Canada.

During a 300-mile race, resulting in seven wrecks but no injuries, fans scatter to remote points of the infield. At the height of the action a couple lie asleep in a red and white Chevrolet. Near the west turn, four men are sitting on a platform built on top of a truck—it is possible to see the whole track from up there—and they are passing a quart of I.W. Harper back and forth. "Go, Double O!" shouts a man in a camouflaged duck-hunting suit. "Go, Double O!"

Now, that is my picture of a good, old-time stock-car fan: a red-faced man in a camouflaged duck-hunting suit, drinking bourbon, hollering, "Go, Double O!" But times and the fans are changing. At 8 P.M., attending a cocktail party given by NASCAR and Pepsi-Cola, I see some of the new-breed fans. A woman in a beige floor-length gown, her hair teased a foot high, approaches two women: "Do you know who's here? The Winchester cigar man! My God, I'm flipping over him!" Soon after, a young woman crosses the floor in an azure dress that is open at both hips, connected by gold chain, showing azure bikini pants underneath. These women will not be in the infield tomorrow with the camouflaged duck hunter. In the VIP lounges, maybe, or the $30 grandstand seats.

Meanwhile, the lions and the lambs are lying down together tonight in the infield. At midnight, making my way through the pickup trucks, the family cars, the motorcycles, and the rented vans, I stop beside a stumpy-nosed wrecker that is filled with firewood. Three men are sitting on logs, warming themselves over a big fire. Who will win tomorrow's race? "David [Pearson], most likely," one of the men answers. "Ol' Cale could do it, too. And Richard." Buddy Baker? "Nah, he don't finish races good." What do you like about racing? "Like about it, how you mean? I like the racing."

The eight kids dancing in the back of the EZ Haul truck are pouring it on now, stereo speakers sound from various points, there is a faint smell of pot in the air, and the young and old move about with no hassles. Some, in fact, are moving about together. A man of thirty-five, sitting beside a big fire with a teen-age girl, says, "Stop and warm awhile. I'm from Birmingham; she's from Tallahassee."

The trucks and cars still pour in.

Sunday

A light rain is falling, it is scarcely daylight, and the infield is still. Here and there, behind a pickup truck or in front of a tent, an early riser puts on coffee or bacon.

Pit crews are already passing through the infield, on their way to the garage area to get ready for the race. But it is some time before last night's celebrants stir much. A young man sits on the back of a pickup truck, drinking beer and listening to a country preacher. Occasionally, a hot car growls on the dirt road—a wide-tired Camaro or a Shelby.

In 14 years there has never been a Daytona 500 rained out, but it appears that this one will be. It is not raining hard, but enough to make the track slippery. At 10:30, the 40 drivers are called together by NASCAR for a meeting, a routine procedure. "Most of you fellows have run this track before and you know what to do," an official says. "When you're going into a turn, keep your eye on your mirror. If a fast car's coming up on you, don't try to get out of his way. Stay in the lane you're in and he'll know how to get by. But I'll tell you this: if you're not running 170, you don't belong in the two top grooves."

By race time, 12:30, the rain has stopped, but the track is wet. It is decided that the racers will run 13 laps under the caution flag at about 80 mph with a pace car preceding them, in order to dry off the track. Then Buddy Baker will run a fast lap to see if it is all right. He does—at 186 mph—and they are off.

It seems that the race will be between Baker and Cale Yarborough. David Pearson, picked to win, goes out with valve trouble after 63 laps. There are 200 laps to run. Benny Parsons has trouble with oil pressure and is out at lap 101. Coo Coo Marlin's engine fails and he's out at 118. Of the 40 cars, 22 will fall out, 18 will finish.

Baker and Yarborough are running right together all the while, Baker obviously faster but Cale "drafting" and hanging directly behind him. A few times Cale passes, but Baker passes him back. Richard Petty is running third, not appearing to threaten the leaders.

In the backstretch on lap 154, Yarborough's engine flames and he is out of the race. Petty is second now, and he is gaining on Baker. Both of them go into the pits to get gasoline and new right-side tires. Their cars get about four miles to a gallon of gas and their tanks hold 22 gallons; thus, they must stop about every 90 miles for gas. Right-side tires get the greatest wear and drivers like to change them at each gas stop. Left-side tires need to be changed only twice during the race. Five pit men change two tires, fill the car with gas, wash the windshield, and give the driver a soft drink in 20 seconds.

With 15 laps to go, Petty is right behind Baker, but Baker still looks faster. Both of them must stop once more for gas, and this could be a crucial move.

On lap 188 Richard comes in and his crew pour in only part of a can of gas. He is out in 8.4 seconds.

On lap 189 Baker comes in. It is 10 seconds before he is out.

Petty has a lead now. With seven laps to go Baker is pushing him hard—probably too hard—and Baker's engine blows. Petty drives the remainder of the race unthreatened, finishing five miles ahead of the second man, Bobby Isaac. Dick Brooks is third and A. J. Foyt is fourth.

It is the 149th time that Richard Petty has won a Grand National race and the fourth time that he has won the Daytona 500. It is unlikely that any stock-car driver will ever match those figures.

Later, in a matter-of-fact voice, Petty explains how—one way or another—he wins races: "They could outrun me a little. My boys beat Baker in the pits. We had handling problems all week. Our hope was that if we couldn't outrun them our boys could put together some good equipment that would last. We did."

It is starting to rain again and to get dark. Among the 103,800 fans, surely some do not know who won the race. Some, in fact, probably don't even know that it is over. But they have been to Daytona. For whatever their reasons, they have been to the Daytona 500.

Hockey

IF KEN DRYDEN'S SO SMART, HOW COME HE'S A GOALIE?

By Nick Seitz

From Sport

Like all great cities in the 1970s, Montreal faces great questions. Can the business community compete with more modern Toronto? Should the 1976 Olympics be canceled? Will French separatists bomb the hotels? Does white wine really go with roast beef? Will Ken Dryden give up hockey for the law?

The last question is the one that really ignites the venerable and cosmopolitan city of 2 million. Will Dryden, freshly minted law degree in hand, forsake *Les Canadiens* in favor of a crusading career protecting consumers? Will he emulate his hero, Ralph Nader, for whom he has worked? Will he decide to stop pollution instead of pucks? Will he end a sensational goal-tending career almost before it has begun?

At Dryden's age, twenty-five, goalies usually are barely starting to master the most challenging job in sports. Dryden already is preeminent, having arrived from somewhere south of nowhere to lead Montreal to the 1971 Stanley Cup, make the All-Star team last season and stand out for Team Canada in its victory over the USSR last fall. Through his team's first 30 games this season, of which he played the amazing total of 27, Dryden allowed an average of just over two goals, had three shutouts, and was the primary reason Montreal was staying ahead of Boston, New York, and Buffalo in a tight-fitting National Hockey League East race.

Goalies are supposed to be different, but Dryden is wildly unique. He is, in addition to being too young and too overworked to be a great goalie, too tall (6-foot-4), too myopic (contact lenses on the ice, regular glasses otherwise) and too intellectual, not necessarily in that order. NHL stalwarts do not come up through American colleges; they drop out of Canadian high schools to play junior hockey. Dryden not only went to an American college, he went to Cornell—in the Ivy League! A lot of fans in the upper seats at NHL games respond to that bit of absurdity by asking, "What's a Cornell?" Cornell has produced many, many farmers, some major political figures (Secretary of State William Rogers) and one editor of *Sport*—but heretofore no NHL goalies. The guy who lives next door to me is a Cornell man and he's always trying to impress me by pointing out that his alma mater has the largest collection of vampire and bat brains in the world, right there far above Cayuga's waters. That is, when he isn't bragging about Dryden.

Dryden has shattered a seemingly impregnable rationale I had evolved to explain to myself why I never became a Joe Namath or Jerry West or Steve Carlton. I don't know about you, but I've always been certain why I wasn't a great athlete. I was too smart. Thought too much. With all due respect to Joe and Jerry and Steve. The better I have come to know Dryden, though, the more normal he makes it seem to wear two heads—consistently turning back the best shooters in hockey but never kidding himself that what happens between two ends of an ice rink defines life. With the upcoming play-offs obsessing most hockey players, Dryden is studying for his bar examinations.

The summer before last, his teammates relaxed from their Stanley Cup conquest by traveling, playing golf, doing innocuous public relations work, partying. Dryden worked with "Nader's Raiders" in Washington for a token fee. The experience crystallized his desire to be a concerned lawyer.

"Nader's a lawyer with a conscience, and there aren't enough of his kind," Dryden says with typically quiet forcefulness. "He has an amazing grasp of many situations and the ability to relate them. He knows where and how pressure should be exerted to do the most good. I learned from him that one man—you or I—can make a big difference in a bureaucracy."

In addition to a large dose of general philosophy, Dryden took away from his Nader exposure an abiding particular interest in improving the lot of fishermen. For Nader he helped unify them so they have a strong voice against industries and government agencies that pollute the waters, destroying the environment. Dryden doesn't fish himself.

Here Dryden is a man of action, there a man of contemplation. He enjoys the higher pleasures of two distinct levels of existence. He couldn't postpone either endeavor, his studies or hockey, without giving it up, his studies because he would lose his academic discipline, hockey because he would lose his reflexes. By doing both, he finds that one stimulates the other.

Dryden's older brother Dave, the Buffalo goalie and a sometime schoolteacher, says, "It's a good situation for Ken. If he were just a hockey player, his intelligence would work against him. There's too much free time to worry if you're as thoughtful as he is. If he's frustrated by hockey, he has school as an outlet."

Dave Dryden's corollary theory is that braininess is not exactly a goalie's best friend. "You can't think too much," he says, giving new life to my bruised rationale for my own lack of athletic success. "You have to contain your intelligence if you're as bright as Ken. Otherwise, you think before you react, and that's dangerous in this game. The players are skating 30 miles an hour and the puck may be coming at you at 120 miles an hour and the element of chance is very great. Playing goal isn't rational or mathematical. You try to get into a nice trance and make moves instinctively."

The quality of mind that *does* help Ken as a goalie, according to Dave, is his photographic memory. He can remember the whereabouts of every opponent on virtually every NHL goal he has allowed. Of course, there haven't been that many, but it's nonetheless a knack matched probably by only Glenn Hall, who can recount five years' worth of goals without missing a man. "The trick," says Dave, "is to concentrate on the puck but still see everything else. It's better to remember where a player likes to be than where he likes to shoot. If you guess where he'll shoot, you can get caught. Jean Ratelle of the Rangers likes to shoot high on your stick side, but as sure as you overplay him, he'll cross you up. It's better to remember that Red Berenson of Detroit likes to give you a head fake and go to the outside. Ken remembers."

Dave, like other goalies in the NHL in the 1970s, does not play nearly as much as Ken. This is the day of the two-goalie system, thanks to pell-mell expansion and its padded schedule and longer, grueling road trips. Ken likes to work, explaining that he doesn't tire physically but occasionally tires mentally. Dave thinks the heavy load is good for Ken, even in a season that will be extra long because of the Team Canada-USSR series:

"You sit in the stands and worry if your substitute looks good or the opposition looks strong. Pretty soon your confidence suffers. Montreal was smart to play Ken last year because it was his first full NHL season and he gained confidence. I think it's wise to keep playing him a lot, because his moves become mechanical and he will avoid slumps." (Last year Dryden led all goalies by playing 64 of 78 games, 3,800 minutes, during which he allowed only 2.24 goals a game and had eight shutouts.)

Ken and Dave first played goal in the streets of Toronto, Ken at three, when he could fit into Dave's hand-me-down goalie equipment. They were the sons of a mother who taught kindergarten and a father in business in everything from cement blocks to Christmas trees and who now, retired, travels the world raising money for civic-club projects that benefit underprivileged children.

Instead of a puck, the neighborhood kids used a tennis ball. That was fortunate for the Drydens, for the tennis ball was in the air continually and developed their glove hands. (A glove stop is best; there is no rebound.) Also Ken notes, dryly, a tennis ball doesn't smart as much as a hard rubber puck when it hits you, or else he might have given up hockey at an early age. As it was, by the time he learned how dangerous playing goal can be, he was hooked.

Always hockey was kept in a reasonable perspective. Once Dave had an out-of-town junior championship game and a school exam the same morning. He took the exam. The example was not lost on Ken.

Montreal got negotiating rights to Ken early, but he shocked the Canadiens by turning down their offer and going to Cornell, where he was recruited and coached by Ned Harkness, now general manager at Detroit. Dryden had seen too many of his boyhood pals turn pro and never make the big leagues, let alone in the powerful Montreal organization, and was convinced that your luck had to be at least as good as your glove hand. I chanced recently to sit next to Harkness, a big, rock-handsome assured man, during a game he was scouting in Madison Square Garden, and at the mention of Dryden he launched into an almost evangelical testimonial punctuated by a fierce assault on two bags of peanuts.

Dryden's record at Cornell was 76–4–1 including a national championship. Harkness said Dryden was an exceptional young man who wasted no time. On road trips, when others horsed around, Dryden read.

Dryden can do more with his glove alone, contends Harkness, than other goalies can do with all their equipment combined.

After graduating from Cornell with a B-average in pre-law, Dryden did a stint with the Canadian National Team, then finally accepted a Montreal contract that assured him he could go to graduate school. Assigned to the minor-league Montreal Voyageurs, he played 33 games in 1970–71 before the Canadiens preposterously promoted him for the play-offs.

For his first act, Dryden shut off Boston, the most awesome offensive juggernaut in the history of the game and heavy Stanley Cup favorite.

In the finals Dryden was too much for Bobby Hull and the rest of Chicago's heavy artillery and he was named the most valuable player in the play-offs. This from a neophyte who hadn't played enough games to be Rookie of the Year—an NHL first and doubtless a last! In 1971–72 he added the rookie award.

The best hope for rival shooters is that Dryden will fulfill the worst fears of Montreal and retire before his hockey prime. This season, however, he has sounded more dedicated to hockey than he ever has before.

"I'm tired of school," he said. "The Russia series put me a month behind in my studies and catching up has been a big burden psychologically. I may take a break from school for a while. Anyway, playing hockey doesn't preclude my doing other things."

My own guess is that Dryden will continue to play hockey at least until he's thirty, also continuing to prepare himself for a Nader-type career later. He is entirely smart enough to appreciate that the fame he is building in hockey will help his law career and that he is accumulating a substantial financial start in life. For the time being, I suspect, the people of Montreal can go back to wondering about the separatists, the next Olympics, Toronto, and the versatility of white wine.

Tennis

THE BITTER LESSONS OF WIMBLEDON '73

By Barry Lorge

From Tennis

For two weeks every year, the All-England Lawn Tennis Championships at Wimbledon become a ritualistic part of English life, like afternoon tea or royal pomp and pageantry. Wimbledon is the national garden party: a civilized, cultivated, gently festive celebration of the joys of being British in the summertime. It's really more an institution than a sporting event, and any threat to its well-being is regarded with almost as much indignation as an attack on the Queen.

It was not surprising, then, that the British public responded with displeasure to a boycott of this year's championships by most of the leading men in the game, and let everyone know their feelings by turning out in near-record numbers.

From central London to the countryside and Fleet Street to Parliament, people rallied to renew the now-familiar platitude that "Wimbledon is bigger than the players." After all, Wimbledon has gone on annually since 1877 except for 1915–19 and 1940–45, and nothing short of a world war is expected to interfere with it. Certainly the British weren't going to let a mere strike spoil their enjoyment of the rites of the season. They put on their stiffest upper lips and vowed to carry on.

A similar reaction to a milder threat had been seen in 1972, when the 32 pros then under contract to World Championship Tennis were barred by the International Lawn Tennis Federation (ILTF). At that time Ian Wooldridge, a columnist for the *London Daily*

Mail, noted that crowds were down only a shade from the previous year and observed shrewdly that "Wimbledon, with its well-pressed suits, picture hats, modulated voices, exemplary manners, courteous officials, machine-turned efficiency, and inescapable strawberries-and-cream could almost function without any tennis at all. It is the last of the great middle-class festivals and nearly 30,000 people a day are clinging to it as though it were their last stand against anarchy."

When 82 members of the Association of Tennis Professionals (ATP) and their sympathizers—including 13 of the original 16 seeds—walked out this year, the danger to the tournament's stature was more urgent, and the response more passionate. "Students of the British character had a field day at Wimbledon," observed Wooldridge. "Our way of life was being threatened, and it really was like 1940 again."

The citizens of Britain rose up to protect their heritage against what seemed a distasteful power play. They resolved to enjoy themselves come hell or high-handedness. The turnstiles clicked and by the end of the fortnight attendance had swelled to 300,172, the second highest total in history.

It didn't discourage the zealots that the men's field was woefully weak, the women got exciting only from the quarter-finals on, and the surrogate heroes the fans created were knocked out along the way. They weren't even daunted when the finals turned up looking like a Communist-Yankee conspiracy: two East Europeans in the men's title match for the first time, and two Americans whom they dislike in the ladies'.

The British hailed Jan Kodes of Czechoslovakia as a worthy champion after he vanquished Alex Metreveli of the Soviet Union 6–1, 9–8, 6–3, even though their match was commonplace. The natives couldn't muster much enthusiasm for either, but at least the bouncy little man from Prague (who had been French Open champ in 1970–71 and runner-up at Forest Hills in 1971) played with the assurance of a fellow who has been in big finals before. Kodes also beat the national hero, Roger Taylor, in a semifinal that would have been called heroic even in a good year, and surely that must count for something.

The Centre Court crowd begrudgingly praised Billie Jean King, the woman they loathe most, after she steamrolled Chris Evert to take her fifth singles title (breaking the post-war record previously held by Louise Brough). They cheered for Miss Evert as the underdog—even though she has the same steely determination and compelling will to succeed that makes Mrs. King so unpopular with a people who prefer gracious losers. But they admitted that Mrs. King's 6–0, 7–5 triumph was the most brilliant and devastating she has ever produced on a court where she has often played spectacularly.

Predictably, though, the greatest accolades were lavished on Wimbledon itself, which was pronounced an unqualified success despite the boycott. Committeemen in their green-and-mauve All-England Lawn Tennis & Croquet Club ties told each other it was so in pat-on-the-back tones. From all quarters came righteous pronouncements that Wimbledon had proved it was above blackmail, and would not be held to ransom.

There is much to be said for the hypothesis that some people go to Wimbledon to watch tennis, and most of the people go to watch some of the people. The social trappings are very important to the British, but that is not, of course, why the tournament has worldwide prestige. Wimbledon is revered internationally because it is considered preeminent, and that reputation can deteriorate very quickly if a large number of the best players stay away.

Some thoughtful Englishmen admitted as much, even as most of their countrymen were extolling Wimbledon's unassailability. "If the standard of play falls off permanently, some of the magic will be gone and everything else will erode eventually," said one businessman.

"It stands to reason that nothing is improved by reducing its standard," said Rex Bellamy of *The London Times*. There is a latent danger to Wimbledon's position, and if its guardians think it is immune, they could be sadly disillusioned.

The boycott was particularly sad because this year's Wimbledon had promised to be such a feast. Defending champion Stan Smith and Ilie Nastase, who played such a wonderful final in 1972, would be trying to repeat against the challenge of the returning outcasts: 1967–70–71 champion John Newcombe; thirty-eight-year-old Ken Rosewall, three times runner-up and again the sentimental favorite in perhaps his final bid for the title; and the rest of the upper echelon—Arthur Ashe, Roy Emerson, Marty Riessen, et al—who have proved so well matched the past two years.

Ironically, the hassle which turned feast into famine really had nothing to do with Wimbledon itself at all. It arose from the suspension of Nikki Pilic by the Yugoslav Tennis Federation (later confirmed by the ILTF although it reduced the duration from nine months to one) for failing to play in the Davis Cup series which Yugoslavia lost to New Zealand in May.

The players considered the suspension unfair and supported fellow union member Pilic by threatening to boycott en masse any tournament from which he was barred. It was a test case in the ATP's opposition to the arbitrary powers of suspension now held by the ILTF and its affiliated national associations. And in a larger context, it seemed that it might be the first in a long series of battles over the control of professional tennis between the ILTF and the ATP, which is a year old and has proven to be the first tennis players' union with real muscle.

The ATP and its chief executive, Jack Kramer, insisted that they never wanted to make Wimbledon the pawn in the struggle; that the ILTF chose the battleground by having Pilic's suspension run five days into the tournament. If it had been reduced by those five days a compromise could certainly have been worked out. But the ILTF was obstinate and many, therefore, believe it was trying to use the position of Wimbledon to fragment the ATP and weaken it.

When a marathon series of meetings, negotiations, and proposals failed to achieve a settlement the week before the championships, the ATP went to the British High Court seeking an injunction to enable Pilic to play. The object, said Kramer, was to buy time: let everyone play Wimbledon, and adjudicate the matter afterward. But Justice Sir Hugh Forbes turned down the injunction request with an unusually long and involved summation that touched on many facets of the case, and assessed the ATP all costs (approximately $15,000).

Disappointed and battle-weary, the ATP board met after the court decision and after protracted debate voted 7–1 (with no abstentions) to go through with the strike. Much of the association's membership undoubtedly wanted to play, but the militant faction argued that the moment of truth had come. If it backed down now, it might never be taken seriously again, but if it struck Wimbledon, every other tournament in the world would know it meant business. Several tortuous sessions followed and, despite exceptionally hostile pressure from the press, the association decided it had to demonstrate its solidarity now. The boycott was on.

By the time the draw was made, two days late, all but three of the ATP members on hand had withdrawn. Nastase said he had to play because the Rumanian federation ordered him to; third-line Australian Ray Keldie, who was recently married, said he needed the money; and Britain's Roger Taylor, who phoned his withdrawal and then quickly rang back to say he had changed his mind, said his conscience dictated that he must play in his own country.

Taylor's decision was extremely difficult—he had to sacrifice the respect of either the people he works with or those he must live with the rest of his life—and his defection was the one that hurt the ATP most. He tried to walk the middle ground, remaining in the tournament but donating all his winnings to the ATP and verbally supporting it, but the other members considered him a traitor, especially since three other Britons (Mark Cox, Graham Stilwell, Gerald Battrick) all withdrew.

In retrospect, it wasn't so much the idea of the boycott as the fact that they went through with it after the court case that damned the ATP in the minds of the British press and public. Up to a point, they had been on the players' side and considered the ILTF the villain for putting Wimbledon on the block.

When all hope of a settlement was lost, the draw was made without the boycotters. Captain Mike Gibson, the referee, bustled in with a new list of competitors, most of whom came from the 128-man qualifying competition at Roehampton. There was obviously no shortage of replacements (the ATP called them "scabs"). "The phone never stopped ringing," said assistant referee Fred Hoyles. This was clearly the chance of a lifetime for some obscure players to be able to someday tell their grandchildren, "I once played at Wimbledon."

The men's qualifying at Roehampton was halted after one round, with the 64 winners put directly into the draw. In addition, a couple of handsful of losers were drawn from a hat. (One, Peter Kanderal, had gone home to Switzerland after losing in the first round, but he was back in a jiffy and became perhaps the first man in Wimbledon history to lose in the qualifying and win a round in the tournament proper.) Wires were hastily sent to players who were not originally accepted directly, but for various reasons had not been able to play the qualifier—including several U.S. collegians who were playing in the NCAA Championships at Princeton, New Jersey, the week before Wimbledon.

A couple of nostalgic names—former champions Frank Sedgman and Neale Fraser—were drafted from other events and placed in the men's singles. (Both lost in the first round, but Fraser, thirty-nine, reached the finals of the men's doubles with John Cooper, and the forty-five-year-old Sedgman took the veterans' doubles title with Don Budge.) Nicki Pietrangeli, the thirty-nine-year-old former Italian No. 1, who had applied to play only in doubles, didn't even know he had been put in the singles. He came to Wimbledon on opening day in civvies, saw that he was scheduled to play, borrowed some gear, and lost in five sets.

At 2 P.M. precisely on a warm and sunny Wimbledon opening day, John Newcombe was losing $2.50 to Tony Roche in a game at the Croham Hurst Golf Club in Surrey, Stan Smith was window shopping on the King's Road, and Arthur Ashe was packing his bags at the Westbury Hotel.

At the All-England Club, the crowds came as usual, the strawberries were outstanding, and the ladies in their summer finery were surpassed only by those who wore very little finery at all. Masses of people milled in the main concourse and wandered the walkways between the back courts, even though the faces there were unfamiliar. Matches such as Ernest Ewert vs Konstantin Pugaev were plentiful.

Times writer Bellamy commended on the "splendid sadness" of it all: the scene was deliciously familiar, but there were important people missing. "It was," he said, "a bit like a coronation without the Queen."

Few of the boycotters ever did come to Wimbledon. Those who remained in London stayed away, and most departed quickly to go home or play in hastily arranged exhibitions. The men on the gates were instructed not to admit the strikers unless they had tickets—"not out of spite," said the club secretary, "but because any competitor who doesn't play becomes just an ordinary member of the public."

Rumanian Ion Tiriac, who was furious with Nastase for playing, came and scoffed at the field. He waved at the scoreboard which indicated that Kodes was playing Ken Hirai on Court 1. "What is a Hirai?" sneered Tiriac. "Is that a brand of chocolate bar?"

Meanwhile, the British manifested that true Dunkirk spirit. When Nastase and German Hans Joachim Plotz stepped onto the green and spongy Centre Court for the first match, a packed house gave them a standing ovation, with the Duke and Dutchess of Kent leading the applause. When Taylor and Frenchman Jean Haillet appeared for their match three hours later and bowed to the Royal Box, the place shook for 45 seconds.

With a remarkable capacity for self-deception, some of the British public and press even convinced themselves that Wimbledon was better without the ATP pros. A *Daily Express* editorial entitled "Glorious Uncertainty" claimed, "This is the Wimbledon where anything can happen, when the youngsters who might not stand much of a chance against the well-drilled automatons of the Kramer circus will be able to play the kind of tennis they enjoy and that can give vast entertainment." Right, chaps. The top pros are old hat, monotonous, overexposed. Give us fresh faces and new blood.

There were also other arguments, repeated and reinforced ad nauseum, that went something like this:

1) We still have Nastase, runner-up last year and the U.S., French, and Italian titlist. Even if he beats Cheddar in the semis and Camembert in the final, no one can call *him* a "cheese champion."

2) We have all the best ladies, and they play more interesting tennis.

3) Wouldn't it be cracking if Roger Taylor became the first British man to win since Fred Perry in 1936!

4) There will always be new heroes, like this Swede, Bjorn Borg —the best seventeen-year old since Rosewall and Hoad. If the men who made their reputations at Wimbledon want to turn their backs on it, there will always be new ones to take their place.

True enough, there was a lot going on at Wimbledon even in this anticlimactic year. Nastase is always fun on court or off, and in the early days he turned up in a variety of disguises, including a vendor's uniform (he sold three ice lollies before being discovered). Alex Mayer, the NCAA champion who beat Nasty in the most stunning upsets since Taylor dumped Rod Laver in 1970, turned into quite an unexpected celebrity as he reached the semis. He played well, coming back from two sets down to oust seeded Jurgen Fassbender in the quarter-finals (his first time on Centre Court), and astounded everyone by saying he felt far less pressure at Wimbledon than in winning the NCAA title for Stanford the week before.

Borg is a self-assured youngster, who set off a rather remarkable wave of hysteria among Wimbledon's teeny-bopper set, which hounded him everywhere he went (after the first day, he needed police escorts to get out of his matches without having his clothes ripped off) and turned the staid old club into a facsimile of a David Cassidy concert. He seemed dazzled, embarrassed, and mildly annoyed by the whole thing, but he reached the quarter-finals before losing to the glamour boy of another generation, the thirty-one-year-old Taylor, in what one paper hailed as "the Battle of the Pin-Ups."

Taylor's run to the semis for the third time (he reached the same plateau in 1967 and 1970) created plenty of excitement among a citizenry that would probably go stark-raving mad if a Briton ever won a singles title again. Taylor was the only one who kept Wimbledon's seasoned ticket scalpers alive ("Nobody wants to know any of the others, and the Borg-boppers can't afford reserved tickets, even at face value," grumbled one tout), but he was always uneasy in his martyr-hero role. His heart never seemed truly in it.

The women's field was strong, but there were few interesting matches during the first week. The problem with the women's field is that there is too much of a disparity at present between the top level and the masses. All eight seeds advanced to their place in the quarter-finals. There were no upsets among the men until the sixth day (Mayer over Nastase) either, making this the first time ever that the seeds have advanced intact to that stage in both the men's and women's events.

There were some great moments and good matches but, on balance, it must have been the dullest Wimbledon in years. In a usual year, Wimbledon has glamour plus more good attractions going on simultaneously than Ringling Bros., Barnum & Bailey. Part of the tournament's inimitable charm is its depth, and that was sorely lacking this year.

Perhaps it was fated that the men's finals should be boring stuff. Metreveli—nervous and double-faulting—lacked the confidence he had shown earlier in thwarting Connors and Mayer with solid, workmanlike tennis. He had seemed supremely eager to win, knowing that this was his best chance, perhaps his only one, to become a Soviet winner at Wimbledon. Kodes said that the title still meant a great deal even if the field was sub-par. Maybe he could have won even if everybody had played, he said. "It was not a good final," he conceded, "but maybe there have been worse."

That summed it up neatly.

In the end, the real class of the tournament was Mrs. King, who had her shaky moments in the quarters and semifinals, but came on gloriously against Miss Evert in the women's singles final. She then won the women's doubles with Rosemary Casals and the mixed doubles with Owen Davidson for her second Wimbledon triple. Her three titles gave her a total of 17 Wimbledon crowns, just two short of the all-time record accumulated by Elizabeth Ryan of the U.S. between the wars.

As play ended, it seemed doubtful that Wimbledon would soon again recapture its old magic—even if it welcomes the boycotters back next year. "The emotional attachment which most players had for Wimbledon has been pretty much shattered," said Bob Maud of South Africa. "Everyone will want to play here again, I'm sure, but in the future Wimbledon will have to come up with prize money commensurate with the rest of the circuit. The players never made demands like that in the past, but they may now."

Wimbledon can again be preeminent—and probably will be—but the British will have to realize that it's more than a garden party.

Olympic Games

THE OLYMPICS: END OF A DREAM

By David Wolf

From True Magazine

The doves soared. Doves of peace. Five thousand freed to fly above Munich's gaudy new stadium where the world's greatest athletes engulfed the field in a colorful sea of flags and national uniforms. Cannons roared and the Olympic flame blazed. The 1972 Games had begun.

From the stands, and to the millions watching on television, it looked beautiful.

"Down on the field, it wasn't so pretty. The doves were shitting all over the athletes," said Al Feuerbach. "People were running and ducking, sticking newspapers over their heads. It was getting in girls' hair and all over guys' uniforms. Kind of prophetic, wasn't it?"

Feuerbach sat on his rumpled bed in the small, cluttered room on the second floor of Building 12 in Olympic Village. He was packing to go home. The closing ceremonies were scheduled for the following afternoon, but like most athletes at the 20th Olympics, he wasn't sticking around.

The T-shirt stretched tight across his massive chest as he reached to pick up a piece of cloth. On it was the number 984. The previous day it had been pinned to his United States uniform when he competed in the finals of the shot put. Feuerbach stared at the cloth, then tossed it to the floor. "I'm not bringing home any souvenirs," he said softly. "This hasn't been something I want to remember."

The twenty-four-year-old Feuerbach had come to Munich expecting to win ("I thought my chances were better than fifty-fifty and almost certain for at least a silver or a bronze"). He had thrown well. But not well enough. His toss of 68 feet 11¼ inches left him in fifth place—just 6½ inches from the gold medal that had been his primary ambition for the last 10 years.

But Feuerbach's disappointment ran deeper. "I honestly believe there are going to be so many victories in my future that I won't even remember the details of yesterday," he said. "I can handle the defeat. But the disillusionment is tougher. The Olympics were always my motivating dream. They aren't anymore."

A thoughtful, articulate graduate of Emporia State in Kansas, Feuerbach is often euphoric about sport—but he is not naive. Cynical about the administration of U.S. amateur athletics long before he made the Olympic team, Feuerbach also was painfully aware of the Neanderthal dictates of the International Olympic Committee, the self-perpetuating oligarchy headed by outgoing president Avery Brundage.

But somehow, Feuerbach had still expected to find the peaceful festival of brotherhood and sport he had dreamed of as a teen-ager lifting weights in his basement in Preston, Iowa (population 950).

Instead, he found a gigantic orgy of nationalism, commercialism, administrative bungling, outright cheating and, finally, bloodshed.

"I never realized how much the Olympics are political springboards for groups and countries," he said with disgust. "When a Russian or East German wins an event, the communists claim it proves their system is superior—which is ridiculous. But the U.S. implies the same damn thing! It's hard for the athlete not to feel he's being used."

Outside, where machine-gun carrying soldiers guarded the entrance to the U.S. dorm, it had begun to rain. Feuerbach swallowed two vitamin C tablets from the open jar on the night table. "I guess athletes are different," he said hesitantly. "I root for Americans. But it's friendship, not patriotism. Sometimes I'll see a foreigner at meets, I'll come to respect him as a competitor and a man—and I'll find myself pulling for him, even against Americans. I think that's good. But there was so little of it here."

Feuerbach stuffed a last sweatsuit into the suitcase, then slammed it shut. Hard. "The disappointment doesn't change my mind about shot-putting," he said. "I love it. But now I'll be psyched for all competition, not pointing for *the* special event. If there's still an Olympics in '76, I'll go to Montreal. I still want a gold. But it won't be the same—ever."

His words were not the isolated response of a lone athlete embittered by personal defeat. Throughout the village a large and growing number of competitors had begun to doubt the value of the Games. But, for several reasons, Feuerbach's reaction is especially significant.

First, he is probably the United States' best prospect in the shot put. Some, in fact, believe that despite his fifth place in Munich, Feuerbach is the finest shot-putter in the world right now.

During 1972, just his second year as a world-class performer, he threw the shot over 69 feet on 11 different occasions—more than double the previous one-year high. George Woods and Randy Matson are the only other men in history to throw past 70 feet in official competition. Just before the Olympics, Feuerbach heaved the 16-pound iron ball 70 feet 7½ inches. It was the third time he crossed the magic barrier and the top throw of 1972.

This winter, along with U.S. teammates Woods and Brian Oldfield, Feuerbach—representing the Pacific Coast Track Club—will compete throughout the country, taking dead aim on his own world indoor record of 69 feet four inches. Next summer, he and the 300-pound Woods are likely to dismantle Matson's outdoor record of 71 feet 5½ inches.

An accomplished weight lifter (full squats with 570 pounds on his back), the stocky, six-foot-one, 255-pound Feuerbach is still a veritable midget in the elephantine world of shot-putting. No world-class competitor is as short or as light.

Feuerbach compensates with coordination, tremendous quickness —and thus acceleration—in the circle, and near-perfect technique. "You give hope to all small men," a British coach told him at Munich. "And you've convinced a lot of coaches they can teach the shot put."

But Feuerbach hasn't had a coach for three years. He is a great shot-putter because he worked and sacrificed—on his own. And that is the second reason why his disenchantment is meaningful. Al Feuerbach is the kind of athlete the Olympics are supposed to be about.

He is totally, joyously, dedicated to his sport—without ulterior motives. Feuerbach doesn't view it as a stepping-stone to a pro football contract, a movie career, a public relations job or a political campaign. He knows his relatively anonymous event will never make him rich or famous.

Nevertheless, he trains full time. He hasn't had a job since he left college three years ago. Each day he throws, lifts weights, or competes.

He's got an attractive girl friend, an old car, and plenty of time for the beach. But the unimposing frame house Feuerbach shares with two shot-putters and a weight lifter in San Jose, California, stands as bleak evidence of his essentially Spartan existence.

"For someone else, my life might seem ridiculous," he admits, a tiny smile creasing his soft, handsome features. "For me, it's exciting and fulfilling. I'm improving my body—the motor pattern and mental efficiency—so I can meet a challenge.

"Sometimes I daydream about ancient Greece. I imagine things being more pure for the athlete, more like what the Olympics *ought to be* now," says Feuerbach, whose knuckles are permanently damaged by the countless practice throws which spread and stretch his fingers. "In the ancient Games, athletes were respected.

"Today people get up-tight because I don't have a job. But would I really contribute more to mankind if I took my business administration degree and became a used-car dealer? I'd rather try to be best in the world at something. And this is what I've chosen."

In East Germany or the Soviet Union, an "amateur" athlete who trains full-time is supported by the state through its athletic governing bodies. He gets a bogus job, a healthy salary, a coach and trainer, access to the most advanced drugs and medical care, and cash bonuses when he breaks world records.

American athletes get nothing—except trouble.

The rules of the Amateur Athletic Union, the internationally sanctioned governing body for U.S. track and field, prohibit Feuerbach from receiving money for personal appearances, coaching, or even writing about the shot put. But Feuerbach won't sponge off his father, a well-to-do Iowa veterinarian. How does he survive? Probably on the meager "expense money" all top track stars get under-the-table from most promoters.

It's hardly a windfall. Last winter a big-name miler commanded $1,000 per meet, but shot-putters were fortunate to get an occasional $250.

As a high school senior, Feuerbach was 20th among the nation's schoolboy shot-putters. But Al weighed just 180 pounds and major college track powers weren't interested.

"The universal consensus—except for me and my father—was I'd done well for a little guy, but I had absolutely no long-range potential," he recalls grimly. "But my father believed you could do anything, if you work hard enough—and even then I felt I'd be in the Olympics someday."

At Emporia State, Feuerbach worked out three hours a day, seven days a week. He lifted weights in the evenings and pitched hay each summer on his father's farm. Eventually, he won the NAIA (small college) championship, but was still no match for internationally ranked behemoths like the six-foot-seven, 275-pound Matson, or Kansas' 300-pound Karl Salb. Friends urged him to give up. "Even my coach would cry for a 'big' putter," he says, the bitterness and hurt still burned in his memory. "But that 'too small' crap just drove me harder."

As recently as 1969, Feuerbach still hadn't reached the mundane distance of 60 feet. But he kept working. "That summer, I watched the U.S.A.-U.S.S.R. dual meet on television at home," he remembers. "Then I went out in the backyard (Preston's only shot-put pit) and had to add 10 feet to my throws to even *pretend* I was in the meet."

One year later, Feuerbach was representing the U.S. against the Russians.

"I'd always lacked strength," Al explains. "I loved lifting weights, but I'd never had a planned program. My junior year, I started one. Soon I was getting bigger. And much stronger. I already had quickness and technique, so my throws suddenly took off."

Today, the once wiry Feuerbach is built like a low stone wall. His biceps are massive and there is no fat on his 40-inch waist. The lifting program was partially responsible. But, with typical candor, he admits there was another factor.

Feuerbach was taking anabolic steroids, sport's most controversial drug.

Steroids are male hormones. When used regularly, they accelerate strength and muscle growth by causing the body to retain protein at an abnormally high rate.

The drug, however, may be dangerous. Many physicians contend steroids cause liver damage, atrophied testes, and cancer of the prostate. Steroids are opposed by the International Olympic Committee, but the IOC has no effective method of detection and—despite the warnings—thousands of athletes (including every top competitor in the discus, javelin, and shot put) take them regularly.

For the shot-putter, the options are clear: use steroids or quit. "I was so naive, I didn't even learn about them till my junior year," says Feuerbach. "My first reaction was negative. Then I saw what they were doing for the guys who were beating me."

Still, he was frightened. But Feuerbach took the drugs anyway. "I guess, subconsciously, I decided that what I wanted—to fulfill my potential and be a champion—was worth the risk and danger," Al reflects. "Now, I don't worry. With a reasonable dosage—like 15 to 25 milligrams a day—I don't think there's any danger.

"I'm not advocating steroids," he emphasizes. "They aren't for kids and too much is dangerous. But I've spoken to about 500 athletes who take steroids and not one had negative reactions. I know I'm in good health—and I definitely don't feel sexually impaired!"

The enlarged physique didn't alter Feuerbach's personality. Still shy, almost gentle, he's uncomfortable making speeches and hasn't had a fistfight since the eighth grade. His aggressions surface where they always did—in the shot-put ring. "I psych myself way up for competition," he says. "I try to manufacture a 'hatred' for my opponents."

By 1971, Feuerbach's primary opponent was world record-holder Randy Matson, the Mexico City gold medalist who had dominated the event so completely his only competition had been boredom.

"I trained for months with just one thought in mind—beat Matson," Feuerbach recalls. "He epitomized the big guys I'd been told I'd never beat. I wanted to destroy him."

In a year, Feuerbach burst from obscurity to set a world indoor record, win the gold medal at the Pan American Games, and beat Matson regularly. He was hailed as shot-putting's brightest new star.

Last spring, huge George Woods, the 1968 silver medalist, came out of retirement with throws equal to Feuerbach's. A soft-spoken, twenty-nine-year-old admissions counselor at Southern Illinois University, the 305-pound Woods believed that only the incompetence of U.S. team doctors had kept him from beating Matson at Mexico City.

The physicians had warned Woods that Olympic rules prohibited his taping a painfully injured wrist. But they neglected to add that the regulation could be waived in the finals if Woods brought a medical certificate onto the field.

"When I found out, it was too late," Woods recalled. "It still galls me. No doctor or team manager told me—and they knew how badly I needed the tape. With it, I'd have won. That's why I'm back."

At the Olympic trials, Feuerbach, Matson, and Woods were heavily favored for the three openings. Then, from nowhere, came Brian "Barney" Oldfield—and the trio was a quartet.

A boisterous, flippant, twenty-seven-year-old extrovert, the six-foot-five, 275-pound Oldfield is a brilliant natural athlete who rarely allows infrequent workouts to interfere with his social life.

A teacher at the Illinois State Training School for Boys in St. Charles, Oldfield unsettled his opponents by competing in flowered Speede swim trunks and a fishnet jersey with deep decoletage. He warmed up with 60-foot puts over his head and side arm, then suddenly exploded a gigantic 72–7 foul.

When Oldfield followed with a career high 68-9½ in the qualifying round, Matson began to come apart. He bombed out in the finals. Oldfield, Woods, and Feuerbach were going to Munich.

"In the end, I felt sorry for Randy. I'd been so nervous myself I had stomach pains and couldn't sleep," says Feuerbach, who finished a strong second to Woods. "But mostly, I felt proud. After all those years, all the putdowns, *I'd* made the Olympic team!"

The euphoria was short-lived. Feuerbach hadn't even left the U.S. before the Olympic Committee ordered him to lie.

While athletes were being processed for departure in Washington, a USOC official handed Feuerbach a lengthy document and instructed him to sign. "It was some kind of oath," Feuerbach recalls. "I had to swear things like I'd *never* taken steroids or amphetamines, never made *any* sort of profit from my sport, wouldn't talk to newsmen without the coaches' permission—I couldn't believe it."

"Just sign," laughed Olympic veteran Jim Ryun. "Nobody even reads it."

"But it's bullshit."

"Sure," said Ryun, "but it doesn't mean anything."

Arriving in Munich, Feuerbach was summoned to a team meeting, where the U.S. men were ordered to sign in the name of every person who visited their dormitory rooms—even their wives.

The rule, of course, was ignored. "But that meeting set the pattern," says Feuerbach. "We were either treated like children or completely ignored. The U.S. officials were old men taking a vacation. They didn't want to get close to a sweaty athlete.

"A lot of athletes wouldn't go near the U.S. trainers," he continues. "When I went to have my back cracked—and almost got my neck broken—I saw why."

One evening, Feuerbach (who must worry about maintaining strength and bulk) tried to locate some cans of high protein food supplement, but was shuttled between three yawning managers and a trainer. "Can't find the storeroom key," a manager mumbled 30 minutes later. "Try coming around tomorrow."

"The Olympic Committee spends huge amounts of money to get our team here," George Woods noted, "but when you need a manager or trainer, or you want some information—like when your event starts—they've gone somewhere."

Even with 168 trainers, coaches, and managers for just 447 U.S. athletes, disastrous foul-ups could not be prevented. The worst occurred when track coach Stan Wright, using an unofficial, 18-month-old schedule, gave gold-medal prospects Eddie Hart and Rey Robinson the incorrect starting time for the 100-meter semifinal. They arrived late and were disqualified.

Most damaging to Feuerbach was a thoughtless administrative decision which placed all three U.S. shot-putters—and three other weight-event competitors—in the same cramped apartment on the second floor of building 12.

A shot-putter's psychological preparation is as important as physical training. Self-confidence is vital. Each man strives to reach the event in the mental state which best allows him to marshal and focus his maximum strength and skill into a few sudden explosions of energy.

For Feuerbach, this means prolonged periods of total concentration and the reduction of opponents to imaginary enemies. "Rooming together is stupid," he snapped early in the Games. "We're competing *against* each other! I can't get the right psych like this."

At first there was friction. Woods, a deeply religious Southern Baptist, and Mormon discus thrower Jay Silvester, badgered Oldfield and Feuerbach about "not being Christians." One night the argument became heated. "I'm more determined than ever to win the gold," Woods shouted at Feuerbach. "Maybe when you're beaten, you'll see the light!"

"Does that mean there's no God if *I* win?" answered Feuerbach, once very involved in the Campus Crusade for Christ, but now indifferent to organized religion. "Well, I think there might be a God, so let's just forget it!"

Until recently Brian Oldfield, whose football and basketball careers at Middle Tennessee State ended before he ever played a game ("The coach wanted me to stop bouncing basketballs off the ceiling—but I wouldn't"), wasn't even relatively serious about the shot. Now, despite his sudden improvement, Oldfield knew he'd be outclassed if Feuerbach and Woods were at their best—so he tried unnerving them with taunts and boasts.

Oldfield called George Woods "fat boy" and "tons of fun." In the crowded Puma shoe store, he laughingly announced, "Some broad told me Al has a tiny dick."

"At least I've got one," Al Feuerbach snapped.

"You think Al's is small," Oldfield continued. "You ought to see George's!"

"But *we* get distance in the shot put," Al replied coldly.

When Oldfield drifted off, Feuerbach glared and said: "He's 80 percent front. Inside, he's scared. There's no way a guy like that can beat me—I *can't* let it happen."

Eventually, however, the pressure of approaching competition, the shared experience, and the constant commotion of the Games seemed to draw the shot-putters closer together.

"They're good guys," Feuerbach conceded. "Brian just wants to be liked and sometimes he's pretty funny. When George gets away from Silvester, he can joke and curse and have fun. We share a TV. We go out drinking together. I'm trying to dislike them, but I can't."

But the strange camaraderie remained fragile, each man still searching for a psychological edge. Woods and Feuerbach worked to undermine Oldfield's shaky confidence ("How will you take it if you don't qualify for the finals?" Al would say innocently). Feuerbach reminded Woods whenever a favorite was upset. Oldfield occasionally asked George: "What's it like to know this is your last chance?"

When Woods began secluding himself in his room, Feuerbach's friend, pole-vaulter Steve Smith, tacked a picture of Feuerbach on Woods' wall. "I won't give 'em the satisfaction of taking it down," said George, staring darts at the photo.

To annoy his teammates, Feuerbach practiced alone and refused to disclose his results. But his own efforts to psych himself were interrupted by Oldfield's constant racket ("The gold will go to the most beautiful body!") and Woods' bellicose pronouncements of invincibility.

"George has to be the favorite," Feuerbach admitted. "He had a 70-foot 1¾-inch the other day and he's throwing 70-foot 2-inch fouls in practice. But can he do it without the foul? The Olympics are a thing apart. The pressure is unbelievable. *Everyone* is at their peak now. We've got to worry about three East Germans and Komar from Poland. You could have a real good day and not even get a medal."

Feuerbach was also throwing well in practice. "But it'll be tougher on him," warned a visiting U.S. college coach. "Al depends on technique. There's little margin for error. Woods is so strong he could screw up under the pressure and still boom one."

As the qualifying round neared, Oldfield grew even more hyper. "Sure I'm scared of doing bad," he admitted, lying on the floor as he watched television, bit his nails, smoked and tossed half eaten candy bars out the window. "But that's gonna jack me up more. I don't need much practice. I'm not into technique, I just go out and explode.

"If I win, no one will ever train," he shouted at Feuerbach's closed door. "But I'm not wearin' a swimsuit this time. They might mistake me for Mark Spitz!"

Even Woods had manic moments. When Feuerbach and Oldfield excluded him from a discussion, Woods kicked Feuerbach's door off the hinges. A sudden urge to "rassle" resulted in a demolished bed and the near-suffocation of Steve Smith. Most often, however, Woods lay in his room and stared silently at the ceiling. "I've handled the pressure before," he said. "Now I'm capable of a gold medal and a world record."

Feuerbach, meanwhile, seemed very subdued. "Partly, I'm building toward going into that stadium completely relaxed," he said. "And partly, I'm finding a lot of things around here depressing."

Each day brought new turmoil. When a preposterous, last-minute IOC decision outlawed the pole he'd used all year, Steve Smith was forced to *borrow* one—and didn't even qualify for the finals. Facing the same handicap, defending champ Bob Seagren blew the gold medal, then angrily shoved the pole at an official.

"Even the food supplement the USOC gives us is bad," Feuerbach noted. "Everybody who drinks it gets diarrhea!"

For a few hours, the gloom lifted, Feuerbach was talking to his San Jose roommate, Lahcen "Sam" Sansame, a shot-putter on the Moroccan team, when a large, brown-skinned man approached. He wore a green cap and a smile. His name was Nagui Assaad and he threw the shot for Egypt.

"Assaad didn't speak real good English," Feuerbach recalls, "but we hit it off right away. He trains in East Germany. We sat there talking about our training methods and what shot-putting meant to us. He's the African record holder, but his country doesn't help him much. He just loves what he's doing. Like me."

Oblivious to the darkness which fell around them, the three large men stood for several hours, talking of their sport and then of themselves. When words were missing, laughter filled the spaces. "Assaad told us he was a Christian," Feuerbach remembers. "Then he said he was a virgin—because he wasn't married yet! He didn't mind when we laughed. I really like him. I felt I'd made a friend. As I walked away, I thought 'This is what the Olympics are supposed to be like.' "

Feuerbach awoke the next morning to learn that Arab commandos had murdered two Israelis. "Attacking defenseless people is chicken shit," he blurted. "They've got to be lower than dogs!"

From his terrace Feuerbach looked out at the village. He could not see the far corner where nine Olympians were held hostage and armed police in track suits encircled the building. Nothing else seemed changed. Athletes played ping-pong, chess, and miniature golf. They sunbathed and traded Olympic pins. That night the discotheque was crowded. Some would later call this callousness.

It wasn't.

The horror nearby never seemed real. Few athletes saw a terrorist or an Israeli. The IOC, which waited an appalling 12 hours before suspending competition, did nothing to inform them. The village loudspeaker continued to play polka music. The most accurate information came over Armed Forces Radio from New York.

"We were all sitting around the radio," Feuerbach recalls, "when Sansame came in and said Assaad had locked himself in his room. The guy was so shook up, he wouldn't even come out for food. Then, I guess, the whole Egyptian team left the village and Assaad went with them. I never saw him again."

In the morning, Feuerbach tried to watch the memorial services on television, but returned to his room, self-conscious because he was unmoved. "The deaths aren't affecting me anymore," he said, frowning. "Next week, they'll make me sick, but now I've got to concentrate. Relax. Get my mind clear to compete. Maybe that's selfish, but I've worked so long I can't let myself be distracted now."

Yet he was distracted. The competitive fire was missing. Weeks later, Feuerbach would realize: "I'd become mentally run-down. I had to fight the idea that losing didn't matter."

The qualifying round standard was just 62 feet. Feuerbach effortlessly tossed the stone near 66, without even removing his sweat shirt. His teammates also moved into the finals with one throw. But first, Woods had an unsettling moment.

An Olympic official threatened to kick him out of the Games.

"All week I'd been trying to get an Olympic medical certificate so I could legally tape my wrist and avoid problems like Mexico City," Woods said back at the dorm, his voice rising with nervous excitement. "The coaches said everything was fine. But when I walked onto the field, this little bald-headed character in a red jacket runs up and hollers, 'Where is your medical certificate?' I thought he meant the one from the *Olympic* medical staff—which I'd been told I didn't need!"

"Aw shit," Woods had mumbled under his breath, "here we go again."

The judge, Adrian Poulen of the Netherlands (who earlier led the move to ban Seagren and Smith's poles), suddenly flushed with rage. "Don't you say 'shit' to me!" he screamed. "I was in the war. I know what those expressions mean!"

"But, sir," Woods began, "I didn't—"

"Don't you tell me," Poulen cried, *"I* tell *you!"*

"Sir," Woods stammered, backing away in confusion, "do you want the medical form from our U.S. doctors? I've got that."

Poulen glared up into his face: "Yes, yes, that one. But don't you say 'shit' to me. I'll have you kicked out of the Games!"

Leaving the stadium, George Woods learned the judge had actually collared an IOC official in the stands and demanded his ouster. "One of our managers saw it," cried Woods, still unnerved two hours later. "They calmed the guy down, but I've been advised to apologize to the little bastard before the finals tomorrow."

"It's good to see it's not bothering you, George," Oldfield needled when Woods recounted the incident a fourth time. "Maybe the little so-and-so has it in for you."

"That's not so funny."

"Then maybe you should protest to somebody right now," Oldfield said seriously.

"Sure," Woods snorted, "but who? We've been here two weeks, and if there's a shot-put coach, I still don't know about it!"

Moments later, Steve Smith brought news that Vince Matthews and Wayne Collett had been banned from the Olympics for life by the IOC.

After finishing 1–2 in the 400-meter run, the day before, the black Americans had caused a small furor by not standing at attention during the victory ceremony and national anthem. Matthews had invited Collett to join him on the winner's platform, where the pair slouched and chatted. When the crowd booed, Matthews twirled the gold medal around his fingers.

Initially some American athletes were offended. "They had a *right* to do it," Oldfield said. "But it was stupid, so soon after the Israelis died." Yet the incident seemed minor until the IOC's classic overkill.

Without giving Matthews and Collett even the pretense of a hearing, Brundage warned: "If such performances should happen in the future, please be advised that medals will be withheld."

In Feuerbach's room the athletes stared at each other in silence. They seemed more shocked than angry—at first. "Brundage is going way overboard, threatening future medals," Feuerbach said finally. "The athlete just has no freedom here. How can those stupid old men think people from all over the world should have the *same* reaction to winning?"

"It wasn't even a real protest," said the usually conservative Woods, who earlier had been critical. "And what about Dave Wottle? Why didn't they take his medal for wearing a golf hat on the victory stand?"

"How about those Australian swimmers carrying their kangaroos and Mark Spitz waving track shoes?" added Steve Smith. "Some guy even wore a wig. But he wasn't black, so it was OK."

Their voices rose in anger and disappointment. "Matthews and Collett worked their asses off to win those medals," said Feuerbach. "But the Olympic Committee act like we owe *them* something!"

"Right!" shouted Woods. "It's like that guy who jumped all over me with his, 'You don't tell me, I tell you!' "

"You ever watch our Olympic officials?" Feuerbach sneered. "They're getting their first ego hits at age sixty, walking around in U.S.A. blazers, always turned sideways so they lead with the shield."

"We ought to find the best facilities and have world championships in each sport," Smith suggested. "The flags and ceremonies are crap. You get the politics cause the Olympics are too big."

"Brundage and his boys won't allow that. They're making too much money," said Woods, a father and husband who has had to paint his shot white so he could practice in the dark after a day at the office. "The AAU and the Olympic Committee make all the rules. They sell TV rights, charge admission, endorse products—and the athlete gets nothing. They're just *using* me."

Then why does he continue? Woods ran a thick hand across his damp forehead. "I keep asking myself that," he said hesitantly. "I suppose it's the motivation to be No. 1 at something—to have a gold medal to look back on. But other guys who represent their countries get some financial help. Americans get nothing. Then everyone jumps on us when we lose. I'm completely disenchanted. The Olympic spirit is a bunch of shit!"

Feuerbach looked up, startled by the emotion in Woods' voice. Woods moved toward the door, then stopped. "I can't say it," he struggled. "Yes, yes I can. I once had a chance to go into football in college—but I wanted the Olympics. Well, I'm here! But I wish I'd gone into football. I had pro potential. I might have gotten a $50,000 bonus. But it's too late now."

In moments Feuerbach was alone. He closed his eyes and tried to gather his thoughts. He hadn't planned it this way. "We're all disillusioned with the Games, but the personal goals are still important," he reminded himself aloud. "I wouldn't take $50,000 to give up the shot put. Tomorrow I'm gonna win a gold medal."

Two hours before the shot-put finals, Feuerbach sat on his bed, pinning the cloth 984 to the back of his jersey. "I'm not very nervous," he said softly. "I don't even know if that's good. But I want to stay like this, everything subdued, till I throw."

Woods was on his bed listening to the radio. Twice he bellowed as though throwing the shot. Otherwise he was silent. For 15 minutes, Oldfield sat alone in front of the television, sucking on a cigarette. "Man, I'm jacked. I'm gonna explode," he rumbled. "Last night I finished a bottle of vodka, went out for four beers, and slept beautiful. Now I'm getting crazy."

Shouting "I'm so fucking strong!" Oldfield rushed to the window and threw eight cartons of fruit juice down at hammer-thrower George Freen, standing innocently across the street.

"Oldfield, you're out of your mind!" Freen screamed as he dodged the splattering.

"Soon you'll all drink from my joint!" Oldfield cried. Then he galloped downstairs and marched in front of the dorm singing, "I feel pretty, oh, so pretty. . . ."

"The handwriting is on the wall," Woods announced from his bed. "Woods will win!" Then he sat up and stared at the picture of Feuerbach. "And maybe a world record, too."

Feuerbach's breathing had begun to quicken. "I'm not worrying about the pressure," he repeated. "This isn't the climax of my career. It's the start."

Feuerbach stood in a passageway leading from the locker room. Behind him in the stadium, the Polish anthem was playing for Wladyslaw Komar—winner of the shot put. "Well," Al said, trying to smile, "that's the Olympics."

Feuerbach had thrown 68 feet 11½ inches and finished fifth. The tall, bearded, thirty-two-year-old Komar had hit 69 feet 6 inches on his first throw and no one could match it.

In truth, George Woods had matched it. His sixth and final throw had hit a marker signifying Komar's new Olympic record. But the judges—after a mysterious silence—spotted the put 13 centimeters short.

An earlier throw, just one centimeter behind Komar, gave Woods another silver medal. But he had not even approached his awesome practice heaves of the previous weeks. "I didn't throw well," Woods would admit the following day. "I felt the pressure. In the back of my mind, I knew I wouldn't get another chance for four years—or maybe I'd never get one. But I resigned myself to second. Now everyone tells me I was cheated, that I actually *won*. What a way for it to end!"

For Feuerbach, there was no doubt. He had been beaten: "It was *there*. Each time, I felt good. I kept expecting a 70 footer. But I just couldn't put it together. Maybe I was dipping my head when I threw. I don't know. There was just no snap. No explosion. It hurts so much because I know I should have won. Nobody threw great. Nobody did anything near what I'm capable of—what I've *already* done. But I guess I'm just not one of those guys who get their names in the history books."

Even before his final throw, with the crowd roaring and TV camera hovering behind the circle, Feuerbach believed he would win. "I wasn't panicky," he recalls. "I felt composed. Maybe *too* composed. I drove across the ring smooth, but I cut it off, pulled away too soon."

He knew instantly that the throw was bad. "Oh wow, goddamn," he moaned under his breath. "I've lost!"

"What went wrong?" asked one of the half dozen reporters encircling Feuerbach in the tunnel.

"I don't know," he said softly. "I'll need time to think this whole thing out. Seven inches really isn't that much. But *fifth* place. . . ."

"Will you look for a job when you get back to San Jose?"

"No, I'll continue to train."

An American athlete stopped Feuerbach in the village to offer condolences—and a barbiturate. Feuerbach smiled wanly and shook his head. "Why do I need a downer," he whispered to himself, "when I'm so down already?"

His face was drained, his eyes were fixed on something very far away. "George seemed to be panicking a little bit," Feuerbach said, reaching the dorm, "but Brian surprised me. He went into that animal psych and really handled the pressure well." Throwing with unexpected consistency, Oldfield had finished sixth with 68 feet 7½ inches.

Still in his sweat suit, Oldfield was pacing about the apartment, mumbling his disappointment with one last burst of braggadocio: "I was strong! I felt good, pretty soon I was sure I was gonna win. But I just wasn't gettin' into 'em proper. My last throw, shit, I had so much goddamn energy—but then it slips off my fingers! But fuck it, I don't even feel bad."

"I do," said Feuerbach, slumping on his bed.

"Yeah, I do, too."

"I'm glad Komar won," Feuerbach said, pulling off his damp sweat shirt. "I've gone out drinking with him a couple of times. He's a decent guy and he's waited a long time for this."

Oldfield suddenly clasped his head in his hands. "Oh man," he groaned. "I just realized: a Polack won the gold medal! I'll never live that down when I get back home."

"Seven inches—that's nothing," Feuerbach mumbled. "One good punch could have done it."

They were staring at each other, but talking to themselves.

Oldfield lifted the window and bellowed out: "Motherfucker! I'm still so psyched. Shot-putting isn't enough to get rid of your energy. There ought to be a fistfight afterward!"

For a moment they were silent. Feuerbach sighed and shook his head. "Poor Woods," he reflected, "he was really suffering out there. And it might have been his last chance."

"Not for us," Oldfield said.

Feuerbach's face brightened as he considered the thought. "I know," he said, sitting up and beginning to smile. "It's just the start, isn't it?"

"Damn right. Komar is even comin' over for indoor season. I'm gonna kick his ass."

Now Feuerbach was standing, his voice once more alive: "Damn, indoor season with Komar, Woods, and you. People up real close, cheering. Oldfield, I'm gonna destroy everybody. *Indoor season!* Man, I can't wait."

Feuerbach tossed his U.S. Olympic uniform into a corner on the floor.

Outdoors

DASH—PROFILE OF A DOG

By H. A. von Behr

From Outdoor Life

It was the first week of the small-game season. Bill, the teen-aged son of a farm neighbor, and I were driving along a secondary road only a few miles from my own place. We stopped the car on the roadside. Bill knew every pheasant swamp and was welcome to hunt on the lands of all the neighbors. He had pointed out a scrubby pasture as a "good spot."

We opened the car door and let out my dog Dash, an eighteen-month-old English setter. He danced around us with all the exuberance of a young hunting dog. Then he dashed out into the pasture toward a low swampy area. Bill and I followed, wondering if the ambitious young hunter would find us a bird.

Dash ranged too far, as most young dogs are bound to do, and my calling him back didn't help, so we followed faster than we liked. Then he stopped suddenly about 300 feet ahead of us—his muzzle forward, his tail straight—and went into a perfect point. Before we caught up to him he broke and moved cautiously forward another 25 feet and pointed again. Shortly before we came up to him, two birds flushed and flew straight away from us—a cock just ahead of a hen pheasant.

It was a long shot but an easy one. I aimed carefully at the cock, trying hard not to hit the hen, and fired. The cock plunged to the ground, and the hen alighted unharmed in a distant cornfield. "You got your bird!" Bill shouted. "I was afraid to shoot at them—too darn close together!"

Within seconds Dash raced to the cock, retrieved, and proudly brought it to my hand. Then my dog sat down to receive my words of praise and a well-deserved pat. It was his first 100 percent performance in the field. Dash had pointed birds before, but he had never completed the job by bringing the bird to me and delivering it into my hands.

It was a great day—Dash's graduation. That fine performance in 1935 was followed by many years of great hunting together. In an entire lifetime a hunter is privileged if he has one great dog. Dash was mine.

I had found him in the barn of a riding academy near Plainfield, New Jersey, where he and his four brothers and sisters were crawling around the warm, soft hayloft. I knew my dog at once. He was the lively male with the big black-and-tan patch over his left eye. I bought him at once.

A few weeks later, when the litter had been fully weaned and the pup could be separated from the bitch, I picked him up together with his pedigree, which listed a longer line of ancestors than the House of Hapsburg can claim. Registered: "F.D. St. Book, Duke of Manhattan, 224922."

I took him with me to the Atelier von Behr, my New York City photographic studio, where he lived out most of his happy canine childhood. Housebreaking presented no real problems, but I climbed the stairs more often than I care to ever again. Dash went through his lively and mischievous "teen-aged" stage in the studio. He chewed up the expensive gloves and hats of fashion models, the belongings of my paying clients, and several pairs of my own slippers.

When he was a year old I felt that I had to do something to bring him up as a hunting dog, which he was from head to tail. I bought for him—and perhaps just a bit for my own use—a 135-acre abandoned farm in the foothills of the Berkshires in Old Chatham, New York. "A good-for-nothing farm" it was called by my neighbors because the fields were poor and the land was hilly and stony. The former owner of the place had finally given up the struggle to maintain it as a respectable dairy farm, but for Dash and me the place became heaven on earth.

Some of the fields were still cultivated by neighboring farmers, but the pastures grew up rapidly in huckleberries, weeds, and bushes. The farm soon became a bird hunter's paradise. There were always pheasants in the swamp on opening day, and elusive partridges and woodcocks in the bushy pines and the hardwood groves along the hillside.

Dash fitted into my way of life graciously. In the city he was as happy as a hunting dog could be in a sophisticated urbane setting. He loved it when people came to the studio, and they always made a big fuss over him. He was beautiful and friendly, and the patch over his eye gave him a certain rakish look. He loved to have his picture taken, and he watched the pretty models and debutantes who came to pose before my camera.

He enjoyed going out to lunch and dinner with me, and he would pull me toward the doors of his favorite restaurants. Luchow's restaurant rated highest with him because the German waiters never forgot to serve him the bones of a Hasenrucken or leftover Sauerbraten under the linen tablecloth. During hot summer weather Dash would pull me into Whalen's drugstore, the only adequately air-conditioned spot on the street at that time.

He often met President Roosevelt's famous dog Fala, a scrappy Scotty, on our walks in Washington Square. Fala would yap and yell when he saw Dash. Dash, in his aristocratic English way, would hardly give the little yapper a second look. With his nose in the air, he would walk away from the insulting little challenger.

The prospect of a weekend in the country helped to make Dash content with his city life. He knew immediately when the time had come for our departure. Just before leaving to get the car for the long trip, I would stuff four or five pipes with tobacco so that while driving I would only have to light them. The moment he saw me stuff more than one pipe, Dash would dance around me in sheer joy. (An even more-enthusiastic performance, accompanied by joyous yaps and barks, always took place at the farmhouse when I put shotgun shells into my coat pocket.)

When we started out for a weekend, Dash leaped into the car and lay there patiently on the seat next to me or stretched out in back, seemingly counting the miles to his Shangri-la. When the car turned off the smooth highway and bounced over the last few miles on dirt roads, he would sit up and look out the side window with intense interest and expectation. When we arrived at our place and the car door was opened, he always leaped out and dashed about in a state of ecstasy—the happiest dog in the whole wide world.

No one ever really teaches a dog to take a scent, follow it, and point. That ability is provided by ancestral genes, but it alone does not make a good hunting dog. The dog must also come to his master upon command. A roaming dog completely out of control is of no use to the hunter. This factor had to be impressed on Dash through strict training.

To teach him that important lesson, I attached a clothesline to his collar. When we headed into the field, I would shout "Heel!" and pull hard on the line. It stopped him and sometimes jerked the wandering setter off his feet. It finally did the trick, but the training took a lot of time and patience. This rough lesson was repeated many times during the summer months, but when Dash's second hunting season started, there was no further need for the clothesline. He responded with unfailing obedience.

My well mannered and properly trained dog made me very popular among local sportsmen, and Dash and I were invited to hunt the choicest pheasant land in the county. A good education pays off! We hunted together over the farmlands of the Berkshire foothills and in the large apple orchards of the Hudson Valley. Dash's performance grew better and better, and we bagged more and more game every season.

After a few hunting seasons, Dash developed his own astonishing strategy. For instance, when a bird ran ahead of us under brushy cover along a stone wall, Dash would run out into the field and make a wide semicircle to the far end of the wall. From there he would cautiously push the bird back along the wall. When the bird was within range of our guns, Dash would flush it on command. That tactic saved me and my companions much tedious tramping along stone walls, and we appreciated it.

There was no doubt that I had a great dog, but I did not always measure up to his talent. I was a fair-to-middling shot. If I missed a bird after all my dog's fine work, he would turn his head and stare at me with sadness in his brown setter eyes. But he forgave me quickly and always started off promptly again in search of another bird.

I wanted very much to take a picture of my pride and joy on point. He was a great ham and seemed to enjoy having his picture taken, but no one can persuade a sporting dog to point unless there is a bird to point at. For a while, we searched in vain whenever my camera was slung over my shoulder.

Finally Dash hit scent, closed in, and pointed in classic fashion.

I unslung the camera, walked around him, and took a good number of pictures. Suddenly two beautiful cock pheasants flew out of the high grass. I swung the camera back over my shoulder, grabbed my double-barreled shotgun, and, in spite of the precious lost time, succeeded in bringing down both birds. It was a rare and wonderful episode.

Dash was also a great house dog. He was friendly with my friends, all of whom held him in affection for his good looks and manners. He was a dependable watchdog and always barked to let me know that a stranger was approaching the premises, but he soon came to recognize all the frequent callers and even greeted the postman and the meter reader in friendly fashion.

Just once, he gave one of my neighbors a rough reception. The man, an elderly farmer, came up to our property along his side of the fence. When the farmer started to climb over the fence Dash went for him, ready to attack, and forced him to retreat. Dash left no doubt about his disapproval of the man's unconventional way of calling on us.

When I took a bride Dash treated her with indifference at first. He barely accepted the mistress of the house, even though she took over the daily task of feeding him. But after some time he began to love her too, even though she did not take him hunting.

His final proof of devotion came on a warm summer day. Dash was hunting woodchucks by himself in a hayfield and drove one of them to cover in a stone wall. His insistent barking finally prompted me to help him. I brought along a crowbar so that I could loosen the heavy boulders in the wall and force the woodchuck out of his hiding place.

A few moments after the woodchuck ran into the field, Dash grabbed him by the neck, shook him, and carried his prey away. He ignored my calls and ran through the house from the back door to the front lawn, where my wife was relaxing in a comfortable chair. Dash placed the dead chuck at her feet in a gesture that meant, "You are my mistress, and I want you to know I love you." My bride was touched by this act of devotion and gratitude.

After our son was born about a year later, Dash soon accepted full responsibility for the protection of the baby. He went on duty near the baby's crib. When baby-sitters came to the house he watched them closely as they attended to the child, but members of the family were permitted to attend the baby without his surveillance. Later he took some poking and ear pulling from the growing infant, but he never growled. When he had taken as much as he could bear he simply walked away.

Dash preferred to travel to the farm by car, but he made the best of it when we had to go by train. The baggage master and the conductors all knew him and always made a big fuss over him. I can still see him sleeping patiently on the dusty wooden floor of the baggage car beside a shipment of baby chicks, a box full of rattlesnakes, or a crated coffin. Traveling in the baggage car did not bother him much. It meant that we were heading for his beloved farm in the Berkshire hills.

Dash loved to swim, which was very evident when I took him with me to visit the well-known writer and historian, Hendrik Willem van Loon at his house in Old Greenwich, Connecticut. We took Dash for a stroll along Long Island Sound. After running up and down the beach, Dash jumped into the water and started swimming. He seemed to be heading for England. I called him back, but he was beyond the sound of my voice. Soon van Loon and I could see only a small dot in the distance. Finally Dash did turn back, and when he reached the shore he was completely exhausted. Dash would probably have been a great waterfowl retriever, but I never took him duck hunting.

At van Loon's house he made friends with the author's dachshund Noodle who was made famous by the book of the same name, illustrated by Ludwig Bemelmans.

During Dash's later years pheasants in our area became scarce because many farms ceased to operate and less corn and buckwheat were grown. So my setter and I turned more and more to hunting partridge (ruffed grouse) in the woods. By that time Dash was older and less eager, so he ranged much closer. He stayed within 100 feet of me most of the time, but we often lost sight of one another in dense underbrush and young pines. Quite often I could not see him when he was closing in on a bird. He was aware of the difficulty, so he would clue me in by producing a strange throaty sound—something like *hach, hach*—to which I replied by smacking my tongue just loud enough to tell him that I was heading his way. When I was close enough and shouted, "Flush!" he would leap forward and put up the bird or birds.

I often missed the cunning, elusive grouse among the thick pine branches, but sometimes I knocked one down. We were a perfectly matched team during many years of difficult hunting.

Dash always pointed in the classic manner with his muzzle up, never low to the ground. He held his point perfectly, frozen like a statue, until I caught up with him and gave the command, "Flush!" Then he lunged forward, and up went the bird.

I did not believe in flushing birds myself. Our hunting grounds were very rough, and I preferred not to have to stumble through brush or swamp at the critical moment. Instead I got my gun and myself ready for the shot. I also felt that letting Dash leap forward on command was a great joy to him—the climax of his work. Perhaps this way of hunting with a pointing dog is rather unorthodox, but I never wanted Dash to compete in field trials.

We hunted together until Dash was fifteen years old. At sixteen he was almost completely deaf and blind, and he was unsteady on his legs. He left me to join his ancestors in the summer of 1950.

Dash had been bred three times to carefully selected, registered bitches, resulting in three large and healthy litters. So he will live on in future generations of setters. Dash was the greatest dog I have ever known.

General

ON THE MOUNTAINOUS APPALACHIAN TRAIL

By George Solomon

From The Washington Post

They began milling outside the Boonsboro gymnasium at 5:30 A.M. Runners, joggers, hikers and hangers-on. By 6:30 there were 1,724 waiting—all sizes and shapes—in sweat suits, jeans, army fatigues, track suits, hiking boots, gym shoes, and penny loafers.

The 11th annual John F. Kennedy 50-mile Hike-Run also attracted one jog-tested dog. On a damp, foggy morning the runners had come to the small Washington County, Maryland, town to overcome the elements, their own limitations, and most of all, a treacherous 50.2-mile course along the mountainous Appalachian Trail and over the Chesapeake and Ohio towpath.

The only requirement was that contestants be at least 10 years old.

From Washington, Baltimore, Frederick, Annapolis, West Point, Manhattan, North Carolina, Indiana, Kentucky, Richmond, the Pentagon, the Capitol, and elsewhere, they'd come to give it their best.

The goal: A white finish line at St. James School. The restriction: To win a trophy, one had to cover the course within 15 hours, by 10 P.M. This was no stroll through the park.

At 7 A.M. Buzz Sawyer, president of the Cumberland Valley Athletic Club, who says he is no sadist, started what could be the world's biggest foot race. Like swarming ants, the runners headed for the first check point at Crampton's Gap, 9.7 miles away. Behind the runners came the joggers. Behind the joggers came the hikers. Behind the hikers came the support troops—wives, husbands, children, dogs, spectators, and cars filled with bandages, extra shoes, jockade, corned beef sandwiches, pickles, and more jockade.

"Are we late?" asked Bedford Chapin of New York City. Chapin had driven down in the morning with a friend, Albert Hilderbrand.

"You're late by 15 minutes," a race official replied. "But go ahead and catch up."

"Fine," Hilderbrand said. "If you start last, you can only improve your position."

The runners appeared at Crampton's Gap, bolting through the fog and mist into a clearing as about 100 people applauded. "Where did all the people come from?" a bewildered contestant asked, running past picnic tables and a woman offering drinks for all.

"What's your number?" a checker asked a tall red-headed runner with a long stride. "No number," he said. "I'm just runnin'."

"Where am I?" another runner wondered as a collegian from Elon, in a daze, began embracing and kissing his girl friend. Two men in "FBI" T-shirts raced past, oblivious to the morning chill.

One woman spectator was beside herself. "I lost my car keys," she said. "After my husband jogs 50 miles, I've got to tell him we've got to walk home to Washington because I've lost my car keys. I'd better find those keys." She did.

The steep rocky hills of the Appalachian Trail were beginning to take their toll, with the dense fog. "People are getting lost," shouted a runner whipping down Weverton Cliffs, which is close to the towpath, 1.8 miles beyond Crampton Gap and nearly three miles from Harpers Ferry.

Christopher Anthony Klein of the Washington Sports Club stumbled over a rock, spraining his ankle and twisting a knee. "We got a guy hurt up here," said a voice on the walkie-talkie.

They brought Klein down the hill and dropped him into a red blanket. "Oh, crap," howled Klein. "I was ahead, but I never saw the rocks. The rocks were hidden under the leaves. Aaaah, I'm hurting. Oh, am I hurting."

The course was beginning to win.

On a hill near Weverton Cliffs, William Eugene Wright of the U.S. Naval Academy was looking for the pickup bus. He had dropped out. "My knees and ankles are killing me," Wright said. At Sandy Hook Bridge, Jon Acton, a Baltimore law student, was in agony. "I've only been walking a month," he said. "I didn't think it would be this hard. These are my brother's shoes and they don't fit too well. I walked 15.9 miles in four hours. That's okay. But now I can't find my wife and I'm dying of thirst."

In the rain and mud, they came trudging off the towpath at Antietam Aqueduct, 27.3 miles from where they all began at Boonsboro Junior High School eight hours before. They looked like they had been walking for three weeks.

"I'm finished physically, mentally, and morally," said exhausted Richard Chopin, a student at the University of Maryland. "I told all my friends I could do the course in six hours. Well, the course did me. When I sat down for lunch, everything cramped up. About six miles back, I asked where the hell was Antietam Aqueduct. No matter how far you walk, you always get the same answer: two miles. Now I can't find my brother. Have you seen my brother?"

"A hell of a workout," said Mike Kramer of Bethesda. "The first 15 miles were the toughest."

The white markers pointed toward a road of about 1,000 yards to the entrance of St. James School. And lastly, 200 agonizing yards to the finish line. Perhaps the longest 200 yards in the world.

Max White, a twenty-two-year-old Virginia law student, was not breathing hard as he ran the final 200 yards to win easily. His time was 5:55.30, bettering the previous record by nearly 20 minutes. The runner-up, Rick Warren, was timed in 6:12.20.

"The longer the race, the better I run," White said. "I would have done better, except I got lost for 10 minutes at the bottom of a cliff."

The rain was falling hard in the darkness. But still they came, their eyes glazed, their legs shaking, their lips trembling. They would not stop.

Five minutes before the deadline, No. 599, Howell Griswold, a fifty-one-year-old schoolteacher, heaved his body across the white line. Jim Ryun had never experienced a happier moment as did Howell Griswold. There were 675 finishers. The dog did not make it.

And finally there was fifty-year-old John McCollum, who came huffing down the path three minutes too late. There was no trophy waiting for McCollum, who howled into the night, "I made it!"

"Nobody has to give me a trophy, or tell me anything. I know I made it," McCollum said. "I would have been faster, but my shoes were too thin, and I couldn't find my wife to get another pair. It was fun, but no man is going to tell me it was easy."

A victory lap was not necessary.

MYTHS AND MISSES

By Furman Bisher

From the Atlanta Journal

Reprinted by permission

Sport is the grand curator of the myth. I mean if it did not happen with the precise dramatic wow you would have it happen, dress it up your own way, spread it around and never change your story. In time it'll become a part of what the revered Apple Pie Society calls the Great American Legend.

A few weeks ago, the Pepsi-Cola Company, dues-paying member of the Apple Pie Society, polled writers and broadcasters of this great nation of ours on the most important sport story of the century. I felt reasonably secure in the feeling that Ellicott Drawbridge Hemingway, the distinguished lexicographer who coined the phrase "Records are made to be broken," would win it in a swoosh.

You are going to be startled to learn that he didn't. Stunned, yet, to learn that Jesse Owens' Olympic Games performance of 1936, "& Treatment," as it says on the final tabulation, did.

"& Treatment" refers to the attitude of Adolf Hitler, who is charged by the legend with having put the big snub on the American Negro. Though Jesse Owens himself repeatedly said it never happened, the fiction has persisted through the years like "Little Red Riding Hood," because it is the way we would have had it.

It hasn't been more than a month ago that I read an article in which Owens resigned himself to his eternal position in sport mythology. "I am tired of trying to set the story straight," he said. "I give up. I just decided to rock along with it. It was easier than denying it."

Another of the great moments in American sport was Bobby Thomson's home run that won the 1951 pennant for the Giants in a play-off against Brooklyn. But even the Pepsi-Cola election authority falls victim to the fictional urge. As the years passed, Thomson's home run has been transferred by errant memory to the World Series, and on Pepsi's election return it comes out "Bobby Thomson's '51 Series Home Run."

Some of the most durable sporting legends are those that never happened, or those that happened one way and have been revised to meet our urgent need of titillation. Athletes who were pretty certain what actually did happen have read what didn't happen so often that they've become willing characters in the revised version.

For instance, Babe Ruth came to believe in time that he actually had pointed to the location in Wrigley Field where he planned to hit his next home run. And why it should have become such a critical matter in the shaping of a new and a free democracy, escapes me.

What really DID happen was, Babe had just bought a new sports car and was taking lessons in the driver's code. The signal he gave was the accredited sports car driver's gig after he has just cut off an old lady at a traffic light. Except that in Babe we find a typical apprentice error. He was using the wrong finger. Dummox!

There are others that have been fictionalized to meet the American standard of acceptance, such as:

"Say it ain't so, Joe."—Supposedly said by an urchin outside a Chicago courtroom when Shoeless Joe Jackson emerged from a hearing on the "Black Sox Scandal." In reality, it was a barefoot midget who, upon seeing shoes on the feet of "Shoeless Joe," was crushed at the dissolution of another fairy tale, whereupon he said, "Say it ain't shoe, Joe."

"Am on my way. Nothing can stop us."—This was a telegram supposedly sent by Blondy Ryan, an obscure infielder who had recovered from illness and was on his way to join the Giants, and which was credited with being the spark that won the 1937 pennant. Actually, Ryan sent two wires that day, one to his intended with whom he planned elopement, and one to the Giants, which said, "Send money, or forget it." Unfortunately, he got his wires crossed. The wedding never took place, but it was a nice pennant.

"They can't touch my boys with a 10-foot pole."—Adolph Rupp is said to have snarled this after members of one of his Kentucky basketball teams had been accused of consorting with gamblers. Actually, he was talking about a coming game with Notre Dame, which had a very tall center named Vladislaw Jabbarski. Reporters were doubting that Rupp's team could handle the Irish, eh, uh, Pole. It was a simple case of a typo. What Rupp said was, "They can't touch my boys with a TEN-foot Pole."

Hooks Awtrey, the well-dressed receiver.—This is a story about a supposed Georgia player who, dressed in street clothes and secreted along the sideline, dashed on the field and caught a pass that beat Auburn in ancient days. Actually, stadium facilities being primitive, there was only one johnny on the premises. Awtrey was a hard-pressed spectator who, seeing a lull in action, decided to take a short-cut across the field. Much to his surprise, just as he reached mid-field he saw a pass headed his way, so he obligingly caught it, raced for the goal line, slammed the ball down, and continued on his course. It was also historic in that this was the beginning of ball-slammingdown after touchdowns. (P.S. He made it.)

"Win one for the Gipper."—Rockne is supposed to have said it to inspire Notre Dame football team while the great Gipp lay dying. A gross exaggeration. This phrase drifted out from behind a hotel room door where Gipp was engaged in a craps appointment. This was his call to the dice.

The Dempsey-Tunney "long count."—It really wasn't a long count at all. It merely shows the effect a foreign influence was having on the fight game at the time. The referee was Yugoslavian and he was counting in his native tongue, plus the fact that someone told him he had a telephone call when he hit "eight." It was his wife with the grocery list, which also had to be taken down in Yugoslavian.

"Lew Burdette throws the spitter."—Said by Birdie Tebbetts when he managed Cincinnati and Burdette pitched for Milwaukee. Later, after Tebbetts transferred to the Braves, he made a clean breast of it all after having the situation thoroughly investigated. "What I find," he reported, "is that Mr. Burdette has a severe case of hives and he has to scratch a lot."

YEAH, BUT WHAT WAS THE SCORE?

By Melvin Durslag

From TV Guide

In pursuit of his occupation as sports commentator for WTAE-TV in Pittsburgh, Myron Cope attended a press conference conducted last fall by the general manager of the Philadelphia 76ers.

Since the Salvation Army headquarters was the location selected for the meeting, it occurred to Cope that a greeting appropriate for the occasion was in order.

Enlisting the Salvation Army band and requesting "Rock of Ages," he brought the Philadelphia official on camera.

"Dear friends," began Myron, "we are gathered here today to pray for the salvation of the Philadelphia 76ers. Ofttimes in recent weeks they have, in spite of good intentions, committed sins against the sport of basketball. They played 17 games and blew 16. Yea, verily, they are a sorry aggregation. . . ."

The scene tended to prove two things: (a) that television has heart, and (b) that its approach to local sports coverage is in the process of change.

Whereas local sportscasts at one time pretty much followed the same pattern—the scores, the national roundup, the filmed interview with the manager of the local Buffaloes—they have taken off today in diverse directions.

The attitudes they assume usually vary with the size of the city and the editorial flexibility of the station manager. Smaller communities are still partial to the straight sportscast, except in those cases where a word of comfort can be offered to the home team.

But in the larger cities and even in some of middle size, viewers are looking at innovations leaning toward irreverence, editorializing, and features that are sophisticated, if not far out.

None of the foregoing is necessarily new to sports journalism. But all are reasonably new to sports on local television, which is breaking out of its old, rigid mold.

Some stations even have brought in women to report on the world of muscle. At KDKA-TV, Pittsburgh, a fresh-looking doll named Lee Arthur, who, for a year and a half on Broadway, played Rivka in *Fiddler on the Roof,* does evening sports news. She doesn't do it with an abundance of knowledge, but then Dandy Don Meredith might play a lousy Rivka.

At KOOL-TV in Phoenix, Arizona, the management has given the sports job to a black lady, Evelyn Thompson, a graduate of Boston University who makes the irrefutable point that "Not too many sportscasters get compliments on their hair."

Describing her show as modestly successful, Miss Thompson explains, "Since I am new to sports, I don't use the cliches the viewers have been hearing for years. I think people are tired of listening to sports hacks."

Jim Bouton, WABC, New York, tends to agree. He insists that the fan wants to be entertained.

"I focus a lot on offbeat stories," says the former big-league pitcher, who once focused on players' bedroom habits in his book, *Ball Four.* "I take the position that people get their fill of hard news on the networks' live coverage."

In search of the off-trail story, Bouton has wandered into the streets of Manhattan to do a segment on stickball. He has allowed himself to be knocked down by girls in the Roller Derby and has roped a calf at the rodeo.

"When I do major sports," reports Bouton, "I favor interviews with those who aren't stars. For instance, I talked one night to Doug Rader, the Houston third baseman. I asked him if he always wanted to be a ball player. He said no. It had been his ambition to be a groundskeeper. Asked why, he answered, 'Because I've always had this affinity for rocks and dirt.' "

A favorite target of Bouton is baseball commissioner Bowie Kuhn.

"He makes so many blunders," say Jim, "that he isn't even fair game anymore. You can always look to him for the obvious. When the Yankee pitchers had their wife swap, I predicted that Kuhn would tell them not to do it again. I was close. He announced that the act was deplorable."

Of course, when Bouton—or other sports reporters—knocks the commissioner on TV, the baseball owners are far more sensitive than they would be reading the same words in their local papers. But sensitivity among owners, coaches, and fans isn't deterring the new order of TV sportscaster, who is suddenly discovering his muscles.

At KING-TV, Seattle, local boat-rocker Ray McMackin attacks the sports establishment periodically. During a siege of foot-dragging on a stadium project, Ray called the community "Bush City by the Sea."

Of course, Seattle reposes on Puget Sound, but minor details don't dampen the spirit of McMackin, who may lack navigational excellence but not firepower. He once advocated the dropping of the national anthem at sports events on the ground it isn't played at theaters or concert halls.

Ray is also a critic of Jim Owens, football coach for 16 years at University of Washington and a local fixture. "The school considers me an outlaw and a cheapshot artist," McMackin explains, "but I maintain it is my job to express opinions, not suppress them. I don't accept Owens' words as gospel."

In western Pennsylvania, his residence since birth, Arnold Palmer is godlike, a fact that fails to impress Pittsburgh's Myron Cope. When Palmer was voted "Athlete of the Decade" in an Associated Press poll, Cope went on the air and guffawed, contending that there is no way any golfer can be called an athlete.

"Socially, my position wasn't enhanced," recalls Myron. "Then one day at Laurel Valley Golf Club, I was teeing up when who should appear but Palmer himself."

Arnold studied Cope, who normally shoots 110, and began a commentary of his own: "I'm anxious to see what a real athlete looks like. Slacks don't fit . . . golf shirt faded . . . grip like a kangaroo with boxing gloves."

In the face of this heat, Myron proved he was a money player. He hit the longest drive of his life—175 yards, of which the first 25 were straight.

But for critical reporting on television, a medal of sorts goes to Eddie Andelman of WNAC-TV in Boston. He blasted his own colleague on the show, sports director Bob Gamere. Dismissing Gamere as a mere decoration, the portly Andelman said: "He's too pretty. No pimples . . . not a blemish."

Still, there are many TV sportscasters who oppose the practice of steady knocking and of developing freaky features.

"I tend to be conservative on the air," says Frank Gifford of WABC, New York, "because fans are interested more in the news than they are in the commentator. The clowns attract attention for a while, but the viewers get sick of them. When it comes to opinionating, I have changed since I started doing local sports in 1962. In the beginning, I didn't feel mature enough on the air to venture opinions. I give them today, but very sparingly. I try to be absolutely sure of my grounds before wading into someone, because the impact of opinions on television is greater than in the newspaper. By that I mean that irresponsible comment on TV can stir more hell."

Last year Gifford devoted a whole sportscast to the demotion of John Unitas of Baltimore. John was benched by the coach, who was ordered by the general manager to use Marty Domres.

"I felt I had license to take a stand here," says Gifford. "It was a situation I understood. I never offer comment otherwise."

At KNBC, Los Angeles, Ross Porter favors the conservative approach too. Porter usually proffers brief observations related to news in preference to strong editorials.

"The trend today is toward opinion," he says, "and I offer more than I used to. But too many people on the air are on an ego trip. They give the impression that the news is secondary to their slanted speeches and their sparkling personalities."

The idea of projecting oneself into the news is defended by Stu Nahan, KABC-TV, Los Angeles, who feels that audiences enjoy seeing a sportscaster in fresh poses.

When Nahan, for instance, did a filmed interview with quarterback Roman Gabriel, he opened playing catch with him. For a feature on the Los Angeles Lakers, he came on tossing free throws. Putting on a Dodger uniform before a game one night, he played pepper with the pros. "Whenever possible," says Nahan, "I believe in doing stories from the scene, not the studio."

Sportscasters on nightly news shows who also do play-by-play for local teams have a special editorial problem. They must walk the ledge of discretion in their news, careful not to offend the team owners. Club owners don't object to criticism, as long as it's directed at someone else.

Nahan has been a play-by-play man over the years in baseball, hockey, and football. Once, while an announcer for the San Diego Chargers, he offered this harsh summary of the team on his sports report: "The Chargers stunk out the place."

Nahan received no comment from the club management, but he admits readily that news commentators must proceed with caution if they want to safeguard their jobs with the teams.

In some areas, sportscasters fall in love with the home teams. At WMC-TV, Memphis, Jack Eaton becomes so enraptured over the Memphis State Tigers that he occasionally appears in a tiger suit, complete with tail. He makes no pretense of being objective.

"I love Memphis State," he says. "I can't say anything bad about it."

Happily, or regretfully, depending upon your viewpoint, Memphians consider him their top sportscaster.

Professional athletes who still play while doing sports news on the side also face an objectivity problem.

For instance, Len Dawson, quarterback for the Kansas City Chiefs, is sports director of KMBC, Kansas City, Missouri. When the Chiefs become involved in sticky stories, particularly of an internal nature, the viewer isn't hopeful of learning the raw details on Dawson's sportscasts.

"Dawson can't become completely objective until he leaves football," says Johnny Morris, former player for the Chicago Bears, who now does sports for WMAQ-TV, Chicago. "I went through the same deal. While I was playing, my news about football, especially the Bears, was very straight. I wouldn't touch a controversial issue. Today, it's a different story."

On several occasions, Morris, whose wife, Jeannie, does sports features on the same channel, has taken on the sacred Bears. He has knocked the ownership for not keeping up with the times and he has criticized the coaching.

"When I attacked the club for trading Mike Ditka to Philadelphia," recalls Morris, "I got a telephone call from George Halas, who was at a loss to understand my attitude. He still saw me as the player, drilled to talk guardedly to reporters. He couldn't believe I had joined them. It was that day that I realized what journalism was all about."

Nor is Mrs. Morris a wilting flower on the air. She has blistered the Chicago Black Hawks for raising prices. She has blasted several pro football teams and accused school authorities of discrimination against women in non-contact sports.

On August 1, the Morrises are taking a year's leave of absence from WMAQ to tour Europe. If viewers miss them, it is safe to assume promoters won't.

A DAY IN THE PRESS BOX

By D. L. Stewart

From The Dayton Journal Herald

"You know," the guy sitting next to me in the press box said, "it really baffles me. I can't understand what all these people are doing here."

The guy had a good point. It was a typical autumn day in Pittsburgh: cold, wet, and ugly. The game was being shown on television. It really made no sense that 45,761 persons should sit in Three Rivers Stadium risking pneumonia to watch the Steelers play the Bengals.

Yep. The guy had a good point. What made the point sort of funny, though, was that the guy was Mike Reid.

Reid, the Bengals' all-pro defensive tackle, wasn't able to play against the Steelers. He thought on Friday that he could play. His injured back felt fine then. But Friday evening he was getting out of his car when something gave out in his back. The next thing he knew, he was lying on the ground, unable to get up.

For almost half an hour he lay there, laughing at his predicament in spite of the pain. Laughing at the notions he had entertained just a few minutes earlier of playing a violent game of football.

Sunday, Mike Reid was scratched from the Bengals' lineup. He wanted to watch the game from the sidelines, but the team doctor wanted him to be someplace where it was warm. Someplace where there was a constant flow of hot air to loosen the muscles in his back. The press box was selected.

And so, on Sunday, I found myself sitting next to Mike Reid, awaiting the showdown between the Bengals and Steelers. What an opportunity. What better way to watch a football game than with an all-pro at your elbow? It was like going to a concert and sitting next to Van Cliburn.

I couldn't wait to hear Reid's expert commentary, his piercing insights. I was tired of sitting in the company of dullards who could only say things like, "Boy, that fumble hurt."

Second down, early in the game. Boobie Clark sweeps the right side, gains four yards and fumbles. The call is close. It seems like a slow whistle to me. I look at Reid, waiting expectantly for his opinion.

"Boy, that fumble hurt," he says.

Play progresses. Reid is silent. It's obvious he doesn't want to be a show-off and dazzle me with more technical talk than I could possibly hope to understand. But I decide to encourage him. Ken Anderson completes a 53-yard pass to Bob Trumpy.

"Say," I say, "isn't that the same play you guys used for a touchdown against Detroit?"

"Don't ask me," Reid shrugs. "I don't know anything about the offense."

Deflated, but not discouraged, I keep my ears open for any meaningful comments as the game continues.

Essex Johnson juggles a pass, catches it, then fumbles at Cincinnati's 13. Another close call by the officials. It might have been an incomplete pass.

I look at Reid.

"Do you know where the word *ukulele* comes from?" he asks.

"No," I confess, trying to make the connection between *ukulele* and what just happened on the field.

"It comes from the Hawaiian word *uku*, which means flea, and *lele,* which means leaping."

"So?" I demand. "What's that got to do with Essex fumbling?"

"Nothing. That's just something I learned in my Funk and Wagnalls."

I thank him for his insight and resume watching the game.

Terry Bradshaw throws a pass that skips off the hands of Franco Harris. Tommy Casanova intercepts and runs five yards, then flips to Ken Riley. The Pittsburgh writers are screaming that it was a forward lateral.

"That's not right," Reid declares. "It couldn't have been a forward lateral, because there is no such thing. That's a contradiction in terms, if you stop and think about it."

Unable to cope with this logic, I turn to the dullard behind me and comment, "Boy, that interception hurt."

Later in the second quarter, Bradshaw is injured trying to run the ball. As he comes off the field, Reid shouts out: "See there, Terry? God is punishing you for those things you wrote about me in your book." (Later, Reid asks for the quarterback's address so he can send him a get-well note.)

Then it's the final minute of the first half.

"The crowd is sure ubiquitous," Reid observes.

"Ubiquitous?" a nearby writer repeats, obviously overwhelmed by the word. Reid chortles softly at the writer's ignorance. I join him in his laugh and make a mental note to look up "ubiquitous" when I get back to the office.

I also make a mental note not to sit next to Van Cliburn at any concerts.

THE DAY OF THE JACKALS

By Stan Hochman

From the Philadelphia Daily News

There were gray blotches around Sparky Anderson's eyes. His hands trembled. His voice trembled too. The words came squeezing out sideways, like there was something raw stuck in his throat.

"Unbelievable," he said raspily. "It doesn't make me angry . . . it makes me ashamed I'm in this country . . . and I'm not too sure New York is in this country."

Anderson is middle America, honest, hard-working, plain. The tide of violence in the big cities shocks him, baffles him, sickens him. He sees the ballpark as a kind of sanctuary where hard work and hustle and determination and clean living are rewarded.

Yesterday, the Mets beat the Reds, 7–2, to win the National League championship. That was bad enough. Anderson could have handled that. The best team doesn't always win. Tom Seaver pitched good for the Mets and the Reds played lousy in a four-run fifth inning and that was that.

But they had to stop the game in the ninth to rescue some women (wives of Reds' players and team officials) from the third base box seats. And they had to stop it again when the jackals down the first-base side crumpled the splintery wooden barriers. The Philistines were spitting all over Anderson's sanctuary.

And then they finally finished the game and the players had to race through the jackals who had come snarling out of the stands to ravage the field. The jackals tore big chunks out of the turf and they snatched bare-clawed at home plate and vandalized anything that could be ripped off or uprooted.

"Can you imagine, in the United States of America, going through something like this?" Anderson asked afterward. "It just shows you what's happening in this country.

"The police were there, but they ignored it. The Mets are wasting their money, hiring those people. If they opened one head wide open, that would settle 'em down. Let the blood flow from that one head. That would do it.

"That's the trouble in America, everyone allowing people to run all over 'em. I asked one cop what was going on. He said, 'What can I do?' I told him, 'What have you got a badge for?' I said, 'Give me that club and I'll show you what to do.' "

There are better solutions than bashing skulls. The jackals don't pay $5 or $7.50 for those downstairs seats. They come snarling down from upstairs in the late innings. If the ushers weren't so lazy, if the cops weren't so overmatched, if the Mets weren't such a bush outfit, the jackals could be kept out of the box-seat area.

"Would they jump out of the second tier?" Pete Rose asked afterward. "Ehhh, maybe they would. Animals. Out of the zoo and into the ballpark."

Rose is the incredible left-fielder for the Reds. In the zoo that was Shea Stadium for three days, Rose was Caruso, he was Nureyev, he was Michelangelo. He was all the wonderful things baseball can be, but seldom is.

He had two hits yesterday. And in the sixth, with his team trailing 6–2, he flung himself onto the dirt warning track trying for an impossible catch on Tom Seaver's double. When he got up, a jackal doused him with beer from the second deck.

"I was mad because Seaver got the double," he recalled. "The beer? Ah, it was making me dizzy the last three innings, from the smell of it on my uniform."

It was gallows humor. Rose walked in the ninth, when the Reds loaded the bases, after the jackals had delayed the game. But Tug McGraw came on and got Joe Morgan to pop up. Then he got Dan Dreissen to bounce to first baseman John Milner. Milner flipped to McGraw, covering first, and Rose scurried for the dugout, a frightened deer fleeing through the jackals.

"I wasn't thinking about my life," he said in that spluttery small-boy way of his. "I was hoping Joe would single and I'd get to third. If Joe got a hit, then Tony (Perez) would come to bat and maybe he'd hit one out and we'd pull it out.

"The thing is, on that last out, I never ran all the way to second.

I saw Milner catch the ball and I ran for the dugout. Suppose McGraw had dropped the throw? They'd have had to come get me in the clubhouse.

"Some weird situations in this series, huh? They talked to me about moving from left to center so the fans couldn't get at me. And then, I can't run hard to second because I'm worried about what the fans might do.

"The thing is, I wanted to win this game so bad, I wanted to beat everybody . . . the Mets and their damn 55,000 fans. The way those people act, they don't deserve to have a champion."

The Reds had gotten out alive. None of the jackals were bold enough to try and interrupt Rose's dash to safety. The players were dazed afterward, numb from defeat, groggy from the wretched scene.

"Johnny Bench was really concerned about Pete," Anderson confessed. "He came up to me in the ninth and asked me if I'd thought about using a pinch runner. I thought if Morgan got a hit, and Perez hit one out, we'd be back in the ball game.

"But John's concern, that's the sort of thing . . . if you're with this club . . . you have to feel good about. There's just a lot of other things that mean more than just winning."

Anderson can console himself with that memory. But the howl of the jackals, whooping and pillaging in that eerie cloud of infield dust, will haunt his thoughts for a while. And the clumsy fifth inning, with the botched plays, will tear at his ulcerated stomach all winter.

On this day, when his dreams for America were dented, it had to be painful for his team to play awkwardly with the stakes so high.

"I don't think," Anderson whispered huskily, "anything can hurt any more than losing . . . not matter how you lose."

FTC: TRUTH OR CONSEQUENCES

By Paul Kaplan

From the Washington Star-News

Two baseball seasons ago, St. Louis Cardinals outfielder Lou Brock did a candy commercial for TV that was easily forgotten by the viewers but will always be remembered by the people in the TV and advertising businesses.

In the ad, Brock roared around the bases and then said with a straight face that he credited his speed to a steady diet of the candy chews.

The ad was hard to swallow. Anyone who has ever been young knows that candy can give you flab, cavities, and acne, but will not make you a major-league base-stealing champion. An investigation was begun by the Federal Trade Commission.

One year ago, in a landmark decision, the government said that Brock can not credit his speed to candy when he and everyone else knows that the credit belongs to exercise, hard work, and the parents who bore him a pair of very firm legs. But for the first time a jock huckster was told to get off the air if he wasn't going to tell the truth.

The FTC pressed on with its investigation and only recently nailed the No. 1 jock culture, the National Football League. The FTC obtained a restraining order against Domino sugar commercials, which billed the product as the "official" NFL and Major League baseball sugar.

"Refined Sugar is refined sugar—one is not better or worse then the next," said Gerald Thain, assistant director of the FTC's national advertising bureau and one of the leaders of the investigation.

"For a company to assert that its sugar is on NFL tables because it is superior is just improper, misleading, and deceptive."

The FTC concluded that it was "monetary considerations" rather than superiority of the product that led the two sports to embrace the Domino theory.

Now Amstar Corp., the manufacturer of Domino sugar, must go through the embarrassing process of using the following corrective clause for one-fourth of its advertising over a one-year period:

"Do you recall some of our past messages saying that Domino sugar gives you strength, energy, and stamina? Actually, Domino is not a special or unique source of strength, energy, and stamina. No sugar is, because what you need is a balanced diet and plenty of rest and exercise."

Partly as a result of the misleading jock ads, the FTC recently came out with a set of proposed guidelines on endorsements and testimonials in advertising. If the guidelines are approved they will become regulations and will go after three broad types of misleading ads:

The testimonial ("I use Flippo car wax because it makes me a better brain surgeon.")—The new guideline would require that the testimonial not only be true, but that there be a cause/effect relationship. In sports, this is the Lou Brock case.

The personal taste testimonial ("I eat Botulism Tuna because I like it best.")—There must appear to be at least some truth in the statement.

In Miami, Dolphins Nick Buoniconti, Dick Anderson, and Larry Csonka did some local advertising for a furniture company. In the middle of the ad campaign it came to the attention of a Florida state attorney that the three football stars were hardly familiar with the merchandise, let alone devoted users of the stuff, as they professed to be. The advertisements were ordered off the air.

The group or team endorsement ("Bailout Airlines pilots drink Reddog Scotch because it keeps them higher longer.")—The new guidelines would require a more stringent standard of truthfulness for endorsements by organizations than by individuals. Detailed information would be required to substantiate the claims. This is the Domino case.

One of the main targets of the FTC is what it refers to as "the man in the white coat." He is a professional actor who puts on a white coat resembling those worn by doctors to endorse one aspirin over another.

People believe "doctors" just like they believe athletes. Both are celebrated members of the community.

"If someone is going to buy a rocking chair because a football player recommends it, he's beyond our help," said FTC attorney Tom Grady.

Grady drew up the guidelines and now he is making final preparations for a move over to the Justice Department. He is concerned that all the investigative work he has done will be lost when he changes jobs in a couple of weeks.

"In government you never know what will happen with a project that's sitting around," he said. "It might wend its way slowly through the bureaucracy or it might not even be assigned to another person. You never know."

Thain, Grady's boss, said the project would not die.

"It will be passed on to someone else," he said. "I'd be surprised if the commission didn't move on this. I think it feels committed to the public on this matter."

But the advertisers and the athletes obviously do not. That is where the FTC comes in.

"It would be nice to see products sold on their merits," Thain said. "I mean Joe Namath could easily show how one popcorn popper offers more than the next one . . . if it really does, that is."

THE SONG AND THE FUSS

By Ray Fitzgerald

From the Boston Globe

Well, I see some college athletes have insulted America again by ignoring the national anthem.

Last year, the outrages occurred before some basketball games and the customers were incensed, because if an athlete is not respectful toward a scratchy recording of "The Star-Spangled Banner," he is probably also making Molotov cocktails in his cellar and not paying attention in class.

Patriotism begins in the gymnasium and don't you forget it.

The latest indecency was Saturday night. Four Eastern Michigan trackmen reportedly slumped on the floor during the playing of the anthem in the Knights of Columbus meet on Long Island.

Luckily the culprits were not lined up and shot on the spot for this flagrant breach of patriotism, but the relay team was disqualified. Timers and judges threatened to leave if the team was allowed to compete.

There were shouts of "Get those commies out of here," which certainly goes to the heart of the matter. If you let kids play footsie with fundamentals, the next thing you know they'll be yelling "Stop the bombing," and where will we be then?

It has possibly occurred to some that the reason a few college athletes no longer stand like ramrods when the anthem is played is that they are no longer thrilled with what the words stand for.

"The rockets red glare, the bombs bursting in air" was okay for Ft. McHenry, but associating those words with the flag today might possibly be embarrassing to some.

But, there is enough divisiveness among us without widening the gap further over such a silly disagreement, especially when there is a perfect solution.

The way to resolve the troubles that result when noncomformists would rather do pushups than stand at attention is to simply dispense with the playing of the anthem. No song, no disrespect.

Where is it written, after all, that "The Star-Spangled Banner" is a must before sports events? Amos Alonzo Stagg got along nicely without it. Richard Nixon never sang it during his years as a sub on the Whittier College football team, and who has ever questioned his patriotism? Never mind, don't answer that.

The anthem wasn't played at a high school game I went to last week and nobody seemed to miss it.

At college and pro events, however, "Oh, say can you see" blares forth as though it were a tradition set forth by our founding father.

The fact is, it wasn't played with regularity at sporting events until World War II, a parlous time that was very big for Uncle Sam posters, war bonds, Praise the Lord and Pass the Ammunition, and other war-inspired patriotism.

The war finally ended, but the playing of the anthem did not. Promotors discovered it was a way of getting the growd together, of building the show to a proper pre-game pitch.

The anthem is a perfect gimmick, as anyone who has been in a jam-packed gym or a stadium filled wtih 60,000 sports fanatics can testify.

". . . home of the brave" has barely died away when the shouts of "Kill 'em Big Red," or whatever, permeate the air. Perfect.

The bigger the event, the heavier the patriotism, so that we have a Super Bowl with planes flying in formation, astronauts waving and allegiances being pledged.

What it all has to do with sports is beyond me. Why athletes should be penalized for actions such as those taken by the Eastern Michigan runners is also beyond me.

They can be called rude, perhaps, or ill-mannered, or thoughtless. But measuring their love of country because they failed to respond to the national anthem—Sorry, no sale at this address.

THE LOVE LIFE OF A PRIVATE SECRETARIAT

By Dick Young

From the New York Daily News

Being a city boy, who learned about boy-girl things by hanging around Bill's candy store on Washington Heights, I never paid much attention to the sex life of the thoroughbred horse.

Then, as time went along, I naturally assumed that a horse was like any other athlete. I mean, if a ball player could make love at night and play ball the next day, or vice versa, why not everybody? My mother, bless her, when she got around to telling me about birds and bees, didn't get to the chapter on horses.

Lately, with all the fuss being made about Secretariat, I decided to ask a few questions, and was I surprised! Not only that, I found out I wasn't the only one. Very few people, outside track people, seem to realize that a horse can't run and make love, both. It has to be one or the other, which explains why there are no horse-groupies.

This didn't make sense to me at first. I mean, if Secretariat has nothing to do between the Belmont and the Travers, why should he just stand around eating and running up bills? Why can't Mrs. Tweedy fix him up with a date or ten? After all, it is two months we're talking about, and Mrs. Tweedy has some classy friends who have some real nice girl horses. Secretariat could, after being formally introduced, of course, spend a few nights in a girl horse's stall and be ready for the next race. Voila, we satisfy everybody. Secretariat is running and siring all at once. As I say, if ball players can do it . . .

Well, the first thing wrong with this kind of thinking, I find, is that the time isn't right. It's mid-June, and horses mate only from February till just about yesterday. American horses, that is. In England, they can go at it till July 1, I am told, because their summers are milder than ours. A stallion can have a heart attack trying to cover a mare in extremely hot weather, which is something else I never heard about happening to ball players. Actors yes.

The reason they limit the yearly lovespan of a horse is that they don't want a foal in December. All horses become a year older on January 1 (I always knew that; what do you think, I'm dumb?). Nobody wants a two-year-old racehorse who is really only thirteen months old. It's giving away too much.

In line with this, you must realize that the gestation period for a horse is 11 months. This means an anxious mother, if she's a horse, counts to 11 on her fingers instead of to 9, which is not easy to do when you have hooves.

"We try to time it so that a colt is born in February," says Johnny Nerud, who has procured for a few mares in his time. "If he is born in June he will wind up racing against horses five, six months older than he is. That's like playing a high school kid against a pro in football."

Why not squeeze the last bit of percentage out of the calendar by aiming for a January delivery instead of February?

"Because nature isn't as automatic as people think," said Johnny Nerud. "You might miss, and the foal will be dropped in December. Besides, the best time to be born is March and April. Everywhere but Florida, the weather is too bad in January and February. The colt doesn't get out to exercise, and loses whatever advantage it might have."

Getting back to my theory of casual love, and the possibility of letting Secretariat double as a stud while waiting for another big purse to come along, that is absurd, I am told. In the first place, you can't just let a boy horse wander into the stall of a girl horse. Girl horses don't slap fresh boy horses in the face. They kick the hell out of them. Secretariat's career, as a runner and lover, could end right there. What's more, the boy horse would kick back, perhaps destroying the mare.

"A horse must be taught to breed, just as it may be taught to race," says Allen Jerkins. "It takes four or five men to help. Three of them hold the mare, and the others help the stallion. He has to learn to put up with that. It's not exactly a natural setting."

"Once a horse has gone to stud," says Johnny Nerud, "it's very difficult to bring him back to racing. He knows there are two ways to make a living, and he likes the second way best."

Besides, there is so much more money to be made by breeding the horse, points out Elliott Burch. "In England, stud syndicates go as high as 42 members. Here, the limit is 32. Secretariat will be kept busy by his syndicate owners, but if he does take on an outsider, it probably would be for $50,000, sudden death."

Sudden death?

"That means one cover, no guarantee, no refunds."

Cover is one of the racing expressions I learned that keeps this from being an x-rated column. I wish to thank Elliott Burch of the Rokeby Stable, John Nerud of Tartan Farms, and Allen Jerkins of Hobeau Farms for this crash course on horses. Next, I shall look into life in the pits with the Ferraris and Porsches and learn what makes little automobiles.

ON COMING IN FIRST

By George Ross

From The Oakland Tribune

A fourteen-year-old kid named Jim Gronen of Boulder, Colorado, won the All-America Soap Box Derby at Akron yesterday only to be disqualified when some snoop found an electromagnetic system in his car to give him a better getaway pull from the steel starting gate.

Littly Jimmy thus ushers in a whole new era of competition in sports.

If we get nothing else out of Watergate, we get the inspiration for a little-league department of dirty tricks for field and arena.

Who wants a kid to grow up to be president when he can grow up to be H.R. Haldeman?

The opportunities for young James Gronen seem endless. A little genius who can wire a home-made soap-box-derby car to beat the other jerks at age fourteen can surely soon be trusted to wire the ladies' room at the White House and expand our knowledge immeasurably. Who knows what those libbers are up to in there?

But one hopes young Jim returns to sender the Junior Plumber Kit he'll get in today's mail from G. Gordon Liddy. He should stick to sports. We need his expertise in the private sector, at this point in time. The commies are gaining on us.

Adaptations of the Gronen jump-starter are endless. Tomorrow's *News Today* brings you what's new around the electrifying beat:

Pebble Beach—Pert Myrt Perkins, thirteen, won the Junior Miss Regional Golf Tournament here today by 17 strokes, one-putting every green but three which she holed with chip shots, only to be disqualified at the Awards Banquet by John Grunge, tourney official.

Grunge said Miss Perkins had toured the course in a blacked-out golf cart the night before play began, placed powerful magnets in every cup, and putted today with a plastic-coated ball bearing.

She forfeited the trophy and sold the patent rights for $763,000 to an unidentified man wearing an Arnie Palmer T-shirt.

Lunchbucket, Pennsylvania—Stockey Cling Czynckworski, field-goal specialist for the Iron Shaft High School football varsity who hadn't made a field goal in two seasons and was 3-for-19 with points-after-touchdowns, kicked the Muckers to a Mid-Penna title last night with a brilliant 6-for-6 performance including booming boots of 49, 33, 42, and 55 yards, the latter an all-time prep record.

League officials have impounded Czynckworski's kicking shoe after an opposing lineman was treated for powder burns and a ringing in his ears.

South Lake Tahoe—It's back to the drawing board for young Ike Walton Tisher III, here today after his third try to land "Old Hog-jaw," a five-foot-long Mackinaw Lake Trout, failed.

"I thought I had him this time," the young nimrod said. "I chummed the hole with steel-cored night crawlers, and cast my electromagnetized Superlure right over him, but I got shorted out on something. Are there electric eels in here?"

San Francisco—Stanley "Slats" Skinner, 6-foot-7, 148-pound grade schooler who had entered his first distance race "to build myself up," was resting comfortably today at Emergency Hospital after colliding with a Market St. bus while leading the annual Bay-to-Breakers Race by a mile and a quarter.

"I'da been all right if the driver hadn't had to stop so suddenly," Slats said through a wired-shut jaw. "I was running well, right behind the bus, when I saw his stop-light go on. I guess I was a little slow squeezing the antipolarity button. Next time I'll split out the magnet."

Fresno—Officials of the annual West Coast Junior Relays, the famed "meet where records are set," are studying results of last night's 12-to-15 Girls Section Finals competition to see if a new mark will be accepted in the javelin throw.

Pretty Jackie Armstrong, fourteen, uncorked a tremendous toss on her first try, which stuck 27 rows up in the stadium seats, narrowly missing an elderly grape grower from Delano.

The versatile Miss Armstrong, daughter of a jet-propulsion physicist from Lemoore, was runner-up last summer in a Junior Achievement Science competition. Her mini-jet model delta-wing aircraft was last seen at 43,000 feet over Winnemucca, Nevada.

FOR THE RECORD

CHAMPIONS OF 1973

ARCHERY

World Champions

Men—Viktor Sidoruk, Soviet Union.
Women—Linda Myers, York, Pa.
Men's Team—United States.
Women's Team—Soviet Union.

National Archery Ass'n. Champions

Men—Darrell Pace, Cincinnati.
Women—Mrs. Doreen Wilbur, Jefferson, Iowa.
Team—Cincinnati Archers.
Women's Team—Henderson A.C. Phoenix.
Junior—Don Dabelow, Galveston, Ind.
Girl—Janet McCullough, Sharpsville, Pa.

National Field Archery Assn. Champions

FREE-STYLE

Open—Bobby J. Hunt, Grapevine, Tex.
Women's Open—Barbara Morris, Frankfort, Ky.
Amateur—Terry Ragsdale, White Oak, Tex.
Women's Amateur—Kathy Cramberg, Dallas City, Ill.

AUTO RACING

World—Jackie Stewart, Scotland.
Can-Am Cup—Mark Donahue, Reading, Pa.
U.S.A.C.—Roger McClusky, Tucson, Ariz.
Trans-Am—Peter Gregg, Jacksonville, Fla.
Indy 500—Gordon Johncock, Franklin, Ind.
NASCAR—Benny Parsons, Ellerbe, N.C.
Le Mans—Henri Pescarolo-Gerard Larrousse, France (Matra-Simco).
U.S. Grand Prix—Ronnie Peterson.

BADMINTON

United States Open Champions

Singles—Sture Johnsson, Sweden.
Women's Singles—Eva Twedberg, Sweden.
Doubles—Don Paup, Long Beach, Calif.-Jim Poole, Northridge, Calif.
Women's Doubles—Diane Hales, Claremont, Calif.-Pam Bristol, Flint, Mich.
Mixed Doubles—Eva Twedberg-Sture Johnsson, Sweden.
Senior Singles—Jim Poole.
Senior Doubles—Jim Poole-Bill Goodman, Wellesley Hills, Mass.
Senior Women's Doubles—Ethel Marshall-Bea Massman, Buffalo.
Senior Mixed Doubles—Jim Poole-Mary Ann Breckell, Los Angeles.

BASEBALL

World Series—Oakland A's.
National League—New York Mets (East), Cincinnati (West), Mets playoffs.
American League—Baltimore (East), Oakland (West), Oakland playoffs.
All-Star Game—National League.

Leading Batter (N.)—Pete Rose, Cincinnati.
Leading Batter (A.)—Rod Carew, Minnesota.
International League—Charleston; Playoffs: Pawtucket.
Pacific Coast—Spokane.
American Association—Tulsa.
National Collegiate—Southern California.

BASKETBALL

National Association—New York Knicks.
American Association—Indiana Pacers.
National Collegiate—U.C.L.A.
N.C.A.A. (Coll. Div.)—Kentucky Wesleyan.
N.A.I.A.—Guilford, N.C.
National Invitation—Virginia Tech.
Atlantic Coast—North Carolina State.
Big Eight—Kansas State.
Big Sky—Weber State.
Big Ten—Indiana.
Ivy League—Pennsylvania.
Mid-American Conference—Miami (O.)
Middle Atlantic—(East) St. Joseph's, (West)—Lafayette.
Missouri Valley—Memphis State
Ohio Valley—Austin Peay.
Pacific Coast Athletic—Long Beach State.
Pacific Eight—U.C.L.A.
Southeastern Conference—Kentucky.
Southern Conference—Furman.
Southwest Conference—Texas Tech.
West Coast A.C.—San Francisco.
Western Athletic—Arizona State.
Yankee Conference—Massachusetts.
A.A.U.—Lexington, Ky.
Women's A.A.U.—John F. Kennedy College.

BIATHLON

World Champions

Senior (20 Kilometers)—Alexander Tikhonov, Soviet Union.
Relay—Soviet Union.
Junior (15 Kilometers)—Jan Szpunar, Poland.

United States Champions

Senior—Dennis Donohue, Worcester, Vt.
Junior—Martin Hagen, Jackson Hole, Wyo.

BILLIARDS

POCKET

World—Lou Butera, Reseda, Calif.
U.S. Open—Steve Mizerak, Woodbridge, N.J.
U. S. Women's Open—Jean Balukas, Brooklyn.
Intercollegiate—Dan Louie, Wash. State.
Women's Intercollegiate—Marcia Girolamo, N.Y. State at Oswego.

BOBSLEDDING

World Champions

Four-Man—Switzerland.
Two-Man—West Germany.

North American Champions

Four-Man—Canada.
Two-Man—U.S. Navy.

BOWLING

American Bowling Congress Champions

All-Events (Classic)—Jimmy Mack, Hackettstown, N.J.
All-Events (Regular)—Ron Woolet, Louisville.
Singles (Classic)—Nelson Burton, St. Louis.
Singles (Regular)—Ed Thompson, Denver.

Doubles (Classic)—Bobby Cooper, Houston-George Pappas, Charlotte, N.C.
Doubles (Regular)—Jamie Brooks-Jim Paine, Houston.
Team (Classic)—Stroh's Beer, Detroit.
Team (Regular)—Thelmal Masters, Louisville.

Women's Int'l. Bowling Congress Champions

Singles—Bobby Buffaloe, Costa Mesa, Calif.
Doubles—Dotty Fothergill, N. Attleboro, Mass.-Millie Martorella, Rochester.
All-Events—Toni Calvary, Midwest City Okla.
Team—Fitzpatrick Chevrolet, Concord, Calif.

B.P.A.A. Open Champions

Men—Mike McGrath, El Cerrito, Calif.
Women—Millie Martorella, Rochester.

BOXING

World Professional Champions

Flyweight—Chartchai Chionoi, Thailand, recognized by World Boxing Association; Venice Borkorsor, Thailand, recognized by World Boxing Council.
Bantamweight—Arnold Taylor, South Africa, W.B.A.; Rafael Herrera, Mexico, W.B.C.
Featherweight—Ernesto Marcel, Panama, W.B.A.; Edre Jofre, Brazil, W.B.C.
Junior Lightweight—Ben Villaflor, Philippines, W.B.A.; Ricardo Arredondo, Mexico, W.B.C.
Lightweight—Roberto Duran, Panama, W.B.A.; Rodolfo Gonzalez, Long Beach, Calif., W.B.C.
Junior Lightweight—Antonio Cervantes, Colombia, W.B.A.; Bruno Arcari, Italy, W.B.C.
Welterweight—Jose Napoles, Mexico.
Light heavyweight—Bob Foster, Albuquerque, N.M.
Heavyweight—George Foreman, Hayward, Calif.

National A.A.U. Champions

106-Pound—Albert Sandoval, Los Angeles.
112-Pound—Richard Rozelle, Columbus, Ohio.
119-Pound—Mike Hess, Albany, Ore.
125-Pound—Howard Davis, New York.
132-Pound—Aaron Pryor, Cincinnati.
139-Pound—Randy Shield, Hollywood, Calif.
147-Pound—William Tuttle, Bowie, Md.
156-Pound—Dale Grant, Tacoma, Wash.
165-Pound—Martin Hagler, Brockton, Mass.
178-Pound—D. C. Barker, Denver, Colo.
Heavyweight—James Chapman, Reno, Nev.

CANOEING

United States Champions

Kayak Singles (500 Meters)—Phil Rogosheske, Alexandria, Va.
Women's Kayak Singles (500 Meters)—Marcia Smoke, Niles, Mich.
Kayak Singles (1,000 Meters)—Rogosheske.
Women's Kayak Singles (5,000 Meters)—Sperry Rademaker, Floral City, Fla.
Kayak Singles (10,000 Meters)—Rogosheske.
Kayak Tandem (500 Meters)—Rogosheske-Bob Mitchell, Catherine, Ala.
Women's Kayak Tandem (500 Meters)—Linda Murray-Nancy Leahy, Washington.
Kayak Tandem (1,000 Meters)—Jerry Welbourn-John Van Dyke, Potomac R.C.
Women's Kayak Tandem (5,000 Meters)

—Marcia Smoke-Patience Vanderbush, Niles, Mich.
Kayak Tandem (10,000 Meters)—Atila Libertini, Connecticut-Jerry Welbourn.
Kayak Fours (1,000 Meters)—Libertini, Van Dyke, Welbourn, Rogosheske.
Women's Kayak Fours (500 Meters)—Niles.
Kayak Fours (10,000 Meters)—Rusty Pelican.
Women's Kayak Fours (5,000 Meters)—Niles.
Canoe Singles (500 Meters)—Andy Toro, Newport Beach, Calif.
Canoe Singles (1,000 Meters)—P. Ross, Yonkers.
Canoe Singles (10,000 Meters)—Ray Effinger, Inwood C.C., N.Y.
Canoe Tandem (500 Meters)—Andy Toro-R. Hahn, Rusty Pelican O.A.
Canoe Tandem (1,000 Meters)—Peter and Gilbert Ross, Yonkers, N.Y.
Canoe Tandem (10,000 Meters)—Peter and Gilbert Ross.
Canoe Fours (1,000 Meters)—R. Diebold-J. Diebold, Don Plakenhorn and Lee Robinson.

CASTING

United States Champions

Grand All-Round—Steve Rajeff, San Francisco.
Angler All-Round—Steve Rajeff.
All Distance—Steve Rajeff.
All Accuracy—Steve Rajeff.
Women's All Accuracy—Mollie Schneider, Jeffersonville, Ind.

CROSS-COUNTRY

National A.A.U.—Frank Shorter, Florida Track Club, Gainesville.
National A.A.U. Team—Florida Track Club.
N.C.A.A.—Steve Prefontaine, Oregon.
N.C.A.A. Team—Oregon.
I.C. 4-A. Team—John Hartnett, Villanova.
I.C. 4-A. Team—Manhattan.
Heptagonal—David Merrick, Pennsylvania.
Heptagonal Team—Pennsylvania.

CURLING

World—Sweden.
U.S.—Winchester (Mass.) C.C.
U.S. Women—St. Paul Bon Spielers.
Canada—Regina C.C.

CYCLING

National Championships

ROAD RACING

Senior (120 miles)—John Howard, Houston.
Veteran (40 miles)—Jim Crist, Colorado.
Junior (40 miles)—Pat Nielsen, Detroit.
Women (32 miles)—Eileen Brennan, Detroit.

TRACK RACING

Sprint—Roger Young, Detroit.
Women's Sprint—Sheila Young, Detroit.
10 Miles—Mike Neel, Berkeley, Calif.
1,000-Meter Time Trial—Steve Woznick, Ridgefield Park, N.J.
4,000-Meter Pursuit—Mike Neel.
Women's 3,000-Meter Pursuit—Mary Jane Reoch, Washington.

Other

Tour de France—Luis Ocana, Spain.

DOGS

Major Best-in-Show Winners

Westminster (New York)—Ch. Acadia Command Performance, standard poodle, owned by Mrs. Jo Ann Sering, Portland, Ore, and Edward B. Jenner, Richmond, Ill.; 3,029 dogs entered.

Trenton—Ch. Wochica Okeechobee Jake, golden retriever, owned by Mrs. Rose Lewesky, Parsippany, N.J.; 3,700.

International (Chicago spring)—Ch. Purston Pinmoney Pedlar, West Highland white terrier, owned by Mrs. B. G. Frame, Indianapolis; 3,095.

Santa Barbara (Calif.)—Ch. Galaxy's Missile Belle, Doberman pinscher, owned by Mrs. Elaine Herndon, Fresno, Calif., and Mrs. N. J. Reese, Los Angeles; 3,935.

Boardwalk (Atlantic City)—Ch. Sunnybrook Spot On, Wire fox terrier, owned by Mrs. Robert V. Clark Jr., Middleburg, Va.; 3,719.

Westchester (Tarrytown, N.Y.)—Ch. Gretchenhof Columbia River, German shorthaired pointer, owned by Dr. Richard P. Smith, Hayward, Calif.; 2,595.

National Bird Dog Champions

Pointers and Setters—Miller's Miss Knight, pointer, owned by Rogers Hays, Pulaski, Tenn.

Open Pheasant—Mission, pointer, owned by Dr. J. M. Bennett, Ridgeland, S.C.

Quail—The Kansas Wind, pointer, owned by Pete Frierson, Clinton, Miss.

FENCING

World Champions

Foil—Christian Noel, France.
Epee—Rolf Edling, Sweden.
Saber—Mario-Aldo Montano, Italy.
Women's Foil—Valentina Nikolova, Soviet Union.
Foil Team—Soviet Union.
Epee Team—West Germany.
Saber Team—Hungary.
Women's Foil Team—Hungary.

United States Champions

Foil—Ed Ballinger, Salle Santelli, New York.
Epee—Scott Bozek, Peabody, Mass.
Saber—Paul Apostel, Fencers Club, N.Y.
Women's Foil—Tatanya Adamovich, Fencers Club, N.Y.
Foil Team—Salle Santelli, New York.
Epee Team—New York A. C.
Saber Team—New York A. C.
Woman's Foil Team—Fencers Club, N.Y.

National Collegiate Champions

Foil—Brooke Makler, Pennsylvania.
Epee—Risto Hurme, N.Y.U.
Saber—Peter Westbrook, N.Y.U.
Team—New York University.

FOOTBALL

Intercollegiate Champions

Eastern (Lambert Trophy)—Penn State.
Eastern (Lambert Cup)—Delaware-Lehigh.
Eastern (Lambert Bowl)—C. W. Post.
Atlantic Coast Conference—No. Carolina State.
Big Eight—Oklahoma.
Big Sky—Boise State.
Big Ten—Ohio St.-Michigan (tie).
Ivy League—Dartmouth.
Mid-American Conference—Miami.
Missouri Valley—North Tex. St.-Tulsa.
Ohio Valley—Western Kentucky.
Pacific Coast A.A.—San Diego State.
Pacific Eight—Southern California.
Southeastern Conference—Alabama.
Southern Conference—East Carolina.
Southwest Conference—Texas.
Western Athletic—Arizona-Arizona St. (tie).
Yankee Conference—Connecticut.

National League

NATIONAL CONFERENCE

Eastern Division—Dallas Cowboys.

Central Division—Minnesota Vikings.
Western Division—Los Angeles Rams.

AMERICAN CONFERENCE

Eastern Division—Miami Dolphins.
Central Division—Cincinnati Bengals.
Western Division—Oakland Raiders.

Super Bowl

Miami Dolphins

Canadian Professional

Grey Cup—Ottawa Rough Riders.

GOLF

Men

World Cup—United States.
World Cup Ind.—Johnny Miller.
National Amateur—Craig Stadler.
National Open—Johnny Miller.
P.G.A.—Jack Nicklaus.
British Open—Tom Weiskopf.
British Amateur—Dick Siderowf.
Masters—Tommy Aaron.
Canadian Open—Tom Weiskopf.
Canadian Amateur—George Burns 3d.
U.S.G.A. Senior—Bill Hyndman 3d.
U.S. Junior—Jack Renner.
N.C.A.A.—Ben Crenshaw, Texas.
N.C.A.A. Team—Florida.
N.A.I.A—Jay Overton, Campbell-Mike Zack, St. Bernard (tie).
Ryder Cup—United States.
U.S. Public Links—Stan Stopa.
Walker Cup—United States.
Western Open—Billy Casper.
Westchester Classic—Bobby Nichols.
U.S. Senior G.A.—Bob Kiersky.
U.S.P.G.A. Senior—Sam Snead.
World Pro Senior—Sam Snead.
World Series—Tom Weiskopf.
World Senior—W. F. Colm.
Tournament of Champions—Jack Nicklaus.
American Golf Classic—Bruce Crampton.
Bob Hope Classic—Arnold Palmer.
Byron Nelson Classic—Lanny Wadkins.
Sammy Davis-Hartford—Billy Casper.
Bing Crosby Pro-Am—Jack Nicklaus.
Vardon Trophy—Bruce Crampton.

Women

U.S. Open—Mrs. Susie M. Berning.
U.S. Amateur—Carol Semple.
British Amateur—Ann Irvin.
Canadian Amateur—Mrs. Marlene S. Streit.
U.S.G.A. Senior—Mrs. David Hibbs.
U.S.G.A. Girls—Amy Alcott.
N.C.A.A.—Bonnie Lauer.
L.P.G.A.—Mary Mills.
North and South—Beth Barry.
World Junior—Suzanne Cadden.
Western Amateur—Katie Ahern Falk.
Eastern Amateur—Lancy Smith.
Dinah Shore-Colgate—Mickey Wright.
Sealy Classic—Kathy Cornelius.

GYMNASTICS

National A.A.U. Champions

All-Round—Yoshi Hayasaki, Illinois U. Yoshiaki Takei, Georgia South (tie).
Pommel Horse—Yoshi Hayasaki.
Floor Exercise—Paul Hunt, Illinois U.
Vaulting—Yoshi Hayasaki.
Rings—Charles Ropiequet, Carbondale, Ill.
Parallel Bars—Yoshiaki Takei.
Horizontal Bar—Yoshi Hayasaki.
Team—New York A.C.

Women

All-Round—Joan Moore Rice, Philadelphia.
Balance Beam—Kim Chace, N. Palm Beach, Fla.
Vaulting—Roxanne Pierce, College Park, Md.
Uneven Parallel Bars—Roxanne Pierce.
Floor Exercise—Joan M. Rice.
Team—Mannettes Gym Club, Philadelphia.

National Collegiate Champions

All-Round—Marshall Avener, Penn St.-Steve Hug, Stanford (tie).
Floor Exercise—Odess Lovin, Oklahoma.
Rings—Bob Mahorney, Indiana State.
Vaulting—John Crosby, Southern Conn.
Pommel Horse—Ed Slezak, Indiana State.
Horizontal Bar—Jon Aitken, Iowa State.
Parallel Bars—Steve Hug.
Team—Iowa State.

HANDBALL

United States Handball Ass'n. Champions

FOUR-WALL

Singles—Terry Muck, St. Paul.
Doubles—Ray Neveau, Oshkosh, Wis.-Simie Fein, Milwaukee.
Masters Singles—Jim Fitzpatrick, New York.
Masters Doubles—Ken Schneider-Phil Elbert, Chicago.
Golden Masters Doubles—Irv Simon, Los Angeles-Earl Russell, Long Beach, Calif.

ONE-WALL

Singles—Steve Sandler, New York.
Doubles—Joel Wisotsky-Lou Russo, New York.

National A.A.U. Champions

ONE-WALL

Singles—Joel Davidson, Brooklyn.
Doubles—Wally Ulbrich-Artie Reyer, Brooklyn.

HARNESS RACING

Horse of Year—Sir Dalrae.
Trotter of Year—Flirth.
2-Year-Old Trotter—Starlark Hanover.
2-Year-Old Pacer—Boyden Hanover.
3-Year-Old Trotter—Flirth.
3-Year-Old Pacer—Melvin's Woe.
Aged Trotter—Flower Child.
Aged Pacer—Mountain Skipper.
Leading Money-Winner—Sir Dalrae.
Leading Driver (Heats)—Herve Filion.
Leading Driver (Earnings)—Herve Filion.
Hambletonian—Flirth.
Yonkers Futurity—Tamerlane.
Kentucky Futurity—Arnie Almahurst.
Dexter Cup—Knightly Way.
Colonial—Flirth.
Messenger Stakes—Valiant Bret.
Cane Pace—Smog.
Little Brown Jug—Melvin's Woe.
Adios—Ricci Reenie Time.

HOCKEY

Stanley Cup—Montreal Canadiens.
National League—Montreal (East), Chicago Black Hawks (West).
World Hockey Association—New England Whalers.
American League—Cincinnati Swords.
Eastern League—Syracuse.
International League—Fort Wayne.
Western League—Phoenix Roadrunners.
Central League—Omaha Knights.
Allan Cup—Orillia (Ont.) Terriers.
Memorial Cup—Toronto Marlboros.
National Collegiate—Wisconsin.
Ivy League—Cornell.
E.C.A.C.—Cornell; Division II: Vermont.
W.C.H.A.—Denver.

HORSESHOE PITCHING

World Champions

Men—Elmer Hohl, Wellesley, Ont.
Women—Ruth Hangen, Getzville, N.Y.
Senior—Ray Miller, Springfield, Ohio.
Junior—Jeffrey Williams, Eureka, Calif.
Girls—Rosemary Gibson, Centralia, Ill.

HORSE RACING

T.R.A. Eclipse Awards

Horse of the Year—Secretariat.
2-Year-Old Colt—Protagonist.
2-Year-Old Filly—Talking Picture.
3-Year-Old Colt—Secretariat.
3-Year-Old Filly—Desert Vixen.
Older Colt and Gelding—Riva Ridge.
Older Filly and Mare—Susan's Girl.
Turf Champion—Secretariat.
Sprint Champion—Shecky Green.
Steeplechase Champion—Athenian Idol.
Triple Crown—Secretariat.

Stakes Winners

Kentucky Derby—Secretariat.
Preakness Stakes—Secretariat.
Belmont Stakes—Secretariat.
Flamingo—Our Native.
Hialeah Turf Cup—Gleaming.
Hollywood Gold Cup—Kennedy Road.
Jersey Derby—Knightly Dawn.
Jockey Club Gold Cup—Prove Out.
Santa Anita Derby—Sham.
Santa Anita Handicap—Cougar II.
Washington D.C. International—Dahlia (France).
Widener—Vertee.

Foreign

Epsom Derby (England)—Morston.
Epsom Oaks (England)—Mysterious.
Grand Prix de Paris—Tennyson.
King George VI and Queen Elizabeth—Dahlia.
Canadian International Championship—Secretariat.
Prix de L'Arc de Triomphe—Rheingold.
Queen's Plate (Canada)—Royal Chocolate.
St. Leger (England)—Peleid.

HORSE SHOWS

American Horse Shows Association

UNOFFICIAL CHAMPIONS

Arabians—Tom F. Ohnemus's Omega Witez. Witez.
Half Arabians—Darryl Larson's F. F. Luckett.
Hackney Ponies—Mrs. Alan Robson's Holiday Debonair.
Amateur Hackney Ponies—Holiday Debonair.
Harness Ponies—Mrs. Robson's Debbie's Fashion.
Amateur Harness Ponies—Debbie's Fashion.
Regular Conformation Hunters—Mr. and Mrs. John H. Leib's Automation.
Green Conformation Hunters—Mr. and Mrs. Kenneth Wheeler's Vim.
Regular Working Hunters—Mr. and Mrs. Wheeler's Gozzi.
First Year Green Working Hunters—Debbie Willson's Market Rise.
Second Year Green Working Hunters—Jane Womble's Third of August.
Amateur-Owner Working Hunters—Penny Loeb's No Alibi.
Small Pony Hunters—Jess Larson's Justa Tinker.
Large Pony Hunters—Hollow Hill Farm's Dressing Drink.
Amateur-Owner Jumpers—Judy Korn's Orange County.
Junior Working Hunters—Nancy Baroody's War Dress.
Junior Jumpers—Keene Tipton's The Intruder.

ICE SKATING

FIGURE

World Champions

Men—Ondrej Nepela, Czechoslovakia.
Women—Karen Magnussen, Vancouver, B.C.
Pairs—Irina Rodnina-Alexander Zaitsev, Soviet Union.
Dance—Ludmila Pakhomova-Alexander Groshkov, Soviet Union.

United States Champions

Men—Gordon McKellen Jr., Lake Placid, N.Y.

Women—Janet Lynn, Rockford, Ill.
Pairs—Melissa and Mark Militano, Dix Hills, N.Y.
Dance—Mary Karen Campbell, East Lansing, Mich.-Johnny Johns, Bloomfield Hills, Mich.

SPEED

World Champions

Men—Goeran Claeson, Sweden.
Women—Atje Keulen-Deelstra, Netherlands.
Sprint—Valery Muratov, Soviet Union.
Women's Sprint—Sheila Young, Detroit.

United States Champions

Men's Outdoor—Mike Woods, West Allis, Wis.
Men's Indoor—Bill Lanigan, New York.
Women's Outdoor—Nancy Class, St. Paul.
Women's Indoor—Michele Conroy, St. Paul-Celeste Chlapaty, Skokie, Ill. (tie).

JUDO

National A.A.U. Champions

139-Pound—David Pruzansky, Passaic, N.J.
154-Pound—Patrick Burris, Anaheim, Calif.
176-Pound—Bill Sanford, Houston, Tex.
205-Pound—Roy Sukimoto, Los Angeles.
Heavyweight—Dean Sedgwick, River Forest, Ill.
Open—Lee Person, Memphis, Tenn.
Grand Champion—Roy Sukimoto.

LACROSSE

Club—Long Island A.C.
N.C.A.A.—Maryland.
Intercollegiate Ass'n—Hobart.
North-South—South.
Ivy League—Brown.
Junior College—Nassau (N.Y.) C.C.

MOTORBOATING

Unlimited Hydroplane Races

Champion Spark Plug (Miami)—Mickey Remund, Pride of Pay 'N Pak.
President's Cup (Washington)—Gene Whipp, Lincoln Thrift.
Kentucky Governor's Cup (Owensboro, Ky.)—Dean Ghenoweth, Miss Budweiser.
Gar Wood Memorial (Detroit)—Chenoweth.
Indiana Governor's Cup (Madison, Ind.)—Remund.
Gold Cup (Tri-Cities, Wash.)—Chenoweth.
Seafair Championship (Seattle)—Remund.
Clearwater Cup (Toledo, Ohio)—Remund.
Spirit of Detroit (Detroit)—Chenoweth.
National Champions—Pride of Pay 'N Pak; Remund.

American Power Boat Ass'n Offshore Races

Hennessy Key West (Fla.)—Bob Magoon.
Le Club (Miami)—Magoon.
St. Petersburg (Fla.)—Sandy Satullo.
Mission Bay (San Diego)—Steve Tagnoli.
Bushmill-KBIG (Los Angeles)—Art Norris.
Long Beach-Ensenada (Calif.)—Magoon.
Sam Griffith (Fort Lauderdale, Fla.)—Norris.
Hennessy Grand Prix (Point Pleasant, N.J.)—Magoon.
Great Lakes (Cleveland)—Willie MacDonald.
Hennessy Cup (Marina del Rey, Calif.)—Norris.
Catalina Challenge (Calif.)—Tagnoli.

San Francisco Cup (Calif.)—Tagnoli.
National Inboard Champion—Magoon.
National Outboard Champion—Randy Rabe, St. Petersburg, Fla.
World Offshore Champion—Carlo Bonomi, Italy.

MOTORCYCLING

U.S. Grand Champion—Ken Roberts, Woodside, Calif.

PADDLEBALL

United States Champions

Singles—Steve Keeley, San Diego, Calif.
Doubles—Dan Alder-Evans Wright, Lansing, Mich.
Masters Singles—Bob McNamara.
Masters Doubles—Diz Kronenberg-Aubrey Olson, Eau Claire, Wis.

PARACHUTING

United States Champions

Overall—Chuck Collingwood, U.S. Army.
Women's Overall—Glorie Porter, Maple Valley, Wash.
Accuracy—John Wolfe, Valdosta, Ga.
Women's Accuracy—Gloria Porter.
Style—Chuck Collingwood.
Women's Style—Susan Rademaekers, Oakland, Calif.

PLATFORM TENNIS

United States Champions

Doubles—John Mangan, Rye, N.Y.-Bob Kingsbury, Scarsdale, N.Y.
Mixed Doubles—Cecil J. North-Mrs. Raymond D. O'Connell, Bedford, N.Y.

POLO

National Open—Oak Brook, Ill.
National 20-Goal—Houston.
National 16-Goal—Boca Raton, Fla.
National 14-Goal—Houston.
National 8-Goal—Maryland.
Intercollegiate—Connecticut U.
Interscholastic—Culver.
Coronation Cup (England)—United States.

RACQUETS

World—Howard Angus, England.
United States Amateur—Howard Angus.
Tuxedo Gold Racquets—Howard Angus.

ROLLER SKATING

World Champions

Singles—Randy Dayney, East Meadow, L. I.
Women's Singles—Sigrid Mullenbach, West Germany.
Pairs—Vicki Handyside-Louis Stoval, Long Beach, Calif.
Dance—Jane Puracchio-James Stephens, Vineland, N.J.

United States Champions

Singles—Mark Revere, Pontiac, Mich.
Women's Singles—Natalie Dunn, Bakersfield, Calif.
Figures—William Boyd, Seabrook, Md.
Women's Figures—Deborah Palm, E. Meadow, L. I.
Pairs—Abe Blass-April Allen, Houston, Tex.
Fours—Wayne Melton-Judy Jerue-Richard Toon and Paula Spangle, Garden Grove, Calif.
Dance (American Style)—Joseph and Marie Guady, Dover, Del.
Dance (International Style)—James Stephens-Jane Puracchio, Vineland, N.J.
Speed—Danny Butler, Springfield, Mo.
Women's Speed—Linda Brooks, Irving, Tex.
Figures (International)—Randy Dayney, East Meadow, L. I.
Women's Figure (Int.)—Deborah Palm.

ROWING

United States Champions

Singles—Jim Dietz, New York A.C.
Singles (½ mile)—Jim Dietz.
Doubles—Jim Dietz-Larry Klecatsky, N.Y.A.C.
Pairs—Jay Forster-Jim Moroney, Vesper B.C.
Pairs With Coxswain—Walt Updegrove-Mike Staines.
Fours—Vesper Boat Club, Philadelphia.
Fours With Coxswain—Vesper B.C.
Quads—New York A.C.
Eights—Potomac B.C., Washington.
150-Pound Singles—Larry Klecatsky.
150-Pound Dash—Bill Belden, Undine, Phil.
150-Pound Doubles—Bill Belden-Fred Duling, Undine.
150-Pound Fours—Mexican National team.
150-Pound Fours With Coxswain—Cambridge (Mass.) B.C.
150-Pound Quads—New York A.C.
150-Pound Eights—Cambridge B.C.

Intercollegiate Champions

Intercollegiate R.A.—Wisconsin.
Dad Vail Trophy—Massachusetts.
Eastern Sprint—Northeastern.
Western Sprint—Washington.
Mid-America—Marietta.
Harvard-Yale—Harvard.
Oxford-Cambridge—Cambridge.

RUGBY

English League Cup—Featherstone Rovers.
Eastern Rugby Union—Old Blue, N.Y.-Sud Americano, Wash. (tie).

SHOOTING

United States Rifle Champions

Small-Bore Prone—Maj. Lones W. Wigger Jr., U. S. Army.
Women's Small-Bore Prone—Schuyler Helbing, Fort Worth, Tex.
Small-Bore Position—Maj. Lones W. Wigger.
Women's Small-Bore Position—Janet S. Hays, Cincinnati, Ohio.
National High Power—Ronald G. Troyer, Williamsfield, Ohio.

United States Pistol Champions

National—Sfc. Hershel L. Anderson, Tracy City, Tenn.
Women's National—Sfc. Barbara J. Hile, Lapeer, Mich.

Trapshooting Champions

Grand American—Dennis Taylor, Muscoda, Wis.
Women's Grand American—Jo Ann Nelson, Lone Tree, Iowa.

United States Skeet Champions

All-Round—Paul LaPorte, Montreal.
Women's All-Round—Karla Roberts, Bridgeton, Mo.

SKIING

World Cup Champions

Men—Gustavo Thoeni, Italy.
Women—Annemarie Proell, Austria.

National Alpine Champions

Men's Slalom—Masayoshi Kashiwagi, Japan.
Men's Giant Slalom—Dave Currier, Madison, N.H.
Men's Downhill—Bob Cochran, Richmond, Vt.
Women's Slalom—Lindy Cochran, Richmond, Vt.
Women's Giant Slalom—Debi Handley, Colorado Springs.
Women's Downhill—Cindy Nelson, Lutsen, Minn.

National Nordic Champions

Jumping—Jerry Martin, Minneapolis.
Men's 15-Kilometer Cross-Country—Tim Caldwell, Putney, Vt.
Men's 30-Kilometer Cross-Country—Bob Gray, Putney, Vt.
Women's 5-Kilometer Cross-Country—Martha Rockwell, Putney, Vt.
Women's 10-Kilometer Cross-Country—Martha Rockwell.
Nordic Combined Overall—Teyck Weed, Etna, N.H.

National Collegiate Champions

Downhill—Bob Cochran, Vermont.
Cross-Country—Steiner Hybertsen, Wyoming.
Slalom—Peik Christensen, Denver.
Jumping—Vidar Nilsgard, Colorado.
Alpine Combined—Peik Christensen.
Skimeister—Kim Kendall, New Hampshire.
Team—Colorado U.

SOCCER

United States Champions

National Challenge Cup—Maccabi, Los Angeles.
National Amateur—Inter, Philadelphia.
North American Soccer League—Philadelphia Atoms.
Junior—St. Elizabeth's, Baltimore.

Other Champions

English Association Cup—Sunderland.
English League Cup—Tottenham.
Scottish League Cup—Hibernian.
Scottish Association Cup—Glasgow Rangers.
European Cup—Ajax of Amsterdam.
European Cup Winners Cup—A. C. Milan, Italy.
European Union Cup—Liverpool, England.

SOFTBALL

Amateur Softball Ass'n Champions

Fast Pitch—Clearwater (Fla.) Bombers.
Women's Fast Pitch—Stratford (Conn.) Raybestos Brakettes.
Slow Pitch—Howard Furniture, Denver, N.C.
Women's Slow Pitch—Sweeney Chevrolet, Chattanooga, Tenn.
Industrial Slow Pitch—Pabst International, Springfield, Ohio.
16-inch Slow Pitch—Chicago Bobcats.

SQUASH RACQUETS

United States Champions

Singles—Vic Niederhoffer, New York.
Women's Singles—Gretchen Spruance, Greenville, Md.
Veterans Singles—Henri Salaun, Boston.
Senior Singles—Floyd Svensson, San Francisco.
Doubles—Jim Zug, Philadelphia-Vic Niederhoffer.
Senior Doubles—William T. Ketcham-Victor Elmaleh, New York.
North American Open—Sharif Khan, Toronto.

SQUASH TENNIS

Singles—Pedro Bacallao, New York.
Doubles—Pedro Bacallao, Vic Niederhoffer, New York.

SURFING

United States Champions

Men—Larry Bertleman, Hawaii Surfing Ass'n.
Women—Laura Powers, Western Surfing Ass'n.
Seniors—Rabbit Kekai, Hawaii S.A.
Masters—Donald Takayama, Western S.A.
Overall—Bob Milfield, Western S.A.

SWIMMING

Men's World Champions

100-Meter Free-Style—Jim Montgomery, Madison, Wis.
200-Meter Free-Style—Jim Montgomery.
400-Meter Free-Style—Rick DeMont, San Rafael, Calif.
1,500-Meter Free-Style—Steve Holland, Australia.
100-Meter Backstroke—Roland Matthes, East Germany.
200-Meter Backstroke—Roland Matthes.
100-Meter Breast-Stroke—John Hencken, Santa Clara, Calif.
200-Meter Breast-Stroke—David Wilkie, Britain.
100-Meter Butterfly—Bruce Robertson, Canada.
200-Meter Butterfly—Robin Backhaus, Redlands, Calif.
200-Meter Ind. Medley—Gunnar Larsson, Sweden.
400-Meter Ind. Medley—Andras Hargetay, Hungary.
400-Meter Medley Relay—United States.
800-Meter Free-Style Relay—United States.
400-Meter Free-Style Relay—United States.
Springboard Dive—Phil Boggs, Akron, Ohio.
Platform Dive—Klaus diBiasi, Italy.

Women's World Champions

100-Meter Free-Style—Kornelia Ender, East Germany.
200-Meter Free-Style—Keena Rothhammer, Santa Clara, Calif.
400-Meter Free-Style—Heather Greenwood, Fresno, Calif.
800-Meter Free-Style—Novella Calligaris, Italy.
100-Meter Backstroke—Ulrike Richter, East Germany.
200-Meter Backstroke—Melissa Belote, Springfield, Va.
100-Meter Breast-Stroke—Renate Vogel, East Germany.
200-Meter Breast-Stroke—Renate Vogel.
100-Meter Butterfly—Kornelia Ender.
200-Meter Butterfly—Rosemarie Kother, East Germany.
200-Meter Ind. Medley—Andrea Hubner, East Germany.
400-Meter Ind. Medley—Gudrun Wegner, East Germany.
400-Meter Free-Style Relay—East Germany.
400-Meter Medley Relay—East Germany.
Springboard Dive—Christa Kohler, East Germany.
Platform Dive—Ulrika Knape, Sweden.

Men's National Long-Course Champions

100-Meter Free-Style—Jim Montgomery, Madison, Wis.
200-Meter Free-Style—Jim Montgomery.
400-Meter Free-Style—Rick DeMont, San Rafael, Calif.
1,500-Meter Free-Style—Rick DeMont.
100-Meter Backstroke—Mike Stamm, Coronado-Navy S.C.
200-Meter Backstroke—John Naber, Los Altos, Calif.
100-Meter Breast-Stroke—John Hencken, Santa Clara, Calif.
200-Meter Breast Stroke—John Hencken
100-Meter Butterfly—Robin Backhaus, Redlands, Calif.
200-Meter Butterfly—Steve Gregg, Wilmington, Del.
200-Meter Ind. Medley—Stan Carper, Portland, Ore.
400-Meter Ind. Medley—Rick Colella, Seattle.
400-Meter Medley Relay—Gatorade S.C., Bloomington, Ind.
400-Meter Free-Style Relay—Gatorade S.C.
800-Meter Free-Style Relay—Gatorade S.C.
1-Meter Dive—Mike Finneran, Columbus, Ohio.
3-Meter Dive—Lieut. Phil Boggs, U.S. Air Force.

Platform Dive—Tim Moore, Ron O'Brien D.S.

Women's National Long-Course Champions

100-Meter Free-Style—Shirley Babashoff, Mountain Valley, Calif.
200-Meter Free-Style—Shirley Babashoff.
400-Meter Free-Style—Keena Rothhammer, Santa Clara A.C.
1,500-Meter Free-Style—Jo Harshbarger, Bellevue, Wash.
100-Meter Backstroke—Melissa Belote, Springfield, Va.
200-Meter Backstroke—Melissa Belote.
100-Meter Breast-Stroke—Marcia Morey, Decatur, Ill.
200-Meter Breast-Stroke—Lynn Colella, Seattle.
100-Meter Butterfly—Deena Deerdurff, Cincinnati.
200-Meter Butterfly—Lynn Colella.
200-Meter Ind. Medley—Kathy Heddy, Summit, N.J.
400-Meter Ind. Medley—Jenny Bartz, Santa Clara.
400-Meter Medley Relay—Santa Clara (Calif.) S.C.
400-Meter Free-Style Relay—Huntington Beach (Calif.) A.C.
800-Meter Free-Style Relay—Santa Clara S.C.
1-Meter Dive—Cynthia Potter, Gatorade S.C.
3-Meter Dive—Carrie Irish, Ron O'Brien D.S.
Platform Dive—Deborah Keplar, Ron O'Brien D.S.
Team—Santa Clara S.C.

National Collegiate Champions

50-Yard Free-Style—John Trembley, Tenn.
100-Yard Free-Style—John Trembley.
200-Yard Free-Style—Jim McConica, So. California.
500-Yard Free-Style—John Kinsella, Indiana.
1,650-Yard Free-Style—John Kinsella.
100-Yard Breast-Stroke—John Hencken, Stanford.
200-Yard Breast-Stroke—David Wilkie, Miami (Fla.).
100-Yard Backstroke—Mike Stamm, Indiana.
200-Yard Backstroke—Mike Stamm.
100-Yard Butterfly—John Trembley.
200-Yard Butterfly—Gary Hall, Indiana.
200-Yard Ind. Medley—Steve Furniss, So. California.
400-Yard Ind. Medley—Steve Furniss.
400-Yard Medley Relay—Tennessee.
400-Yard Free-Style Relay—Tennessee.
800-Yard Free-Style Relay—Indiana.
1-Meter Dive—Tim Moore, Ohio State.
3-Meter Dive—Tim Moore.
Team—Indiana.

TABLE TENNIS

World Champions

Singles—Hsi En-ting, China
Women's Singles—Hu Yu-lan, China
Doubles—Stellan Bengtsson-Kjell Johansson, Sweden.
Women's Doubles—Maria Alexandru, Rumania-Miho Hamada, Japan.
Mixed Doubles—Liang Ko-liang-Li Li, China.
Swaythling (Men's team)—Sweden.
Corbillon Cup (Women's team)—South Korea.

United States Champions

Singles—Dal Joon Lee, Parma, Ohio.
Women's Singles—Violetta Nesukaitis, Toronto.
Doubles—Dell Sweeris, Grand Rapids, Mich.-Alex Tam, Kalamazoo, Mich.
Women's Doubles—Judy Bochenski, Eugene, Ore.-Patty Cash, San Diego.
Mixed Doubles—Violetta Nesukaitis-Errol Caetano, Toronto.

TENNIS

International Team Champions

Davis Cup—Australia.
Wightman Cup (Women)—United States.
Federation Cup (Women)—Australia.

Wimbledon Champions

Men—Jan Kodes, Czechoslovakia.
Women—Mrs. Billy Jean King, Emeryville, Calif.
Men's Doubles—Jimmy Connors, Belleville, Ill.-Ilie Nastase, Rumania.
Women's Doubles—Mrs. King-Rosemary Casals, San Francisco.

U.S. Open Champions

Men—John Newcombe.
Women—Margaret Smith Court.
Men's Doubles—Owen Davidson-John Newcombe.
Women's Doubles—Margaret Court-Virginia Wade.

United States Clay-Court Champions

Men—Manuel Orantes.
Women—Chris Evert, Fort Lauderdale, Fla.
Men's Doubles—Frew McMillan, South Africa-Bob Carmichael, France.
Women's Doubles—Patti Hogan, La Jolla, Calif.-Sharon Walsh, San Rafael, Calif.

Other Foreign Open Champions

Australian Men—John Newcombe, Australia.
Australian Women—Mrs. Margaret Court, Australia.
Italian Men—Ilie Nastase, Rumania.
Italian Women—Evonne Goolagong.
French Men—Ilie Nastase, Rumania.
French Women—Mrs. Margaret Court.

TRACK AND FIELD

Men's National Outdoor Champions

100-Yard Dash—Steve Williams, San Diego T.C.
220-Yard Dash—Steve Williams.
440-Yard Dash—Maurice Peoples, D. C. Striders.
880-Yard Run—Rick Wohlhuter, Chicago U. T. C.
3,000-Meter Steeplechase—Doug Brown, Tennessee.
One-Mile Run—Len Hilton, Pacific Coast Club.
3-Mile Run—Steve Prefontaine, Oregon T.C.
Six-Mile Run—Gordon Minty, Golden Triangle T.C.
120-Yard High Hurdles—Tom Hill, U. S. Army.
440-Yard Hurdles—Jim Bolding, Pacific Coast Club.
High Jump—Dwight Stones, Pacific Coast Club.
Pole Vault—Mike Cotton, Florida T.C.
Long Jump—Randy Williams, Beverly Hills Striders.
Triple Jump—John Craft, Chicago U. T. C.
Shot-Put—Al Feuerbach, Pacific Coast Club.
Discus Throw—Mac Wilkins, Oregon T.C.
Hammer Throw—Ted Bregar, Navy.
Javelin Throw—Cary Feldman, Club Northwest.
Decathlon—Jeff Bennett, Oklahoma City.
A.A.U. Marathon—Doug Schmenk.
10-Kilometer Walk—Randy Mimm, Penn A. C., Phila.
15-Kilometer Walk—Jerry Brown, Boulder, Colo.
20-Kilometer Walk—John Kelly, California.
25-Kilometer Walk—John Knifton, New York A.C.
50-Kilometer Walk—Bill Weigle, Boulder, Colo.

One-Hour Walk—Roger Mills, England.

Three-Mile Walk—John Knifton.

Women's National Outdoor Champions

100-Yard Dash—Iris Davis, Tennessee State.

220-Yard Dash—Mabel Fergerson, West Coast Jets.

440-Yard Run—Mabel Fergerson.

880-Yard Run—Wendy Koenig, Boulder, Colo.

Mile-Run—Francie Larrieu, San Jose Cindergals.

2-Mile Run—Eileen Claugus, Sacramento, Calif.

100-Meter Hurdles—Patty Johnson, Club Northwest.

400-Meter Hurdles—Gale Fitzgerald, Atoms T. C., Brooklyn.

Mile Walk—Esther Marquez, Sports United.

440-Yard Relay—Tennessee State.

880-Yard Medley Relay—West Coast Jets.

Long Jump—Martha Watson, Los Angeles T. C.

High Jump—Deanne Wilson, South Coast T. C.

Javelin Throw—Kathy Schmidt, South Coast T. C.

Discus Throw—Jean Roberts, Delaware Sports.

Shot-Put—Maren Seidler, Daley Y. F., Chicago.

Team—Los Angeles T. F.-Atoms T. C., Brooklyn (tie).

Men's National Indoor Champions

60-Yard Dash—Hasely Crawford, Phila. Pioneers.

60-Yard High Hurdles—Rod Milburn, Southern U.

600-Yard Run—Fred Newhouse, Phila. Pioneers.

1,000-Yard Run—Marcel Philippe, Fordham.

One-Mile Run—Martin Liquori, New York A. C.

Three-Mile Run—Tracy Smith, Athletes in Action.

One-Mile Relay—Sports International.

Two-Mile Relay—Chicago U. T. C.

Sprint Medley Relay—Essex County College.

One-Mile Walk—Ron Daniel, New York A. C.

High Jump—Dwight Stones, Los Angeles.

Pole Vault—Steve Smith, Los Angeles.

Long Jump—Randy Williams, Southern Calif.

Triple-Jump—John Craft, Chicago U. T. C.

Shot-Put—George Woods, Los Angeles.

35-Pound Weight Throw—George Frenn.

National Collegiate Outdoor Champions

100-Yard Dash—Ed Hammonds, Memphis State.

220-Yard Dash—Marshall Dill, Mich. State.

440-Yard Run—Maurice Peoples, Ariz. State.

880-Yard Run—Skip Kent, Wisconsin.

One-Mile Run—Dave Wottle, Bowling Green.

Three-Mile Run—Steve Prefontaine, Oregon.

Six-Mile Run—Charles Maguire, Penn State.

3,000-Meter Steeplechase—Doug Brown, Tennessee.

120-Yard Hurdles—Rod Milburn, Southern U.

440-Yard Hurdles—Robert Primeaux, Texas.

440-Yard Relay—Memphis State.

Mile Relay—U.C.L.A.

High Jump—Reynaldo Brown, Calif. Poly.

Pole Vault—Dave Roberts, Rice.

Long Jump—Finn Bendixen, U.C.L.A.

Triple Jump—Milan Tiff, U.C.L.A.

Shot-Put—Hans Hoglund, Texas, El Paso.

Discus Throw—Mac Wilkins, Oregon.

Javelin Throw—Sam Colson, Kansas.
Hammer Throw—Jacques Accambray, Kent State.
Team—U.C.L.A.

VOLLEYBALL

U.S. Volleyball Ass'n. Champions

Open—Chuck's Steak House, Santa Monica, Calif.
Women—E. Pluribus Unum, Houston.

Other National Champions

Y.M.C.A.—Columbus, Ohio.
Y.M.C.A. Senior—Balboa Bay (Calif.) Club.
National Collegiate—San Diego State.
N.A.I.A.—Graceland.

WATER POLO

World—Hungary.
A.A.U. Indoor—San Jose State.
A.A.U. Outdoor—Concord, Calif.
A.A.U. Women's Outdoor—Coral Gables, Fla.

WATER SKIING

World Champions

Overall—George Athans, Kelowna, B.C.
Women's Overall—Lisa St. John, Fall River Mills, Calif.
Slalom—George Athans.
Women's Slalom—Sylvie Maurial, France.
Jumping—Ricky McCormick, Independence, Mo.
Women's Jumping—Liz Allan Shetter, Groveland, Fla.
Tricks—Wayne Grimditch, Pompano Beach, Fla.
Women's Tricks—Maria Victoria Carrasco, Venezuela.

United States Champions

Overall—Wayne Grimditch, Pompano Beach, Fla.
Women's Overall—Liz Allan Shetter, Groveland, Fla.
Slalom—Kris LaPoint, Castro Valley, Calif.
Women's Slalom—Liz Allan Shetter.
Tricks—Tony Krupa, Jackson, Mich.
Women's Tricks—Liz Allan Shetter.
Jumping—Ricky McCormick, Independence, Mo.
Women's Jumping—Linda Leavengood Giddens, Eastman, Ga.
Senior Overall—Dr. J. D. Morgan, Key West, Fla.
Senior Women Overall—Thelma Salmas, Novato, Calif.

WEIGHT LIFTING

United States Champions

114.5-Pound—Donald R. Warner, York (Pa.).
123.5-Pound—Dwight Tamanaha, Los Angeles.
132-Pound—Roy D. Moore, York, Pa.
148¾-Pound—Dan Cantore, San Francisco.
165¼-Pound—Fred Lowe, York, Pa.
181¾-Pound—Michael Karchut, Chicago.
198½-Pound—Phil Grippaldi, York, Pa.
242-Pound—Bob Bednarski, York, Pa.
Super-Heavyweight—Jacob Stefan, Los Angeles.
Mr. America Contest—James R. Morris, Los Angeles.

WRESTLING

U.S. Wrestling Federation Champions

105.5-Pound—Wayne Holmes, Ohio W.C.
114.5-Pound—Dale Kestel, Michigan W.C.
125.5-Pound—Yoshiro Fujita, Int. W.C.
136.5-Pound—Darrell Keller, Int. W.C.
149.5-Pound—Mike Young, Treasure Valley.
163-Pound—Stan Dziedzic, New York A.C.

180.5-Pound—Greg Hicks, A.I.A.
198-Pound—Willie Williams, Mayor Daley Y.F.
220-Pound—Buck Deadrich, S.F. Olympic Club.
Heavyweight—Mike McCready, A.I.A.
Team—Mayor Daley Youth Foundation, Chicago.

National A.A.U. Free-Style Champions

105.5-Pound—David Range, Ohio W.C.
114.5-Pound—Dale Kestel, Michigan W.C.
125.5-Pound—Don Behm, East Lansing, Mich.
136.5-Pound—Dave Pruzansky, New York A.C.
149.5-Pound—Lloyd Keaser, U.S. Marines.
163-Pound—Carl Adams, Ames, Iowa.
180.5-Pound—John Peterson, Wisconsin W.C.
198-Pound—Ben Peterson, Wisconsin W.C.
220-Pound—Russ Hellickson, Wisconsin W.C.
Unlimited—Chris Taylor, Ames, Iowa.
Team—New York A.C.

National Collegiate Champions

118-Pound—Dan Sherman, Iowa.
126-Pound—Mark Massery, Northwestern.
134-Pound—Don Rohn, Clarion State.
142-Pound—Dan Muthier, Navy.
150-Pound—Jarrett Hubbard, Michigan.
158-Pound—Wade Schalles, Clarion State.
167-Pound—Bill Simpson, Clarion State.
177-Pound—Rich Binek, Iowa State.
190-Pound—Greg Strobel, Oregon State.
Heavyweight—Chris Taylor, Iowa State.
Team—Iowa State.

YACHTING

North American Yacht Racing Union Champions

Mallory Cup (Men)—Dr. John Jennings, St. Petersburg, Fla.
Adams Cup (Women)—Mrs. David Larr, Sewanhaka Corinthian Y. C., Oyster Bay, N.Y. Crew, Mrs. James C Miller 2nd and Carolyn McCurdy.
O'Day (Single-handed)—Jim Hahn, Annapolis Md. Naval Sailing Ass'n.
Sears Cup (Junior)—Glen Brown, Houston, Tex.
Prince of Wales Trophy (Inter Club)—M.I.T. Nautical Ass'n.

Ocean and Long-Distance Racing

Annapolis-Newport—Equation, John T. Potter, Oyster Bay, L. I.
Chicago-Mackinac—Bay Bea, Pat Haggerty, Sturgeon Bay, Wis.
Marblehead-Halifax—La Forza del Destino, Norman Raben, Mamaroneck, N.Y.
Fastnet (England)—Saga, Brazil. Erling Lorentzen, skipper.
Trans-Pacific (Los Angeles-Honolulu)—Chutzpah (Class D), Stuart Cowan, Hawaii.
Miami-Nassau—Cascade, Jerry Milgram, Boston.
Trans-Atlantic (Cape Town-Rio de Janeiro)—Stormy C. B. Bruynzel (Class 1).

WHO'S WHO IN BEST SPORTS STORIES—1974

WRITERS IN BEST SPORTS STORIES–1974

THE PRIZE WINNERS

DAVID KLEIN (Peter Pan's Unexpected Birthday), winner of the news-coverage award, is a columnist for the *Star-Ledger* of Newark, N.J. and associated Newhouse Newspapers. In addition, he is the author of 14 books, including *The New York Giants: Yesterday, Today and Tomorrow*. He has also contributed to most of the national periodicals. He attended the University of Oklahoma and Fairleigh Dickinson University in New Jersey. He has appeared in *Best Sports Stories* on many occasions.

RAY DIDINGER (Larry Brown: King of the Hill), winner of the news-feature award, joined *The Philadelphia Bulletin* in 1970 after spending a year with the *Delaware County Daily Times* as a news reporter. He covers the Philadelphia Eagles and the National Football League beat. In the past three years he was honored by the Pennsylvania Newspaper Publishers Association as the author of the finest sports column of the year. This year he was honored by the Philadelphia Press Association in the Best Human category for his profile of Larry Brown. He is a graduate of Temple University and is making his second appearance in *Best Sports Stories.*

JIM HAWKINS (Baseball's Wildest Owner), winner of the magazine award, has covered the Detroit Tigers for the *Detroit Free Press* for the past five years. A 1966 graduate of the University of Wisconsin, he began writing sports for the *Milwaukee Sentinel* while still in school. Later, he wrote for the *Wilmington* (Del.) *News-Journal* and the *Baltimore Evening Sun,* concentrating there on golf as well as college football and basketball. In 1969 he was selected Sportswriter of the Year in the state of Maryland. He has merited other inclusions in *Best Sports Stories.*

OTHER CONTRIBUTORS (In Alphabetical Order)

Bob Addie (Weiskopf Conquers Himself), one of the fine veteran writers in the country, won the feature award of *Best Sports Stories* in 1963 with his moving account of blind children at a baseball game. He was graduated from the University of Alabama and began his newspaper career with the old *New York Journal-American*. Later he went to *The Washington Post,* for which he is now a sports columnist. In 1967 he was president of the Baseball Writers Association of America. His stories have appeared many times in *Best Sports Stories.*

Dave Anderson (The Greatest Is Now the Tiredest) is a sports columnist for *The New York Times* and was the winner of the news-feature award of *Best Sports Stories* in 1972. He also won the 1965 magazine award with his profile of Sugar Ray Robinson. He was born in Brooklyn and began his newspaper career with the now defunct *New York Sun.* After his graduation from Holy Cross in 1951, he went to work with the *Brooklyn Eagle,* also defunct, and then to the *New York Journal,* likewise defunct. As a columnist and reporter for *The Times,* he covers the entire range of sports.

Charles N. Barnard (Penn State's Joe Paterno), a free-lance writer after many years as editor of *True* magazine, is a frequent contributor to numerous magazines. Some include *Signature, Reader's Digest, McCalls,* and *Better Homes and Gardens.* He is also author of a book, *The Winter People,* about his sentimental return to his summer Cape Cod home in the midst of winter to get a new perspective. This is the third time that an article by Barnard has been selected to appear in *Best Sports Stories.* He is happy about this, he says, since "I am not basically a sportswriter at all."

Ira Berkow (The Smell of the Ball) is the sports editor of Newspaper Enterprise Association and writes a three-times-a-week column for the Scripps-Howard feature service. He holds a bachelor's degree in English from Miami (Ohio) University and an MSJ from Northwestern University's Medill School of Journalism, where he graduated in 1963. He is co-author with Walt Frazier of the recently released book *Rockin' Steady: A Guide to Basketball and Cool,* published by Prentice-Hall.

Furman Bisher (Myths and Misses) has been honored by *Time* magazine as one of the outstanding sports columnists in the country. He is sports editor of the *Atlanta Journal* and has merited many appearances in this series of anthologies. He has written for many major periodicals and has authored a number of sports books, his latest (and fifth) being *Arnold Palmer—The Golden Year.*

Al Cartwright (The Drive on the Record), after long service as sports editor of the *News-Journal* in Wilmington, Del., has switched to a thrice-weekly general column, *A La Carte.* Formerly with the *Reading* (Pa.) *Times, Dayton* (Ohio) *Herald,* and the *Philadelphia Record,* he has been a frequent contributor to *Best Sports Stories.* He has also won the Headliners Club award for his consistently fine writing. He also was the first winner of the Thoroughbred Racing Association's annual writing award.

LOU CHAPMAN (Mays Has the Last Laugh) has been with the *Milwaukee Sentinel* for more than 25 years. He has covered two major league sports—the baseball Braves and Brewers and pro basketball Hawks and the Bucks. He is a graduate of Marquette University and won six writing awards from the old Hearst organization. He contributed to the *Saturday Evening Post* and the *American Weekly* and is presently a correspondent for the *Sporting News.* He also has co-authored a paperback book on the Milwaukee Braves. This is his second appearance in *Best Sports Stories.*

MELVIN DURSLAG (Yeah, But What Was the Score?) began working for the *Los Angeles Examiner* in 1938 while still in high school. He was graduated from the University of California in 1943 and after service in the Air Force went to the *Los Angeles Herald-Examiner.* At various times he has been rewrite man, make-up man, and sports editor for his newspapers. Major national magazines have published his work since the early fifties, but now he does most of his sports pieces for *TV Guide,* in which this story appeared. He has been reprinted in *Best Sports Stories* on numerous occasions.

JOSEPH DURSO (Baseball's Tenth Man), who writes for *The New York Times,* is a Phi Beta Kappa from New York University with a master's degree from Columbia. After three years in the Air Force and three years in radio news and sports, he came to *The Times* in 1950. He has been assistant to the national news editor there and assistant city editor. He was also an associate professor in the Columbia Graduate School of Journalism. He is the author of two books, *Casey* and *The Days of Mr. McGraw.* This marks his third appearance in *Best Sports Stories.*

DWAIN ESPER (The Knicks Upset the Form Charts) has been a member of the *Pasadena Star-News* sports staff since 1965. He has won the Associated Press and California Newspapers Association Awards for best sports stories. He formerly was with the *Hayward Daily Review, Imperial Post Press, San Francisco News,* and other California papers. He is well known for track-and-field public announcing and his colorful commentary for football, basketball, and track. He has appeared in *Best Sports Stories* on numerous occasions.

BOB FEENEY (What Price Indy Glory) has been with the *Buffalo Evening News* since 1937, covering all sports, and has a two-a-week outdoor column. He also has specialized in motor racing as well as working on the copy desk for a time. He became a sportswriter at age nineteen. He holds records in cross-country and is also a classic league bowler. This is his first appearance in *Best Sports Stories.*

NELSON FISHER (The Saga of Secretariat Lights Up Again) is one of the West Coast's fine writers particularly known for his Derby articles. He composes a daily full-time column for *The San Diego Union* and lays claim to the fact that as a selector he picked 12 out of 15 races at Caliente one fine Labor Day. He has appeared in *Best Sports Stories* many times.

RAY FITZGERALD (The Song and the Fuss) is a graduate of Notre Dame and this past year he has been writing five sports columns a week for the *Boston Morning Globe* on a varied and delightful collection of subjects. He has had the honor of being voted Massachusetts sportswriter of the year a number of times. He has merited many inclusions in *Best Sports Stories.*

TED GREEN (Golf Paralysis . . . Form Analysis) is a newcomer to sports writing. After a year in law school he embarked on a journalistic career at UCLA and worked as an intern at the *Los Angeles Times.* At present he is a staff writer there. He is involved in the magazine approach to his newspaper chores and analyzes the sporting areas from top to bottom. He is kept busy in all areas of athletics and is doing what makes him most happy. This is his initial appearance in *Best Sports Stories.*

BOB GREENE (Nate Archibald Is Ten Feet Tall) writes a general column for the *Chicago Sun-Times* and for distribution to the *Sun-Times/Chicago Daily News* wire service. He was graduated from the Northwestern University Medill School of Journalism in 1969 and joined the *Sun-Times* immediately. He was given his own column in 1971. His book *We Didn't Have None of Them Fat Funky Angels on the Wall of Heartbreak Hotel and Other Reports from America* was published by Regnery that same year. This is his third appearance in *Best Sports Stories.*

WILL GRIMSLEY (The Square Who Became Champion) has covered the globe in pursuit of stories for the Associated Press desk. He has reported on five Olympic games, made 12 trips to Australia on Davis Cup tournaments, and has had numerous reportorial chores in every major world capital. He has authored three books: *Golf: Its History, People and Events; Tennis: Its History, People and Events;* and *Football: Greatest Moments of the Southwest Conference.* He also was supervising editor of *Century of Sports,* a popular book that sold close to 100,000 copies in 1971. This marks his fourth appearance in *Best Sports Stories.*

JOE HEILING (All Runs Unearned) has covered the Houston Astros and major league baseball for *The Houston Post* for the past eight years. He recently completed a one-year term as national president of the Baseball Writers' Association of America. He is a three-time winner in the Texas Headliners Club awards and twice has been a first-place winner in Associated Press competition. He is a graduate of Victoria College in Texas. This is his fourth appearance in *Best Sports Stories.*

DAVE HIRSHEY (What It's Like in the Bushes) was graduated from Dickinson College in 1971 with a major in English. He went to work at the *New York Daily News* and at the age of twenty-one became the youngest sports reporter in New York. He started out by covering soccer, roller derby, and racing. He now covers all sports, specializing in college football, college basketball, and tennis, as well as general features. He is an occasional contributor to *Sporting News* and other publications.

STAN HOCHMAN (The Day of the Jackals) was named sports editor of the *Philadelphia Daily News* in 1971 after 12 years as a baseball writer and columnist. He is a former schoolteacher who left the classroom for the sports desk. He has worked for many papers throughout the country and his fine writing has merited him 12 appearances in a row in *Best Sports Stories.*

PHIL JACKMAN (Where's Ken Venturi?) is making his third appearance in *Best Sports Stories.* He is a graduate of Providence College and upon his graduation in 1958 he worked for the *Worcester* (Mass.) *Telegram* until he joined his present paper, *The Baltimore Evening Sun.* In 1968 he was voted Maryland Sports Writer of the Year. Although he does suffer a great deal with the misfortunes of the Colts and Orioles, he continues to flagellate himself with this beat and continues to thrive by making himself a host of readers.

PAUL KAPLAN (FTC: Truth or Consequences) is a graduate of the University of Florida and University of Miami Law School, who enjoys writing more than practicing law. He has been with the *Miami News* for three years, doing mostly features while covering pro basketball (ABA Floridians), boxing, and golf as primary beats. This is his second appearance in *Best Sports Stories.*

DAVE KINDRED (The Recruiting of Kent Benson) is a native of Atlanta, Illinois, and a graduate of Illinois Wesleyan. He has been sports editor of the *Louisville Times* for three years, a member of the paper's Washington bureau for one year, and sports editor of *The Louisville Courier-Journal* since July, 1973. His stories have appeared in *Best Sports Stories* twice.

TONY KORNHEISER ("Very Bad, Very Rough, Damn Dirty Basketball") is twenty-five years old and has been working at *Newsday* on Long Island for the past four years. A 1970 graduate of Harpur College in Binghamton,

N.Y., he taught school in Newark before joining the *Newsday* staff on his 22nd birthday. Some of his work has appeared in *Sport, New York* and *Street and Smith* magazines. He lives with his wife Karril and their dog Sundance in Long Beach, N.Y., and most of his free time is spent keeping his indoor plants alive—which seems to be a losing battle. This is his second appearance in *Best Sports Stories.*

HAL LEBOVITZ (Little Boy Lost) is a graduate of Western Reserve University who started his career as a high school chemistry teacher but then became a sportswriter because of his avid interest in athletics. He started writing for the *Cleveland News* and then went to the *Cleveland Plain Dealer,* where he is now the sports editor. His column "Hal Thinks" is supplemented by his "Ask Hal" column, and both have earned him numerous writing honors. He is a past president of the Baseball Writers Association of America and has been included in *Best Sports Stories* many times.

DICK LIEN (The Giant among the Champions) is beginning his 11th year as a member of the sports staff at *The Peoria Journal-Star* after graduation from Bradley University in 1964. He was named an assistant sports editor in 1971. For the last six years he has specialized in college basketball. His story on UCLA's 1972 national collegiate basketball championship appeared in *Best Sports Stories* that year. This makes his second appearance in this anthology.

BARRY LORGE (The Bitter Lessons of Wimbledon '73) is making his second appearance in *Best Sports Stories.* He was graduated from Harvard, class of 1970, and in spite of his interest in the study of government he went to work with the *Worcester* (Mass.) *Telegram and Gazette.* His beat was mostly tennis and he also free-lanced for *Sport* and many other magazines. He has covered tennis in over a dozen countries and is working on a book to be published in the fall by Harper & Row. At present he is an associate editor of *Tennis* magazine.

WILLIAM MCILWAIN (Speed, Sex and Heroes) was born in Lancaster, South Carolina, and has been a writer and newspaper editor all of his adult life. He was editor of *Newsday* until 1970 when he left to become writer-in-residence at Wake Forest University. McIlwain was a collaborator in the writing of *Naked Came the Stranger* and *Legends of Baptist Hollow.* He is the author of *The Glass Rooster,* a novel, and of *A Farewell to Alcohol*—his most recent book. His writing appears frequently in leading American magazines. He is presently managing editor of *The Bergen Record* and was before that deputy managing editor of the *Toronto Star.* This is his debut in *Best Sports Stories.*

NEIL MILBERT (The Greatest Race Horse in History?) works for the *Chicago Tribune* and covers mostly thoroughbred racing, boxing, and pro football. He is proudest of his new accomplishment—as a selector he had eight winners on a nine-race card at Hawthorne. He is a graduate of Marquette University and his previous newspaper affiliations include the *Jersey City Journal,* the *Ottumwa* (Iowa) *Courier,* and WEMP radio in Milwaukee. This is his second appearance in *Best Sports Stories.*

HUBERT MIZELL (A $500,000 Tournament . . . and Who Cares?) is a columnist and feature writer for the *St. Petersburg Times* and a contributing editor to *Golf Digest* magazine. He is a native Floridian who served a stint as a sportswriter for the Associated Press in New York. His assignments have included the World Series, Super Bowl, 1972 Olympics, Pan American Games in Colombia, and many top auto-racing events as well as major golf championships. This marks his first appearance in *Best Sports Stories.*

EDDIE MULLER (It Took Him 4 Minutes 35 Seconds) is San Francisco born and has worked for Hearst's *San Francisco Examiner* for his entire newspaper career. He has been boxing editor since 1930 and was the only boxing writer on a major American newspaper to pick George Foreman to knock out Joe Frazier. He has won six first-place awards in the annual Press Club competition. He was the originator of the Golden Glove tournament in 1931.

DWAYNE NETLAND (The Vikings Mine the 49ers) is a graduate of the University of Minnesota and after some newspaper stints in Austin, Minn. and Madison, Wisc. he went to the *Minneapolis Tribune,* where he covers a host of Minnesota sports including the Vikings and golf. He has appeared previously in *Best Sports Stories.*

PHIL PEPE (The Mets Run Out of Miracles) is a graduate of St. John's University in Queens who in 1957 became a member of the *New York World-Telegram* staff, covering the Yankees and college sports. In 1967 he moved to the *World Journal Tribune* as a three-days-a-week columnist; then he free-lanced until 1968, when he joined the staff of the *New York Daily News.* He is the author of five sports books, including *From Ghetto to Glory,* on Bob Gibson, Cardinal pitcher. He has appeared in *Best Sports Stories* many times.

EDWIN POPE (The Horrors of Training Camp) was born in Athens, Georgia, and maintains he fumbled his way through the University of Georgia. Nevertheless he has established a warm readership as a columnist and reporter with his paper, *The Miami Herald,* of which he became the sports editor in 1957. His former newspaper work was with the *Atlanta Constitution,* the *Atlanta Journal,* and United Press International. He is the author of four books: *Football's Greatest Coaches; Baseball's Greatest*

Managers, Encyclopedia of Greyhound Racing; and *Ted Williams: The Golden Years.* He has merited many appearances in this anthology.

George Ross (On Coming in First) works for *The Oakland Tribune* and is a journalism graduate of the University of Nevada. He began with the *Tribune* in 1950 and became its sports editor in 1961. He holds a pilot's license, flies regularly to all important assignments, and recently added a glider rating to his airman's certificate. This is his first appearance in *Best Sports Stories.*

Jay Searcy (17 in a Row on a Shoestring) attended East Tennessee State University and joined the *Chattanooga Times.* He became that paper's sport editor in 1960. He has been on the sports copy desk of *The New York Times* since August, 1972, writing occasional features. He is a former winner of the Sportswriter of the Year Award in Tennessee. This marks his second appearance in *Best Sports Stories.*

Nick Seitz (If Ken Dryden's So Smart, How Come He's a Goalie?) is making his eighth appearance in *Best Sports Stories,* but this time as the golf editor of *Golf Digest.* He is a graduate of the University of Oklahoma, where he majored in philosophy. He then, at the age of twenty-two, became editor of the *Norman* (Okla.) *Transcript.* He has won numerous prizes in golf and basketball writers' contests.

Blackie Sherrod (Nightmare for the Longhorns), the executive sports editor of *The Dallas Times Herald,* has garnered just about every important sportswriting prize in the country. To name a few: the National Headliners Award; seven citations as the outstanding sportswriter by newspaper, radio, and TV colleagues; and over a dozen inclusions in *Best Sports Stories.* As a master of ceremonies and banquet speaker, he has made a reputation almost equal to his writing. He also has his own radio and TV programs.

Mark Shrager (1,001 Sure Fire Ways to Lose a Race) is a twenty-four-year-old graduate of UCLA and is only a few units short of an M.A. in political science/public administration. He is currently an administrative aide in the budget division of the Los Angeles unified school district and writes as a free lance in his spare time. With this piece—the third he has had in *Turf & Sport Digest*—he is making his first appearance in *Best Sports Stories.*

George Solomon (On the Mountainous Appalachian Trail) has been a staff writer for *The Washington Post* for the past two years. He is a graduate of the University of Florida's School of Journalism and Communications. He joined the *Post*'s sports department upon the demise of the *Washington Daily News* in July, 1972. Previously he had worked for five years at the *Fort Lauderdale News and Sun-Sentinel.* He is the author of many free-lance articles and a recently published book, *The Team Nobody Wanted: The Washington Redskins.* This makes his third appearance in *Best Sports Stories.*

BOB STEVENS (History Is Relived) joined the *San Francisco Chronicle* directly after his graduation from high school and has been with the paper ever since. This is his 39th year as a writer, all of them spent in the sports department of the *Chronicle.* He has been covering baseball, major and minor, for the paper since 1939. He is the past president of both the Pacific Coast League Baseball Writers and Baseball Writers Association of America and also scored two All Star games and two World Series. His work has appeared many times in this anthology.

D. L. STEWART (A Day in the Press Box) has been with *The Dayton Journal Herald* for seven years, covering golf and the Cincinnati Bengals. Prior to that he worked for two years with the *Mansfield* (Ohio) *News Journal.* He is a native of Cleveland and a graduate of Ohio University. This is his first appearance in *Best Sports Stories.*

PHIL TAYLOR (Tommy Aaron Is Finally No. 1) is a veteran of more than 35 years in the newspaper business. Besides serving as sports editor of *Stars and Stripes* (1948–50), he has covered every major sport as member of the sports staffs of the *Tacoma News-Tribune, Seattle Star, Seattle Times,* and *Seattle Post-Intelligencer.* He has been with the *Post-Intelligencer* since 1951 and at present is its golf editor and football writer. He also writes a column. Taylor is a two-time winner of the National Golf Writers' competition. This is his third appearance in *Best Sports Stories.*

WELLS TWOMBLY (Super Hero) is sports columnist for the *San Francisco Examiner,* turning in six columns a week. His sports reporting has appeared in newspapers in all parts of the country, in this order: East—*Willimantic* (Conn.) *Daily Chronicle;* West—*North Hollywood Valley Times Today;* South—the *Houston Chronicle;* North—the *Detroit Free Press;* and then back to the West to the *Examiner.* In 1970 he won the news-coverage prize in *Best Sports Stories* and was named by *Newsweek* as one of the young sportswriters who is changing the face and style of sportswriting. His book about George Blanda won warm acclaim.

H. S. VON BEHR (Dash—Profile of a Dog) is a photographer who has done considerable writing for magazines. He has also been a teacher of photo journalism at New York University. Born in Germany, he came to the United States in 1924 and established his own photo studio in New York City in 1931. He was elected a Fellow of the Royal Photographic Society of Great Britain in 1941. A farm he bought in 1933 at Old Chatham, New York, has been the setting for many of his outdoor articles. This is his first appearance in *Best Sports Stories.*

MAURY WHITE (The Unbelievable Happens) is a sports columnist for *The Des Moines Register* and has been with the paper since finishing four years in the navy during World War II. A former football and basketball player at Drake, he was selected on the Sports Illustrated Silver Anniversary team in 1966. He is a past president of the Football Writers Association of America and has won awards in the Basketball and Golf Writers Association contests. He has appeared a number of times in *Best Sports Stories.*

DAVID WOLF (The Olympics: End of a Dream), now a contributing editor of *True,* where this article appeared, did his undergraduate work at the University of Wisconsin and then received his M.A. in journalism at Columbia School of Journalism, where he was awarded the Grantland Rice Fellowship. He then became a sports reporter and editor with *Life* magazine. In 1966, after an intensive investigation, he cleared basketball player Connie Hawkins of involvement in the 1961 basketball scandals. This is his second appearance in *Best Sports Stories.*

DICK YOUNG (The Love Life of a Private Secretariat) joined the *New York Daily News* in 1941 and appeared in the first edition of *Best Sports Stories* in 1944. He was at that time one of the youngest sports reporters in New York City. Since then he has become one of the two most consistent winners in this series with five *Best Sports Stories* awards—two prizes in news-coverage (in 1959 and 1960), two for news-features (1957 and 1966) and one in the magazine category (in 1955). He writes a daily column for the *News* entitled "Young Ideas," and baseball is his major sport.

PHOTOGRAPHERS IN BEST SPORTS STORIES—1974

THE PHOTO WINNERS

BILL SERNE (Innocent Bystander) is the winner of the action photo award of *Best Sports Stories* in his first appearance, at the age of twenty-four. He is a graduate of Kent State University and went to work for the *Tampa Tribune* photo department immediately after graduation in 1972. In college he was photo editor for the *Kent Stater* for two years and prior to that was a sportswriter for a year. He says he realized that his pictures told people more than his stories, so he turned to photo journalism.

JOSEPH BAKER (Double Play), winner of the feature-photo award, is also making his first appearance in *Best Sports Stories.* He has been staff photographer for three New Jersey dailies, including three years with the *Newark Star-Ledger.* He started his career as a youngster stringing for New York dailies and wire services and has worked as photo editor for a string of 11 Long Island weeklies. He is currently free-lancing.

OTHER PHOTOGRAPHERS (In Alphabetical Order)

MICHAEL A. ANDERSON (Play Ball!) is making his fifth consecutive appearance in *Best Sports Stories.* A general assignment photographer for the *Boston Herald-American,* he has been named Press Photographer of the Year by the Boston Press Photographers Association for two of the last four years. He also served as treasurer of the National Press Photographers Association.

ERNEST W. ANHEUSER (Game Called on Account of Mud) has an artistic background, including studies at the Chicago Art Institute. During World War II he turned to photography as a profession. He is now on the staff of *The Milwaukee Sentinel.*

ANTHONY BERNATO (Up the Wall) started with the old *New York Daily Mirror* and in 1963 moved to the *Philadelphia Bulletin,* where he mainly covers sports. A full-sized newspaper gives him much more space and fuller rein, than a tabloid, he says. This is his third appearance in *Best Sports Stories.*

JOHN E. BIEVER (Alphonse and Gaston Are Brewing a Boo-Boo) won the action photo award a year ago with his picture, Confrontation of the Giants, and is making his fourth appearance in *Best Sports Stories.* A recent graduate of the University of Wisconsin (Milwaukee), he is a free-lance photographer and works with his father, Vernon Biever, who has also appeared in *Best Sports Stories.*

DONALD BLACK (Vaulting a Viking) has been a staff photographer with the *Minneapolis Tribune* since his graduation from high school in 1952. He has won awards in contests conducted by the *Inland Daily Press,* the Associated Press, and *Page One.* This is his second appearance in *Best Sports Stories.*

CLINT GRANT (Behind the Eight Ball) has been with the *Dallas Morning News* for 25 years. Primarily a feature photographer, he specializes in animals and children but has won awards in sports photography, nationally and locally. This is his first appearance in *Best Sports Stories.*

CHARLES G. KIRMAN (Mud Pack) received a bachelor of science degree with honors in the field of professional photography from Rochester Institute of Technology in March, 1972, and since then has been employed as a staff photographer for the *Chicago Sun-Times.* He was discharged from the Navy in 1968 and has received several local and state photography awards. This is his first appearance in *Best Sports Stories.*

KENT KOBERSTEEN (Nothing Corny about This Cornhusker) has been a staff photographer for the *Minneapolis Tribune* since 1965. Prior to that he attended the University of Minnesota. His fine photography has merited six inclusions in *Best Sports Stories.*

JOHN LONG (A Study in Frustration) has been with the *Hartford Courant* for just under three years, photographing any and all assignments. He has a bachelor's degree in English from Catholic University and before becoming a photographer was a high school English teacher for three years. This is his first appearance in *Best Sports Stories.*

RICHARD MACKSON (Break My Jaw, Will Ya!) is, appropriately enough, a full-time pre-dental student at Santa Monica College who free-lances for the *Santa Monica Outlook.* In college photography competition he has won first place in sports two years in a row.

RAY MATJASIC (Pro and Progeny) has been with the *Cleveland Plain Dealer* for 35 years, the last nine of them as chief photographer. He was a marine combat photographer in World War II and was wounded on Saipan while shooting pictures of the landing there.

FRED MATTHES (Mane Event) started as a student in photography at City College of San Francisco and has been a staff photographer at the *San Jose Mercury-News* for 12 years. His first job was with International News Photo and he spent a couple of years in industrial photography after INP merged with United Press.

WILLIAM MEYER (The Clock Tells the Whole Story) is a twenty-four-year-old staff photographer for *The Milwaukee Journal.* He has been with that newspaper for two years since graduating from the University of Wisconsin (Milwaukee). He competed in track-and-field sports and won college division All-America honors for the discus in 1970.

RICHARD OLSENIUS (A Rare View of a Rear View) started as a staff photographer for the *Minneapolis Tribune* in the fall of 1970. A Minneapolis native, he attended Gustavus Adolphus and the University of Minnesota. This is his first appearance in *Best Sports Stories.*

AL ROBERTS (The Stackup) is a twenty-six-year-old veteran of *The Knoxville Journal* photo staff and a familiar face on the sidelines at University of Tennessee football and basketball games. This is his first appearance in *Best Sports Stories.*

RONALD E. SCHIFFERLE (Where Is that Marker?) has been a staff photographer for the *Buffalo Courier-Express* for 20 years and has won a number of photo awards. Before coming to the paper he served three years in the U.S. Navy. This is his first appearance in *Best Sports Stories.*

SEYMOUR SNAER (Hang Gliders) is a veteran photographer with the *San Francisco Examiner* and the recipient of many distinguished awards as Photographer of the Year. He is a pioneer in newspaper color photography and his exciting shots have appeared many times in *Best Sports Stories.*

AL STEPHENSON (Georgia Poetry) has been working for the *Atlanta Journal Constitution* since 1971. He was in graduate school at the University of Georgia when he decided to become a photographer. This is his first appearance in *Best Sports Stories.*

PAUL TEPLEY (The Windup) started his career working for UPI and in 1964, after seven years with the agency, became a press photographer for the *Cleveland Press.* He is a graduate of Cleveland State University and is making his fourth appearance in *Best Sports Stories.*

JOHN TITCHEN (Three on a Wave) has been with the *Honolulu Star-Bulletin* since 1959. He began his newspaper photography career with the *Sydney* (Australia) *Daily Mirror.* His work has appeared often in *Best Sports Stories.*

JIM VINCENT (Technical Talk Is Not Nice Talk) has been a staff photographer for *The Portland Oregonian* for seven years. Prior to that he was with the *Oregon Journal* for 11 years. This marks his sixth appearance in *Best Sports Stories.*

DICK YARWOOD (Flying High) has been a staff photographer for *Newsday* for almost eight years. He is a native New Yorker, having been born in Queens, and is twenty-seven years old. Currently he is secretary-treasurer of Region 2, National Press Photographers Association.

THE YEARS BEST SPORTS PHOTOS

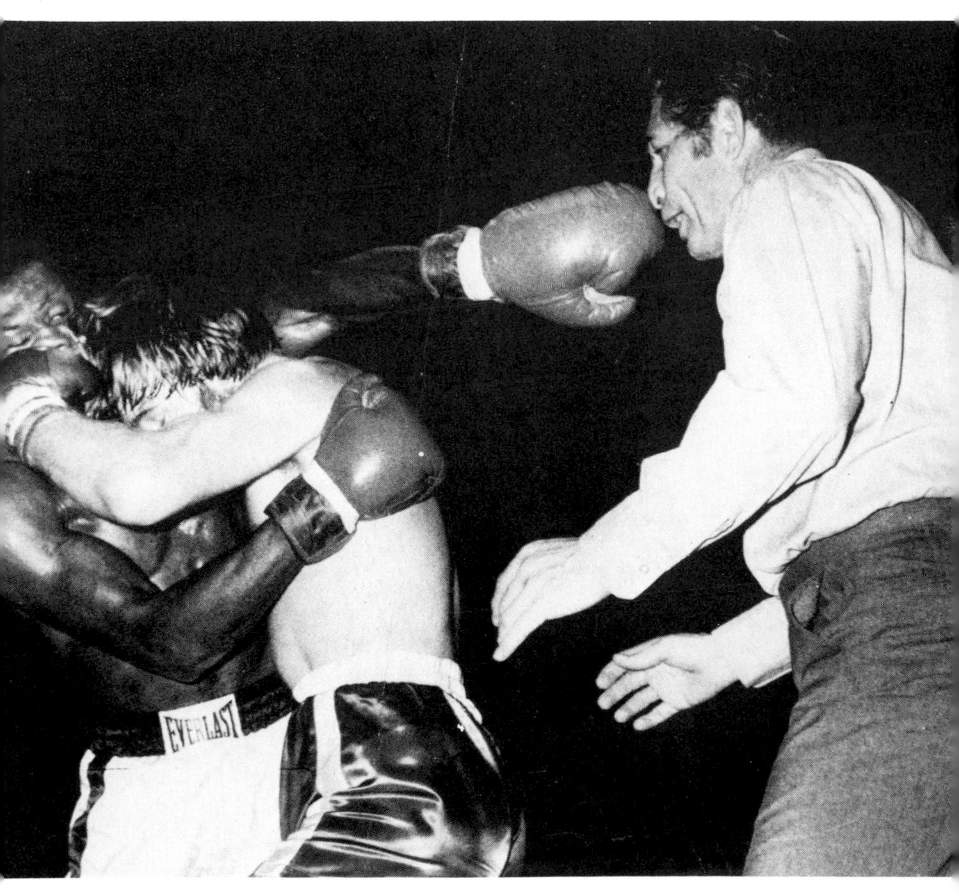

INNOCENT BYSTANDER

by Bill Serne, *Tampa Tribune*. This is the winning photo in the action division and it shows a misdirected punch thrown by Willie Chaney that connected with referee Lee Sala instead of opponent John Pinney. Sala was not hurt and Pinney went on to win the fight, split decision in Curtis Hixon Hall, Tampa, Florida. Copyright ©, 1973, The Tampa Tribune Company.

DOUBLE PLAY

by Joseph Baker, *Passaic Herald-News.* This is the feature photo winner of *Best Sports Stories* and was taken on the sidelines of a high school baseball game in Passaic, New Jersey. It ran on page one of the newspaper and placed first in the New Jersey Press Photographers Association competition. Copyright ©, 1973, Joseph Baker. Reprinted by permission.

UP THE WALL

by Anthony Bernato, *Philadelphia Bulletin*. Dell Unser of the Philadelphia Phillies leaps high against a wall trying to catch Ted Simmons' fly ball which went for a triple in a Phillies-Cardinals game in June. In the foreground is shortstop Larry Bowa looking on. Copyright ©, 1973, by Bulletin Company, Philadelphia.

FLYING HIGH

by Dick Yarwood, *Newsday*. In the last game of the National League playoff between the New York Mets and the Cincinnati Reds, Reds' catcher Johnny Bench goes up in the air to catch a relay as the Mets' Felix Millan scores. The Mets won the game and the pennant. Copyright ©, 1973, Newsday Inc.

ALPHONSE AND GASTON ARE BREWING A BOO-BOO

by John E. Biever, *The Milwaukee Journal.* The Milwaukee Brewers' Don Money (front) and Tim Johnson both miss a pop foul off the bat of the New York Yankees' Bobby Murcer for an error. The photo was made at a Milwaukee–Yankee game at Milwaukee in June. Copyright ©, 1973, *The Milwaukee Journal.*

GAME CALLED ON ACCOUNT OF MUD

by Ernest W. Anheuser, *The Milwaukee Journal*. This scene was shot at a high school baseball game in Milwaukee. Copyright ©, 1973, *The Milwaukee Journal*.

PLAY BALL!

by Michael A. Andersen, *Boston Herald-American.* Unable to wait any longer for opening day of the baseball season, two exuberant youngsters duck under a partially opened bleacher gate at Fenway Park in Boston. Copyright ©, 1973, The Hearst Corporation.

WHERE IS THAT MARKER?

by Ronald E. Schifferle, *Buffalo Courier-Express.* Umpire Tom Hensley brings a new element into football—a snow shovel, as he tries to find the yard marker and hash marks in Buffalo's new 80,000-seat Rich Stadium in a game between the Buffalo Bills and the New England Patriots. The Bills won by 37–13 as O. J. Simpson gained 219 yards during the snowy game. Copyright ©, 1973, *Buffalo Courier-Express.*

VAULTING A VIKING

by Donald Black, *Minneapolis Tribune.* Redskin running back Larry Brown is vaulting over Viking Bobby Bryant in the first half of a game which the Vikings won 27–20. On the next play Brown went in for the first touchdown of the game. Copyright ©, 1973, *Minneapolis Tribune.*

MUD PACK

by Charles G. Kirman, *Chicago Sun-Times*. Rick Kapryan of Gordon Tech High School displays the mud which he accumulated in a game against Loyola Academy at Chicago's Gordon Tech field. Copyright ©, 1973, *Chicago Sun-Times*.

NOTHING CORNY ABOUT THIS CORNHUSKER

by Kent Kobersteen, *Minneapolis Tribune.* Nebraska's Brent Longwell goes for a first down despite an attempted tackle by Minnesota's Kevin Keller during the Cornhuskers 48–7 victory at Minneapolis. Copyright ©, 1973, *Minneapolis Tribune.*

A STUDY IN FRUSTRATION

by John Long, *Hartford Courant*. Alex Webster, then coach of the New York Giants, watches as his team loses to the Vikings in the final game of the season at the Yale Bowl, New Haven, in December. Copyright ©, 1973, *Hartford Courant*.

A RARE VIEW OF A REAR VIEW

by Richard Olsenius, *Minneapolis Tribune*. Somewhere under this mass is a Viking halfback named Chuck Foreman. He obviously gained very little on this play. Copyright ©, 1973, *Minneapolis Tribune*.

THE CLOCK TELLS THE WHOLE STORY

by William Meyer, *The Milwaukee Journal.* The winning shot for Northwestern in its Big Ten game with Wisconsin at McGaw Hall in Madison. Wisconsin was ahead 73–72 with only one second remaining when this winning jump shot was taken. Copyright ©, 1973, *The Milwaukee Journal.*

TECHNICAL TALK IS NOT NICE TALK

by Jim Vincent, *The Portland Oregonian.* Kennedy McIntosh (forty-three) of the Seattle Super Sonics yells foul and gets a technical foul from referee Mark Mana during NBA Portland Trail Blazers–Seattle game. Copyright ©, 1973, *The Oregonian,* Portland, Oregon.

THE STACKUP

by Al Roberts, *The Knoxville Journal.* Tennessee's Larry Robinson (bottom), Auburn's Gary England (center), and Tennessee's Wayne Tomlinson (top) form a three-tiered pileup during a Vol–Tiger basketball game last February. Copyright ©, 1973, *The Knoxville Journal.*

THE WINDUP

by Paul Tepley, *Cleveland Press*. Cleveland Cavaliers' Bill Fitch, furious over the officiating in a game with Atlanta at the Cleveland Arena, grabs a chair and prepares to hurl it onto the court in a game in Cleveland. He let fly the chair more than 22 feet and luckily he missed. Copyright ©, 1973, *Cleveland Press*.

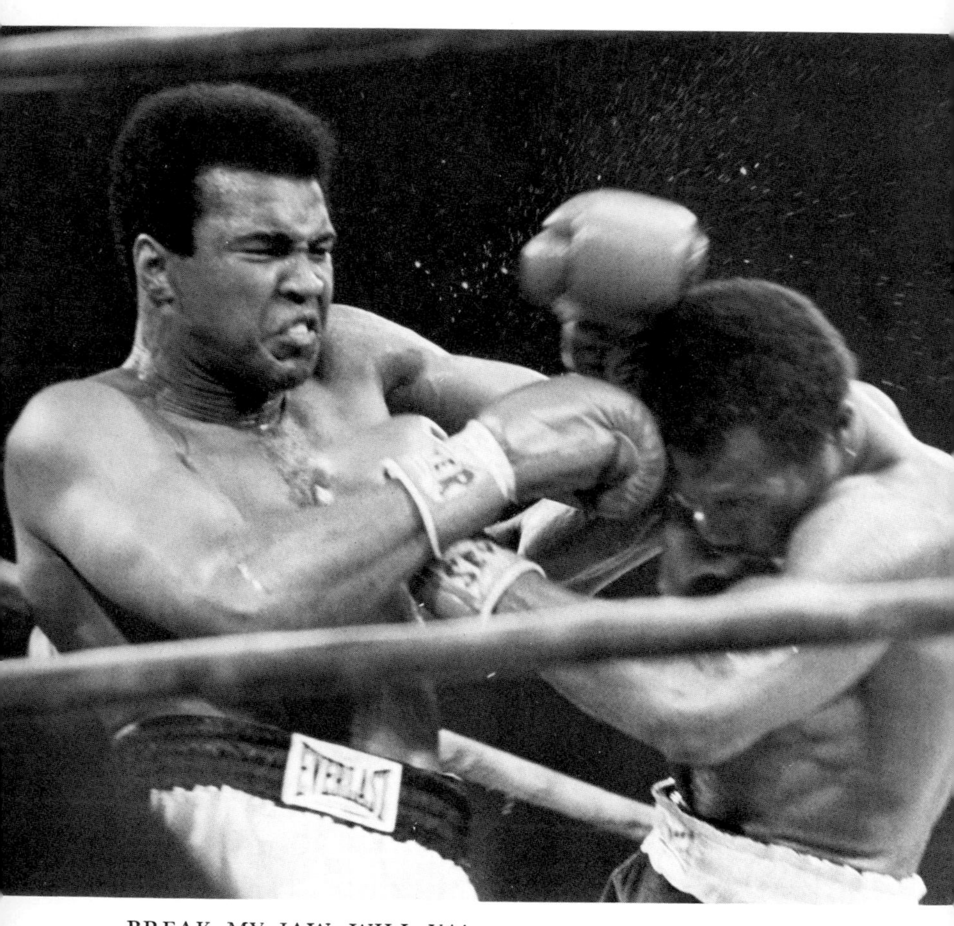

BREAK MY JAW, WILL YA!

by Richard Mackson, *Santa Monica Outlook*. Muhammed Ali smashes Ken Norton in the head during the battle of the broken jaw. Ali won a split decision. Copyright ©, 1973, United Western Newspapers, Inc.

PRO AND PROGENY

by Ray Matjasic, *Cleveland Plain Dealer*. Jack Nicklaus greeted by his son after winning the PGA championship of 1973 at the Canterbury Club outside of Cleveland. Copyright ©, 1973, *The Plain Dealer,* Cleveland, Ohio.

THREE ON A WAVE

by John Titchen, *Honolulu Star-Bulletin*. Rory Russell, left, Richard Harvey, right, and Eddie Aikau, bottom right, come through with good rides in a heat of the Duke Kahanamoku Hawaiian Surfing Classic. Copyright ©, 1973, *Honolulu Star-Bulletin*.

MANE EVENT

by Fred Matthes, *San Jose Mercury-News*. Gene Upshaw and Otis Sistrunk of the Oakland Raiders show their two completely different hair-styles prior to a football game last fall. Copyright ©, 1973, *San Jose* (Cal.) *Mercury-News*.

GEORGIA POETRY

by Al Stephenson, *Atlanta Journal-Constitution.* Horses going over a hurdle at the annual Atlanta Steeplechase. The card of nine races is staged for charity and this was the Gallant Man Purse. Copyright ©, 1973, Atlanta Newspapers Inc.

HANG GLIDERS

by Seymour Snaer, *San Francisco Examiner*. A three-man flight over San Francisco Bay is beautifully caught by the photographer.

BEHIND THE EIGHT BALL

by Clint Grant, *Dallas Morning News*. Pat Barta doesn't have a vocabulary yet but he does make bad English shots. Copyright ©, 1973, *Dallas Morning News*.